# CONSCIOUS SEEING

## Transforming Your Life through Your Eyes

# CONSCIOUS SEEING

## Transforming Your Life through Your Eyes

ROBERTO KAPLAN, O.D., M.Ed.

BEYOND
WORDS
Publishing
I N C

Beyond Words Publishing, Inc.
20827 N.W. Cornell Road, Suite 500
Hillsboro, Oregon 97124-9808
503-531-8700
1-800-284-9673

Editors: Hal Zina Bennett and Laura Carlsmith
Copy editor: Michael Ashby
Proofreader: Nelda Street
Managing editor: Julie Steigerwaldt
Design: Principia Graphica and Dorral Lukas
Composition: William H. Brunson Typography Services
Line Drawings Emily Strelow

Printed in the United States of America
Distributed to the book trade by Publishers Group West

*Library of Congress Cataloging-in-Publication Data*
Kaplan, Robert-Michael
    Conscious Seeing : transforming your life through your eyes /
    Roberto Kaplan
        p.   cm.
    ISBN 1-58270-048-6 (pbk.)
    1. Vision disorders — Alternative treatment.   2. Visual training.
3. Personal development.   4. Psychology.   5. Consciousness.   I. Title.
    RE48 .K325   2002
    617.7 — dc21

                                                                00-068887

The corporate mission of Beyond Words Publishing, Inc.:
  *Inspire to Integrity*

The individuals in this book are composites of current and former patients, participants in workshops, and individuals I have worked with throughout my career. Names and other identifying characteristics have been changed to protect individual privacy.

# Contents

Contents

# Acknowledgments

Thanks to all of you; my parents Mark and Hilly; numerous teachers; my children Julia, Symon, and Daved; beloved friend Gabriela; my U.S. editor and book consultant Hal Zina Bennett; and the publishing staffs in both Germany and the United States, who have so generously contributed to cocreating this book. Bless you all on your journey to conscious seeing.

# Introduction

Down through the centuries, poets have referred to the eyes as *the windows to the soul*. This metaphor has sparked the imaginations of people everywhere; for there is something in this poetic notion that strikes us as true and real. The lover gazes into the eyes of the beloved and often, without knowing why, feels a distinct quickening of their relationship. The newborn and mother connect with their eyes and instantly—some say "electrically"—their lifetime bond is established. The more we contemplate these experiences, the clearer it becomes that our eyes offer us a way to learn more about who we are, the inner visions that drive us, and even what we might want to change in order to live more fully.

I have always been fascinated by the notion that the eyes provide access to the soul. But there is yet another dimension to my own interest, since I am also an eye doctor. A lifetime in this profession, closely examining literally tens of thousands of eyes, has given me the opportunity to explore what the eyes express and what they can teach us about our own inner vision. In addition, I have come to understand how the eyes, as extensions of the brain, can provide each of us with "in-sights" concerning the perceptions we have formed about life and the world around us. It is my poetic interest, combined with my professional experience with the eyes, that has brought me to the discoveries I have recorded in this book. As you will find, what I share here confirms what the poets have said, that the eyes truly are the windows to the soul. I am not just speaking of what the lovers project to their beloveds when gazing into their eyes. The fact is that the eyes actually do reveal objective information about ourselves—our emotions, our state of health, our way of perceiving the world. Therein is an invaluable source of knowledge, which, until now, has been greatly neglected.

The poet George Santayana said, "It is not wisdom to be only wise, / And on the inward vision close the eyes..." (*O World, Thou Chooseth Not*, 1894) In this book, the focus is definitely on what Santayana calls "the inward vision" of the eyes. In these pages I've described a path for exploring what your eyes can tell you about your own life, and provide clues for how to transform aspects of your present life that you would like to change. In that respect, this is not a book about vision improvement—yet, as you move through this process of exploration that I've outlined, many of you will also discover that your eyes in fact will change and your vision of the outer world will become clearer, making you less dependent on corrective lenses. There's a gift beyond that, however: the gift of inner wisdom.

For the past thirty years, I have been examining the mechanism of vision not just as an eye doctor but as a person intrigued by the inner workings of human perception. At first I practiced my profession by following conventional thinking and what I'd learned in optometry school; that is, if the patient couldn't see clearly I prescribed corrective glasses. I sincerely believed that this approach was going to solve their problems. In most cases it did. However, I became more interested in the cases that were not helped. Why did patients suddenly say they couldn't wear their contact lenses anymore? Why, at age forty, did patients complain of small print becoming blurry? Why did some patients have such severe reactions to their new glasses, in some cases even having their lives quite disrupted? The why's propelled me to explore more deeply the science and wisdom of vision. This book is the result of turning my attention more fully and completely to these kinds of issues, and not limiting my exploration to vision correction only.

In these pages I describe my journey into the science and wisdom of conscious seeing. To the prescribing of spectacles I have added new dimensions of healing. Modified lens prescriptions, coupled with seeing practices, become a therapeutic means for my patients to wake up to their true potential, to *consciously see*.

The eye, after all, is a perfect model for understanding how human perception is the key to transformation and change. When we look carefully at all that we know about the eye, we can take a more active part in creating our own experiences of the world beyond our eyes. We learn that in the blur or fuzziness of what we once may have described as "poor vision" new doors of perception may open to us, revealing the thoughts and emotions that become invisible when our vision is sharply focused. That may seem contradictory at this point, but by the end of this book you'll know why it is not.

This book is the compilation of many things — my experiences as a photographic artist, eye doctor, shaman, and human being — one who strives to evolve, to be conscious in my actions and daily living. The incredible insights shared by my patients and workshop participants have all motivated my own personal evolvement, even while dedicating myself to helping them.

# 1

## *The Anatomy of Seeing*

*Look with eyes of what is and not what isn't.*

—THE AUTHOR

The American mathematician and philosopher, Alfred North Whitehead, was one of the great explorers of human consciousness. He pointed out, for example, that the beauty we find in nature is much more the product of human perception than it is of the object itself. In that insight we take our first step on our journey to deepen our understanding of the eye and the nature of perception. Dr. Whitehead said, "The poets are entirely mistaken. They should address their lyrics to themselves, and should turn them into odes of self-congratulation on the excellency of the human mind. Nature is a dull affair, soundless, scentless, colorless; merely the hurrying of material, endlessly, meaninglessly."

If Dr. Whitehead is correct, and it is my belief that he is, then we must accept the fact that what we *think* we are seeing most assuredly tells us more about ourselves than it does about the external world. That concept is, in fact, at the heart of the world's greatest psychological and spiritual teachings. But, you may ask, how can the eye serve us as a metaphor for applying these principles in our everyday lives? To begin that process, let's look at what we know about eyesight.

When scientists try to explain the phenomenon of human sight, they often begin by comparing the eye to a camera. They explain that just as with the lens of a camera, light enters through a small opening,

1

the pupil centered in the *iris*, which opens or closes to adjust the amount of light that enters. Light striking the back of your eye (the *retina*) produces an image in your brain. Similarly, when light strikes the back of the camera, an image is recorded on film. But there is much more than this involved with the anatomy of seeing. If we are to understand the process of conscious seeing, we need to explore how the person uses his or her eyes and brain together to make it possible for us to see, and this takes us quite beyond the simplistic camera analogy. What we quickly discover as we explore the human anatomy of sight is that light entering our eyes triggers a complex of events within our minds that involves our entire lives. And it soon becomes clear that good vision is much more than visual acuity. It shapes our very lives, determining not just how accurately we see the light, color, and imagery that pass before us but how we experience our lives and how we interact with the world around us. We discover that genetics, our behavior, our earliest memories of life, all impact how we use our eyes and what we see. The most exciting part of all, perhaps, is that by looking more deeply into the anatomy of sight you will discover that you can improve your eyesight and vastly expand your awareness of the world around you, the quality of the choices you make, and even how you interact with others in your life.

Let us go back to the analogy of the camera for a moment. You have focused your camera lens on the image you want to capture. You've clicked the shutter. Light enters the camera, exposing the film. Once the film is exposed, you can no longer influence the image. What you have recorded on the film can be changed through computer or darkroom manipulation, but that process, however artistic it might be, is still a mechanical one. So how is human vision different?

Millions of sensations and nerve impulses in your eye are sent into your brain. At this point there are complex interactions between your brain and your mind[1] that produce images you recognize as

---

[1] As I use the terms here, and throughout this book, "brain" refers to the physiological functions that the brain performs, whereas "mind" refers to those functions that make up our life experience, including our personal vision of life, what we value, our memories, thoughts, and so forth.

your house, your car, the lakeside resort you visited last summer, your mother's face, in short whatever it is that you are viewing. Light, shaped into these recognizable images, stimulates and interacts with your memories of past events. In this respect, vision is anything but passive.

It's important to understand that much of how we see is a learned process. We don't simply come into life knowing instantly how to make sense of the light striking our retinas. In early childhood what our minds see may mean little or nothing to us. The light-stimulated impulses racing from our retinas to our brains are just sensations with no meaning beyond that. As we learn and mature, through childhood into adulthood, we start to interpret these sensations and begin to elaborate on what they mean.

Imagine the millions of sensations that have streamed into your brain during your lifetime. Consider how your mind had to master the process of decoding all those nerve impulses and making sense of what was otherwise only a chaotic stream of light and color. Our minds filter and interpret these sensations. They even make judgments that determine what is acceptable and unacceptable; that is, what we will allow ourselves to see and what we will reject or deny. Our minds decide on what incoming information they will permit to enter the deeper parts of ourselves, and so it is here, in this process, that we discover what I am calling "conscious seeing."

A friend recently related a story that beautifully illustrates this point. Jerry had been in therapy for several months and had recently learned that relationship problems he'd been having were related to events that occurred around the time of his birth. When he was born, his mother was anesthetized due to some life-threatening health complications. As a result, his mother was unconscious when he was born and sedated for two days thereafter, so he never bonded with her. Instead he was left in the hospital nursery, fed from a bottle, and rarely held until his mother was able to receive him three days after he was born. He jokingly commented that he bonded with the fluorescent lights high above his crib.

3

Through further research into human bonding Jerry discovered that there is a particular pattern of behavior that people who did not bond when they were infants tend to exhibit in adulthood. When Jerry learned all this, he better understood why people he was closest to often complained that he was "distant and remote." It is also interesting to note that Jerry was fiercely independent and farsighted. Through the help of his therapist he set out to learn ways to trust the present and move beyond these limiting patterns.

One day Jerry was visiting his best friend's place, where he had been hundreds of times in the past. As he walked in, he noticed a large framed photo on the wall facing the entrance. The image he saw stopped him in his tracks. It was a photo of his friend holding his baby daughter at the time of her birth. It captured the dramatic moment of eye contact and bonding that can happen between newborns and their parents. For Jerry, it was a moment of great revelation. He asked his friend's permission to remove the photo from the wall, then sat down in the nearest chair and stared at it for several minutes.

"This is an incredible picture," Jerry exclaimed. "When did you get it?"

"Why, it's been right there on that same wall for at least seven years," was his friend's bemused reply.

In spite of the fact that Jerry had passed the photo hundreds of times in the past, and in spite of the fact that the photo had always been in clear sight, Jerry had never seen it before. Something within his own mind had prevented him from seeing and experiencing the content of the picture. It was only after his revelation about events around his own birth, and his own lack of bonding, that he was suddenly able to see what had been there all along.

We see from this and similar experiences of our own that when comparing our own eyes to the eye of the camera, there is a whole world of other functions involved with human sight than with the eye of the camera. And so it becomes necessary to look at this difference and to understand which of the functional parts of our eyes are like cameras and which are not. The camera, like our eye, has many components. It is these components working together that determine how the light is distributed to produce a coherent image on film, or on the retina.

The front of your eye; that is, the part you see when looking into a mirror—from the outer transparent covering (the cornea) to the iris and pupil—is the part that you are probably most familiar with. Why? Because you can see it as you stare into the mirror. As you move past the pupil you start to reach into the relatively unknown. It is dark back there. Unless you look through a special instrument called an ophthalmoscope, the back of your eye is invisible. And what you will see at the back of the eye is the orange-red color of the retina.

Most of us associate invisibility with darkness, or at least an inability to perceive what is there. What we are unaware of remains outside the realm of our present consciousness. And so it was for my friend Jerry in the story I just told you. Becoming aware precedes conscious seeing. This is the process of *experiencing the indiscernible*, whereby we open up to possibilities that are not in our immediate field of vision. If we are to enter into conscious seeing, it is necessary to become aware of how light affects us within, as well as what it tells us about what's "out there."

Let us for a moment consider the path by which light travels from outside us to within us. First, light in the form of waves of energy enters the plane of the cornea, which is the outermost part of the eye involved with focusing the light. The iris (opening) and sclera (white of the eye) are the visible structures. Traveling through the pupil, we enter the focusing lens of the human eye. The cornea, iris, sclera, and pupil are visible, while the lens and retina are invisible to the outside eye looking in.

In our everyday lives, we find analogies for the visible and invisible, the light and the dark. During the daylight hours, most of us are awake, visibly *doing* our lives. At night we slow down, becoming more *being* than *doing*, as we prepare for entering the *invisible*, which we encounter when we sleep. While my purpose for these analogies may not be immediately obvious to you, keep them in mind as you read on, paying particular attention to the growing role of the invisible in the evolvement of conscious seeing.

Turn your attention now to the space behind the lens of the eye, where you will find a vitreous jellylike substance and finally the amazing structure of the retina. The retina covers a large surface area at the back of the eye. It has a unique and exquisite nature, quite unlike any other part of the body. Within the retina are 100 million light-receptive structures, known as the *rods* and *cones*. Each one of the photoreceptors is responsible for detecting one particle of the focused or unfocused light. The rods are specifically designed to let us see during darkness, and when we activate them we become aware of the invisible. Camera film cannot do this. If we use film that is fast enough to see in semidarkness, it cannot also capture the imagery that exists in better light. Yet the human eye has one retina that does it all. It's like a multipurpose film, if you will. The cones, as distinct from the rods, function best in light. The cones need light to provide sharp focus and acute sight. There is the highest concentration of cones in one particular area of the retina, known as the *macular* region. In the center valley of the macula is the fovea centralis. It is in this region that our most acute sight is made possible.

In the book *The Eye: Window to the Soul*, the author, Leal Wertenbaker, states:

> Each waking second the eyes send some 1 billion pieces of fresh information to the brain. These fragments of light converge in the mind as images of stunning subtlety. The eyes can sense about 10 million gradations of light and 7 million different shades of color; they are responsible for about 75 percent of all we can perceive.

Imagine a beam of light traveling from the early morning sun. It passes through the cornea to your retina. For help visualizing this, turn to photograph 2 on page 116. The image of the light passing through the eye and the rays that help form a sharp focus illustrate a process of transformation that occurs in the human eye. Light striking the structures of the eye represents an energetic process.

First the visible parts of the eye receive the light. The pupil constricts in the presence of light. This happens because one of the iris muscles, the sphincter, responds to light, and this action causes the iris to get larger. Imagine a round window with light beaming through it; suddenly, the window becomes smaller and smaller, until only a single, narrow shaft of light is coming through.

It is easy to take this reaction to light for granted since we experience it in action nearly every moment of our lives. But this muscular action holds a very important metaphoric message. It takes light to produce this constriction. Light is a form of energy. Energy has the ability to bring about a change in function. When a part of the body changes from one function to another, a transformation results.

> *It is the action of the eye's fire, which reaches out to grasp,*
> *and so to apprehend the world.*
> —ARTHUR ZAJONC,
> *Catching the Light: The Entwined History of Light and Mind*

In the preceding example, the pupil of the human eye becomes smaller. This happens without any thought or effort at control on your part. You don't have to adjust a lever to produce this change, as you would on a camera. An automatic control from your brain brings about this pupillary constriction. The newest, auto-focusing cameras produce a similar action, with a photoelectric eye adjusting the opening behind the lens, adjusting how much light will enter. But it still takes the person operating the camera to make certain adjustments to match the speed of the film.

It has always interested me why the pupil of the human eye becomes smaller. The rays need to light up the macular area in order to bring about sharp sight. The pupil size is set by the iris constricting and dilating muscles.

The cornea, pupil, lens, vitreous fluids, as well as the length of the eyeball, all have an impact on focusing the light as it travels through the various structures. This changing of the focus of light is a process called *refraction*. Light is focused as sharply as possible

7

toward the fovea, and simultaneously light is less focused and scattered throughout the retina. This marvel of visual science, which works with the retinal and foveal distribution of light, is vitally important in understanding the principles of conscious seeing.

Light enters through the small opening of our eye, then flows into the vast darkness of inner space. Imagine there are two areas of space: one outer, one inner. Outer space is what we perceive as existing outside ourselves, beyond the visible portion of our eyes. Our perceptions of the outer world can be likened to watching a movie. While we are viewing the movie it is as if the action is all taking place outside us. However, the content of the movie is affecting us on the inside; within our inner space we are relating to the movie from another point of view. The imagery and sensations we are receiving are mingling with our history, our life experiences, and other variables; it is through what's already in our minds that we interpret and are affected by the light and imagery that come from outside us.

For a moment, think of the darkness inside your eye as invisible space. As light travels from the outside into this darkness, it can demand us to change. What we perceive as being outside us is a transformative energy, and the deeper it goes into the invisible, the greater the impact it will have on us. You might compare this journey of light into the deeper, invisible regions of our being as something akin to traveling into the depths of an uncharted cave or snorkeling around reefs previously unexplored. Either of these adventures will generate energy and excitement. As you go deeper there is more to see. Going below the surface of the outward appearance is called *depth*. And it is here that the invisible becomes known to us.

> *Two lights brighten our world. One is provided by the sun,*
> *but another answers to it — the light of the eye.*
> *Only through their entwining do we see;*
> *lacking either, we are blind.*
> — ZAJONC, *Catching the Light*

The integration of our inner lives comes about when we connect the visible and the invisible. In the movement toward integration, we observe and we sense. The human eye is designed for this form of integrated vision, and this integrative process is what I am calling conscious seeing. It is here where we enter a world, a universe beyond the analogy of the camera's eye, a place where we discover that the eye does much more than process light.

# 2

## *The Eye as a Metaphor*

## The Eye as a Projector

The eye of the camera cannot also be a projector. A projector needs information, such as a transparent slide upon which there is an image, or a video that contains electronically stored information that can be converted to light. The lenses in the projector transmit the information onto a screen where it can be viewed by people outside. In this way, invisible data—from film or electronic files—becomes visible.

Is it possible that the human eye projects something? This question has been posed since the earliest investigations of human psychology and science. And in spite of the fact that it has been shown to be true, there are still some who would never consider the eye to have the ability to project. This is understandable if your only frame of reference is your observation of what is obviously visible, such as we have with the analogy of the camera's eye. But we have begun to explore how and why the eye is much more than a camera. To understand how the human eye can be a projector we must begin using our eyes to see deeper than what is only on the surface, deeper than the obvious external appearance of things. I'll explain in the following.

During my formal training in optometry and visual science, my colleagues and I became skilled in the use of an instrument called a *retinoscope*. This device is comprised of a lens and a sharply focused light that is held in front of a patient's face. While the patient is encouraged to look off into the distance, the physician observes a light reflex from the retina, reflected in the plane of the pupil. We learned this technique to help us measure the refractive condition of a patient's eye, from which we determine the measurements and needs to prescribe corrective glasses.

One day I heard a doctor talking about the reflexes in people's eyes when they think or visualize. This fascinated me. Was it possible that this reflex I was seeing in the eye could be affected by the person's thoughts or feelings? I began asking patients questions while I performed my retinoscopy. I had them look at two or three distances, with varying degrees of focus—from fuzzy, soft focus, to sharply focused—while I measured and recorded what I was seeing. My colleague who reported the changes in reflex was right. The degree of reflex motion and color differences I saw in the retina were dependent on the patient's participation. If the person was trying to see, was unfocused, wasn't concentrating, or changed his or her thought sequences, the retinal reflex changed. If I had the person remember a particularly pleasant event in childhood, the reflex became brighter, with less motion. From this depth I could see that the person's thoughts and feelings were influencing the light presence in his or her eyes. The person's mind and brain interaction was literally dictating the amount of light that was to be projected through the eye.

The visible, physical changes in the eyes have fascinated psychologists for years. By carefully observing, one can see varying emotions displayed through the eyes and surrounding facial structures. Young people have bright eyes. Elders have gray, misty eyes, for example. People who are newly and passionately in love have more vibrant, lively eyes than their less passion-smitten counterparts.

Other evidence to support the idea that the eye can act like a projector has recently surfaced in clinical practice. Patients diagnosed with multiple-personality disorders have been tested via retinoscopy as they pass through different personality states. As you might have guessed, the retinal reflex physically changes from one personality to another. The eye reflects the changes projected by the different personalities. The eye becomes the projected image of the consciousness of the personality behind the eye.

In spite of these clinical findings, some of which have been published in the visual science literature, there are hundreds of thousands of ophthalmologists and optometrists all over the world using retinoscopy on a daily basis who are only seeing their results from a refractive-error perspective. They look through their retinoscope as if they are viewing the surface of the ocean. This is not wrong. They are just missing the depth of possibility. The new paradigm of vision care is to look below the surface, go beyond the obvious, and reveal the unknown. It necessitates putting on goggles and snorkel, and daring to travel into the depths. There is a whole new world waiting to be discovered, demanding a willingness to evolve.

To see with depth we must examine what I call our "constructed" life. To be conscious, to see consciously, demands that we look more deeply into who we think we are. Perhaps this is why it is easier to stay on the surface. If we do not venture too deeply, we needn't face the imagined sharks below. But it may not be the sharks we fear. Perhaps we avoid the depths for fear that we might discover our own magnificence. Is this an illusion? We shall see.

## The Eye as a Printer

By now it is clear that the human eye does not function independently of the brain. The eye can be likened to Mother Earth floating in outer space. She is influenced by the moon, the sun, distant planets, the stars, and celestial phenomena that scientists have only begun to imagine. Even though the eye seems to be somewhat isolated as an external organ, its lifeblood is dependent on the brain. The eye is literally a natural extension of the brain, extending outward and forward—literally a specialized appendage of the brain. The eye is connected to the visual cortex via the optic nerve, emerging from a vibrating, complex assemblage of neurons, similar to a sunflower reaching toward the light of the sun. Healthy functioning of the eye relies upon the nerves and blood supply from the brain. Consider this supply of blood to be a vital energy that is passed down from the brain as food and exercise for the eyes; for it is exactly this.

For a moment turn your attention to the printer that is connected to your computer. It receives its instructions from your computer; likewise your eye receives instructions from your brain and ultimately from your mind. By looking at what comes out of your printer, you can determine the nature of the information in your computer. Similarly, the eye structure—mainly the retina and the conditions of the eye that determine whether one is nearsighted, farsighted, and so forth—can, like the printer, reveal the instructions that are being sent from the brain (computer) to the eye (printer). As a clinician, I have spent thirty years examining eyes and observing how factors beyond what is visible to the human eye have an impact on the quality of a person's vision. In other words, sometimes the visual problem comes from behind the retina, not from in front of it; our sight is the product of the mind, not just the external world and the physical eye.

Once I was convinced that vision problems were not all in the portions of the eye in front of the retina, it didn't make much sense to me to keep diagnosing only what was wrong with the eye—as to whether the person was nearsighted or farsighted, or that they were suffering from some other pathology. Evidence kept mounting that the human eye was like a computer printer, in that it was telling me something about the invisible capacities of vision. It became obvious to me that the conditions I was seeing in the eye were messages from the brain and its life partner, the mind.

Here are some examples from my patients' files that led me to this conjecture: For one patient, increased pressure in the eye (called glaucoma) coincided with the time when the patient's career or family life was loaded with demands and pressures. For another, the diagnosis of cataracts (clouding of vision due to opacification of the lens of the eye) occurred during a time when the patient was confused about the future. The onset of myopia for some patients (difficulty making out small details at a distance) came during times of family disharmony, when the patients were not able to deal with what they were witnessing in the home. A baby's right eye began turning in when his father left the family home. A retinal detachment started in another patient's eye when he became conscious of his "detachment" from his former feelings of love for his spouse.

As I inspected more closely the life circumstances that patients were facing when I discovered their eye irregularities, it became apparent to me that the intimate connection between the eye, brain, and mind needed to be further explored. Other investigators supported this notion. In the earliest writings of behavioral optometry, the founding American clinician, Skeffington, linked his vision findings with the research of Hans Selye, the researcher of human stress and how it affects various organ systems of our bodies. When there are intervening stressors, the reflexive and fast-acting autonomic nervous system makes adjustments for the body to cope with distress. The eyes are one of the many organ systems that are affected. In his clinical teachings, Skeffington showed how optometric measurements of the eyes "print out" these autonomic nervous system changes. For example, when a person is in distress, the focusing of his or her ciliary muscle and lens become sluggish. The ability to maintain attention when reading a book or doing work on a computer screen is diminished, for example. Nearsightedness can develop as a result. A person's ability to maintain effective connections with day-to-day events, and to view his or her life in an integrated, stereoscopic[2] manner, decreases during periods when stress is mismanaged.

In modern primary vision care, eye doctors routinely examine the retina with an ophthalmoscope, a special instrument that enables them to look at the complex structure (the retina) at the back of the

---

[2]As I use the term here, *integrated stereoscopic* refers to viewing our lives not in simplistic, linear terms but in terms that allow us to take into account the many influences that affect how we ourselves, as well as other people, experience our lives.

eye to detect early signs of bodily health problems. Diseases such as hypertension or diabetes, for example, show up quite clearly in the blood vessels and other structures of the retina. The condition of the body, recorded by the brain, prints out the subtle information in the retina of the eye. This is a clear demonstration of the integrative nature of the eye, brain, and mind—that the human organism functions in an integrative manner. This theme is one of the keys of conscious seeing, and I will be expanding upon it in later chapters.

It is not just physicians of the eye who have noticed that the condition of the retina can predict illness in other parts of the body. The system known as "iridology" has quantified the relationships between illness and how it is mirrored in the iris. Many physicians the world over use iridology as part of their diagnostic procedures. Indeed, it is almost as if, with the eye, nature has provided us with this chart, or "printout," of all that is going on in the body.

By extending our *printer/computer* metaphor we can learn a lot about ourselves from information revealed through the eye. I propose that the eye discloses valuable *invisible* information not just about conditions such as hypertension and cardiovascular dysfunctions but about the brain, mind, and human consciousness itself.

At first it may seem that I am walking on thin ice here, between speculation and what has been scientifically established. However, what I describe here comes out of my own as well as many other physicians' clinical research. And here I would like to remind the reader that the visual sciences, which are now well established, came out of what was once viewed by science as "clinicians' crazy notions." In this work on conscious seeing I admit that the following proposals may only be judged by what is visible, real, and possible by today's standards. I happen to be one of those clinicians who has delved more deeply into my observed findings for thirty years, with tens of thousands of patients. By conventional methods this would be considered a good clinical trial. I am taking this opportunity to present my clinical findings, leaving the basic research of my proposals to the visual scientists.

## The Brain: Computer Chip

In today's advanced technological world many of us have experienced the marvels of a computer chip. Information can be programmed and stored in an electronic memory. This memory can then be accessed to perform a variety of functions, such as keeping track of time, remembering appointments, switching on the coffee machine, sending faxes while we are sleeping, and doing complex mathematical computations.

These external examples are metaphors for reflecting on what is possible within the confines of our brain. Wasn't it a human brain and mind that conceived of the idea of a computer chip in the first place? Outside discoveries, such as cellular phones, palm-sized computers, and "game boys" are themselves like computer printouts that provide tangible evidence for our brains' creative capabilities. In the same way the eye can print out what is happening in the brain. My digital video camera reveals immediate images to me, in vibrant color, and guides me in understanding how my brain works. When I take a moment to consciously see what is happening outside of myself, I can more deeply know how my inner workings operate. The brain can be viewed as a landing pad for the arrival of sensory information. As the deeper layers of the brain are penetrated the sensations are more deeply and more idiosyncratically organized. This integration helps the mind make sense out of chaos.

An example comes to mind. Optometrists can create a pair of glasses that will give the wearer the impression that the world is twisted sideways or upward. Light coming into your eyes is shifted by prisms and mirrors. For a while, there is much confusion. Your brain receives these new sensations of light, and, through the millions of interconnecting networks of nerve complexes, the computer chip within your brain attempts to sort out this new information and interpret what exactly is going on. Very soon everything appears quite normal again, and the wearer of these prisms sees the world as he or she always has. To flip the vision of the world right side up, the brain and mind must take into account many more factors than sight alone: factors such as gravity, the coordination of the musculoskeletal system, and the speed and distance between the observer and objects around him.

The outer level of the brain is the surface, like the skin of the body. At this level of the brain, the neocortex, the computer chip, works at an elementary level. Sensations are collected and stored. Instant by instant the electrical and chemical impulses from the eyes and other senses are methodically stored in memory. In the deeper layers of the neocortex the data become more systematically organized. Like the tissue below the surface of the skin, the deeper layers of the brain are increasingly complex, and it is here that the impressions of light are now reorganized into lines and shapes. The initial light becomes more complex images that will later be interpreted by the brain and mind.

The role of the brain is to understand by acquiring visual-motor experiences, that is by correlating visual information with information from the large muscles of the body—your arms and legs— including your response to the pull of gravity, the size and position of your body, and each part of your body's relationship to the whole. What you see is linked to the motor actions of your body, which relate what you are seeing to your physical presence.

## The Mind: Super Software

In our everyday lives, light striking the retina can be likened to a video camera. Streams of images are brought into the brain, where they are structured in a sequence of moving images to coincide with time passing, rather than as a single snapshot from a still camera. Your ability to receive and make sense of this stream of images will in part be determined by your state of mind. For instance, if you are in a state of fear and anxiety, your level of receptivity will be diminished, and with it your ability to make sense of the light will be lessened. This suppression of light we experience while in a state of fear is linked with survival reflexes that have evolved within the nervous system. The brain's capacity for regulating what it is seeing is partly determined by the mind. The human mind will emotionally process the incoming light, and this will help determine how much of the light will be allowed to come in. If you are seeing a situation that activates uncomfortable emotions, perhaps associated with similar experiences from your past, you will likely block some of the incoming impressions. We believe that this is necessary for our survival, for we want to avoid being drawn back into a dangerous or painful situation that we have experienced in the past. When we cross paths with a tiger in the jungle, we don't, for example, stop to study its beautiful stripes or sit down and reflect on our previous experiences of being clawed by a cat as a child; we rally all our forces, start moving our legs, and do our best to make it to safety.

The following story can help deepen your understanding of how you experience light, the eye, the function of your brain and mind, and the evolution of consciousness and sight.

## The Cave Reveals

Sara was a third-year medical student. As part of her course of study she was required to learn about the elaborate workings of the brain. Much of the process involved memorizing names of the various parts of the brain and studying its intricate neural pathways. Sara was fascinated by this information and excelled at her studies. She also enjoyed the heated classroom debates about the role of the mind.

Many of Sara's professors believed that the mind is separate from the brain. Their opinion was that the mind is the domain of psychiatrists, philosophers, and priests. They cautioned that students not pay too much attention to their patients' mental and emotional lives. To be a good doctor, they believed, one need only understand the physical body and know what to do to repair its malfunctions. "Do not become emotionally involved with your patients' problems," was the motto of her professors.

Sara's father, Daved, was an archaeologist, and he invited her on a trip to Israel. He didn't tell her too much about the nature of their journey ahead of time, other than to say they would have an opportunity to spend time together.

During their stay in Israel, Daved took Sara to the site of an archaeological dig. As they walked among remnants of an ancient civilization, Daved pointed to a small hill and told Sara the mound was called a "tell." At first glance, Sara thought it looked like an ordinary "little mountain." As she and her father walked toward the tell, Daved spoke from years of experience, guiding Sara's untrained eyes to notice the shapes of the rocks. He pointed to scooped-out holes in the surfaces of the rocks, and Sara noticed that puddles of rainwater had collected in them. Her father explained that this was where the early settlers of the region had washed their clothes and their cooking materials. Sara realized that she would not have understood the significance of those holes had her father not pointed it out to her.

As she walked, Sara thought about how a tendency to look only at the surface of what we see around us leaves us with a superficial awareness of what life offers. She wondered how this shallow way of seeing the world develops and allowed her mind to travel back to her own experience as a young woman.

Sara's memories took her back to when she was twelve years old, an unhappy time in her life. In fact, the two previous years had been extremely difficult. Her mother, Sophia, had passed away after a long illness. During the time of her mother's illness, Sara's father had dedicated himself to helping his wife enjoy her final years, and Sara, an only child, was left alone much of the time. As a result, she became quite introverted.

Sara remembered spending many unhappy hours alone in her bedroom. She would pull the bedcovers over her head and read with a flashlight for hours. In this way she could bury the pain she felt about her mother's illness and departure. "Why did she leave me when I needed her so much?" she remembered wondering as a young girl. Sara remembered how her way of looking into the world changed. She was no longer interested in what was happening outside of her. Instead, she focused on what was inside her head. Deep in fantasy, in the dreaming and thinking world of her mind, Sara could escape her painful feelings. She devoured books and hardly spoke about her inner world to anyone. It was her secret.

Shortly before her thirteenth birthday Sara put on her first pair of glasses to compensate for nearsightedness and astigmatism.

In her late teens and into her twenties Sara was involved in personal development work, which helped her begin to deal with the emotions she had suppressed. By her early thirties her eyeglass prescription had stabilized. She continued to deal with her outside life by looking through contact lenses. This provided her with clear, projected eyesight. However, her vision as she experienced it in her mind, behind her eyes, remained pretty much as it had been early in her life—the inward perceptions of the young girl buried in her secret world under the blankets. As Sara walked alongside her father among the tells, she realized that she had not changed her inner behavior since she was twelve years old, turning inward to a world of books and fantasy. Moreover, her eyes had matched this behavior by adapting to a way of seeing that mimicked her inward projection: nearsightedness.

For many years, Sara had given her eyes very little thought. She functioned very well with her contact lenses and glasses, and was an excellent premedical student. But recently she had begun to question the relationship between her inner, emotional world and her vision. "What happens to my brain when I look through my contact lenses?" she wondered. "Is it possible that relying on the prescription glasses forces me to look at the world without experiencing the depth of what I am seeing?" Sara wondered if this was why she had looked so shallowly at the rocks her father pointed out. Was this a nearsighted, astigmatic way of seeing? Was it possible to broaden one's way of seeing? Sara's studies had taught her that the brain is highly adaptable, that in many cases the healthy part of the brain would take over functions of a damaged part of the brain, for example, even though it previously had little to do with those functions. Was that true for vision as well? Could the brain change the way she used her eyes?

Sara looked off into the distance, where her eyes feasted on the rich green, fertile valley of the Galilee. She was struck by the contrast between the desert tell and the luscious valley. That day she was not wearing her contact lenses. For a moment, she slipped off her prescription sunglasses. "How do I really see without any glasses?" Sara wondered. The details in the valley were not visible. With her glasses, the –3 diopter lenses had brought those details into clear focus for her. The light rays passing through the prescription lenses were sharply focused and directed to the foveal area in the retinas of her eyes. Her brain recorded that light. Sara remembered that, in the beginning, the light reaching the brain is merely a sensation, a raw impression. Making sense of that raw impression was the function of the brain, like a computer chip, translating and making sense of millions of light sensations. From chaos would emerge meaning. But how was that meaning affected by the prescription lenses that artificially focused the incoming light?

For a while, Sara continued to explore her vision without any lenses before her eyes. Objects close to her were clearer. In the distant valley, details were more like an impressionistic flow of colors. She noticed how the light reaching her eyes from far away, without the influence of her prescription lenses, was a meaningless blur. Clearly, her brain needed some help to learn how to deal with those sensations of light to give meaning to her vision of the distant world. Then, the miracle of knowing what is true outside of her self would become a reality.

Sara reflected on a lecture given by one of her professors, a theoretical researcher in neuroscience. "There is a visual part of the brain," he told his students.

It is the processor of impressions and a portal to other mechanisms in the brain that prime the accumulated sensations of light to migrate to the mind. These sensations are the provider of the necessary elements, ingredients, and components that allow the mind to construct images and thus allow us to have experiences with the content provided by those images.

It was this professor's contention that experience helps mold the intricate relationship between the brain and the mind; and it is the structure of experience in the mind where the "seer" and the "seen" meet.

Sara and Daved walked a little further, until a wall-like structure appeared before them. Daved explained how the rearranged rocks were a reconstruction of part of a village. This unassuming mound of rocks was the covering of what had once been the famous settlement known as Yodfat. As Sara's father directed her through the tell, he was preparing her to look more deeply at the obvious things of life. Sara began to understand that the way we interact with our environment through our eyes can be likened to the structure of the brain. We can look at our world and see only the superficial layer of things. In that way we use only the beginning of the brain's organizing potential. While our lives can work at that level of seeing, we miss the depth of experience that might otherwise be available to us. Sara was about to discover what it was like to experience vision, and her world, at a much deeper level.

Father and daughter stood in front of a half-opened cave. Daved beckoned to Sara, inviting her to enter the mysterious space with him. At first it seemed very dark. Her retinal rods became activated for night vision. Within seconds, the cave seemed to fill with candle-light. The remarkable ability of the eyes to adjust to the dimmer light inspired Sara to respect her vision more. She vowed to become more aware of how her eyes work miracles every moment of every day. This was an important step toward conscious seeing.

As they made their way down into the cave, Sara looked around at the walls. Layer upon layer of colorful and extraordinary fossilized stones had woven themselves into the structure of the wall. She scanned the patterns from the entrance up above and traced the layers downward. Every stone was a piece of history. People had lived in this place. Events had taken place. Ancient wisdom was stored in the organization of this cave. Daved pointed out the paint-like markings on various rocks, and the grooves carved into the stone by time.

Sara flashed back to her eyes and her brain. She knew that the layers of the brain are structured in the same way as history had been scribed on the walls of this cave. Each millimeter of depth in the brain corresponds to an ability to handle a more complex organization of recorded sensations of light. Accessing this deeper organizational level makes it possible to have a deeper experience of what we see. We can go through life never seeing below the surface, or we can go deeper into the brain and take advantage of the rich source of data in the brain's computer chip. When that happens, what we know deep down inside ourselves, what we have gathered from our unique life experience, we can see on the outside as well.

Sara and Daved walked deeper into the cave. The rods in their eyes struggled to adjust to the ever-diminishing light. The passageway narrowed. The smell of the cave had its own record of time. Daved led Sara by holding her hand. Soon they entered a deeper cave. From high up in the roof a beam of light penetrated the darkness. Sara looked up to see a small, partially covered opening where the sunlight was streaming through. Once again, they were able to make out the details of the cave.

The combination of the smells of the cave and her own excitement caused Sara to feel dizzy. She took off her glasses and relaxed into the blurriness. She breathed deeply. Sitting down on a flat rock, she motioned her father to join her. Meanwhile, her dizziness persisted and the walls of the cave appeared to be moving. The sensation was like riding in a car speeding out of control. She lay back on the cave floor, rolling her sweater to make a pillow for her head. Her father lay down next to her. Sara let out a long, relaxing sigh. A stillness settled in around them. After having her eyes closed for a minute, Sara again looked around at the cave. She could feel herself being transported in time. Hundreds of years passed by.

Sara placed her hands flat on the floor, holding on as if she were riding in that speeding car. Questions floated through her mind. "Where am I going? What is happening?" The outer stillness comforted her. She remained relaxed and let her thoughts go, allowing herself to flow into the experience.

She turned her head toward her father. A tremor moved through her body. The man next to her was not her father, but someone with long hair and a long beard. Flowing strands of hair curled from his temples, down alongside his cheeks in front of his ears. His magnetic eyes pulled her awareness to him. His voice spoke in a strange English dialect. Sara was enraptured.

"Look up to the opening of the cave," the strange man instructed her. Without questioning, as though in a trance, Sara turned her attention to the narrow opening up above.

"Listen to my voice. Do not speak or ask questions. You are here to be transformed. You are consciousness ... listen ... look ... be present and you will be conscious. Then real seeing will be yours."

## The Pathway of Vision

Sara entered a deeper state of inner awareness. A space inside her chest awakened. She breathed deeply and entered that space. Now it was as if she were inside her own eyes looking out. The small opening of the cave was the pupil of her eye. Sara was inside the cave, inside her eye, looking out. It took a moment for her to realize the significance of what was happening. An echo of the man's strange voice resonated from the walls of the cave, drawing on the energy of the rocks and the wisdom of the cave's consciousness.

"Conscious seeing is to *be* your eyes," uttered what now appeared to Sara to be the voice of the cave. She felt as though she were sitting at the back of her eye, observing the sunlight streaming in. She was inside her left eye. A beam of light was bending its way toward her point of observation. She was seated in the center of her retina, in the fovea. From this position she was able to focus directly on the light beam. She breathed a deep breath and let the light in. Sara entered a part of her awareness where she held a deep understanding, where she was able to access universal knowledge. Thinking was easy. There was a logical order to events. There was an orderly flow of clear, precise thoughts.

Sara noticed there was also light off to the right, in her peripheral vision, filling the retina of her left eye. The light striking the outside part of the retina seemed to stimulate the thinking part of her nature. She took in this light, closed her eyes, and breathed more deeply.

With open eyes Sara became aware of the light streaming in from the left of where her eyes were focused. This triggered a surge of emotion. A sense of space opened inside her body. She felt free. Time melted away.

The strange voice spoke again. "Each pulse of light reaching your eye carries a message of universal consciousness. The light pulses are part of divine creation. Light awakens seeing. Stay present and you will see more."

Sara shuddered at the sound of the voice. What had happened to her father? She was about to call out his name when the whole cave filled with what seemed like an explosion of light. Sara remembered her father holding her hand at a fireworks show when she was a little girl. In her memory, she flashed back to an image of him standing on her right. Her mother was holding her left hand. She felt her own words somewhere in the back of her mind. "I feel unified in the presence of both my parents' love." Sara kept this image alive as if it were an afterimage lingering on her retina.

The cave seemed to be moving now. It felt as though she were being transported to a deeper part of her left eye, the eye she was sitting in. Sara opened her eyes for a brief moment. There, off to the right, she realized that her father was sitting inside her right eye. He waved at her, sending her a welcoming greeting.

The cave voice echoed once again. "You hold within you the memory of integration, of the union of your parents. Merge your left eye with your right eye in a divine marriage. This will prepare you to travel to the deepest level of your wholeness. You will become your true nature."

"How is all this possible?" Sara asked herself. "I visit a cave in Israel and it is speaking to me! No, it is my father playing tricks on me. He did that when I was a little girl. It must be the air I am breathing. It is like a drug and I am hallucinating. Is this safe? I'd better see if Dad is all right."

She reached toward her father, and as she felt his hand the light in the cave became brighter. She heard a rushing sound, and felt like she was back in the speeding car, out of control, moving backward very fast.

Sara traveled down her optic nerve through a series of tunnels, carried by a cocoon of light. Again the cave spoke to her:

> You are light. Master how to receive light without reaction. Flow with incoming light like water moving in a river. Each light image reaching your eye is competing for recognition. It is your mind that will later give each of them meaning. Be present with the light. Your hundreds of millions of rods and cones are sensitively detecting the fragments of image focused by your cornea and lens. It is this electrical chemical signal that is carrying the visual information. Stay with the light as long as you can. Each step in your journey gives you the possibility of transforming yourself further. The light traveling through your eye is undergoing the same transformation. As the light signal travels further and further along the visual pathway toward the visual cortex, the information increases in complexity. Integration takes place in preparation for your mind to make sense of the signals. More potential for understanding and wholeness becomes available.

## Construction of the Mind

The voice stopped. There was silence. Sara felt as though she were rolling and turning. She was in an invisible space like a black hole of outer space, a vacuum. She was inside the cavity of her own mind. She was aware of so much and, at the same time, Sara was *inside* her awareness. She was there, at that place in the mind where the experiences arising from the light signals and their images are organized and content arises. With more life experience, this content generates boundaries and the boundaries solidify as objects. As the mind reorganizes these objects again and again, the mind starts generating meaning. Sara realized that the mind is the organizer of her brain. She sensed that she was in a part of her mind that gives rise to the meaning of her personal, professional, and community life.

In the next moment Sara opened her eyes and was back in the cave. She remembered everything clearly. Her father was next to her, in the same position as the right eye in her journey. Sara recalled that the images from each eye unite more and more, the further into the brain and mind one travels. Daved moved toward Sara and hugged her. He looked at her with knowing eyes. He had experienced what Sara had just gone through. They both knew that all was well and that it was time to leave the cave. They walked to the entrance and sat down on the wall, and talked for hours about their experience.

## Expanding Consciousness

> *Your brain is a data processor.*
> *It tells you what it perceives, not what it really is.*
> —NEAL DONALD WALSCH, *Conversations with God*

In conscious seeing, as Sara experienced in the above story, the question arises, Where did her expanded vision occur? Was it in the brain, the mind, or even beyond? If it occurred in the brain, how could she have perceived what she did from a vantage point that was not the same as the location of her physical body? We have to ask, Is human perception limited to that small mass of gray matter we call the brain that resides inside our skulls? Are the brain and the mind the same thing? And where does consciousness itself come from? These are points of great interest to scientists, transpersonal psychologists, and shamans, as well as philosophers.

It is my intention to present a sampling of the necessary facts and provide my personal and clinical findings to let you have your own experience and draw your own conclusions regarding these matters. Given the space constraints of this book and its specific focus on eyesight, we can't go into exhaustive detail about the nature of human consciousness. But since conscious seeing involves the transcendent potentials of human consciousness, it is necessary for us to explore this fascinating aspect of the human experience enough to show its relationship to achieving better vision. If the topic of the brain/mind and human consciousness stirs your interest, I encourage you to explore other books on the topic, which I've listed in the back of this book.

There is a new frontier of science that involves investigating human consciousness. This has come about, in part, because biological research as well as the neurosciences have been able to unravel so many of life's secrets. For approximately the past 100 years, as we have attempted to apply the mechanical model to explain human existence, scientists have attempted to explain the human mind in terms of chemical and electromagnetic events occurring inside the hunk of tissue that is housed inside our skulls. However, while scientists and medical researchers have been able to make much progress in terms of understanding the nervous system, they have failed with this approach to explain human consciousness.

The most advanced consciousness research suggests that the physical brain structure, as we know it, is probably part of a vast, nonphysical phenomenon that is generally called the mind. The mind harbors complex thoughts, feelings, and emotions. The mind is where sensory input from our eyes, ears, nose, tongue, and skin contributes to these functions. All of this information comes together when we are able to recognize a person's face, which in turn sets in motion feelings and emotions we may associate with that face. Moreover, we can probe our minds and, with the aid of new electronic instruments, measure activity occurring within our brains when we are experiencing certain thoughts, feelings, and emotions. However, it is our consciousness interacting with activities—like seeing a familiar face—that permits these measurable events to even occur. Without our participation these mental functions within the brain would simply not exist. If we subtract our interaction with the world around us, the brain is nothing more than a physical mass of intertwining sausage.

Exploring vision requires much more of us than simply measuring the physical structure of the eye. Much more is involved with our vision. Human consciousness itself is involved, and that means that a strictly mechanical approach to vision is tantamount to explaining the entire experience of being human in terms of chemical and electromagnetic events in our brains. Deeper vision involves considering the whole person, each with his or her own unique blueprint of consciousness. Indeed, conscious seeing involves much more than the manner in which light comes into our eyes. Conscious seeing requires us to develop a deeper understanding of what I call the *mind's eye*. While part of the mind's eye involves the brain, we can move beyond the brain, into the vision of human consciousness that exists outside any measurable time or space. Consciousness embraces the self but allows us to experience our identity within the larger universe, and all of this impacts our mind's eye. Over time these outer reaches of consciousness can change the shape and condition of the physical eye, what I refer to as the camera eye, which acts as the printer of the brain, giving us a clear readout of our total life experience.

Through the mind's eye there are unlimited invisible influences that affect your vision. Here in a place that many would describe as "intangible," seeing is a sense, like intuition or love, a level of vibration and changing energy that eludes rational explanation. And so it is here that we cultivate conscious seeing. It is here that you can discover how your personal consciousness is able to direct your outer vision.

Many consciousness researchers have noted that the mind is observable only by its owner. An outside observer simply cannot know what is possible within the scope of another person's mind. However, in the field of transpersonal psychology, which considers human experience beyond our mechanical model of consciousness and the universe, demonstrates that experiences like Sara's not only occur but that they are real. Moreover, in this field of study, we prove beyond a shadow of a doubt that human consciousness extends beyond physical boundaries. Stanislav Grof, M.D., author of *The Holotropic Mind: The Three Levels of Human Consciousness and How They Shape Our Lives*, is one of the leading researchers and proponents of this discipline. He states: "We are not just highly evolved animals with biological computers embedded inside our skulls; we are also fields of consciousness without limits, transcending time, space, matter, and linear causality...." He further points out that "the world we create from our personal mythology and sensory data, what we call our 'inner world,' is a mere stepchild of that infinite consciousness."

In the chapters ahead we will be exploring the many ways in which your vision is more than what is happening inside your eyes and head. Your journey will lead you much deeper. We'll be learning how our individual consciousness can put us in touch not only with our immediate environment and with parts of our own past but also with events that are quite beyond the reach of our physical senses. Indeed, human consciousness, and the mind's eye, can give us glimpses of regions beyond our physical location, even into other historical eras, into nature, and into the vastness of the cosmos itself.

Sara's experience gives you a hint of the depth of this form of seeing. There are more stories and practices ahead that will allow you to experience firsthand that your vision is much more than what is processed by your camera eye. You are going to step beyond what you thought was consciousness, to move into a realm described nearly a hundred years ago by world-renowned philosopher William James: "Our normal waking consciousness, rational consciousness as we call it, is but one special type of consciousness, whilst all about it, parted from it by the filmiest of screens, there lie potential forms of consciousness entirely different..." Conscious seeing can be your way of entering this deeper realm of seeing, living, and being your self.

## Exercise

Spend at least five minutes a day for a month or more gazing at photograph 3 on page 117. Experience the light in your eye and around you, as Sara did. Read her story for twenty-one days so you can better imagine and then replicate the experience of being an observer and being touched by all levels of consciousness. In doing so, you are preparing the way for your conscious seeing.

# 3

## *Seeing, Not Looking*

## Looking: The Logic of Thinking and Doing

Your first understanding of vision may have been similar to mine. Like most people, you may think of vision simply as the way your eyes function; that is, what allows you to see. We take vision for granted in this way, adopting the belief that the images we perceive in our brains are exact replicas of what we are looking at in the external world. If the images appear blurred we think no further than to assume something is wrong with our eyes. At the level of mainstream conventional eye care, this simplistic approach to vision is generally adequate. If your eyes no longer allow you to see clearly you visit the eye doctor, who helps you by giving you a prescription for glasses, or provides medication or surgery. However, conscious seeing means stepping beyond this narrowly defined approach of eye care to broaden the scope of your vision.

Long ago, in the days when we humans hunted for our food, most of us had to maintain our sharp vision as part of being good hunters. The ability to see our prey far in the distance was the mark of the good hunter and a considerable asset in the matter of survival. In the modern world we obviously don't require this level of visual acuity, and as a culture we have lost the skills that our distant ancestors may have once possessed. However, there is no reason that we can't reclaim this capacity.

I call the skill of maintaining sharp eyesight, which is part of conscious seeing, *looking*—and I distinguish looking from *seeing*. When we direct clear vision through the fovea centralis (the central valley of the macular area of the retina) then we are *good lookers*.[3] Our vision is focused on what is close at hand.

What is the difference between looking and seeing? Seeing is triggered by the light impulses that reach the peripheral retina. In doing so, seeing is not about clarity and sharpness so much as it is about stimulating those parts of consciousness we refer to as intuition, "sensing," and creativity. To see is to have feelings about what we are perceiving, not merely to register the presence or absence of an object or person. Seeing is an active process, one that calls upon the participation of the seer on many different levels. This is the process that Alfred North Whitehead was referring to in the beginning of chapter 1, where he speaks of what the excellency of the human mind brings to the dullness of nature. In order to practice conscious seeing we need to link looking with seeing. This is what I referred to as "integrated vision" in my earlier book, *The Power Behind Your Eyes*, referring to the process of being able to clearly see the object before us while being aware of what we are bringing to our perception of that object through our thoughts and feelings. As easy as it may sound, integrating looking and seeing is a complex process that calls for deep self-awareness.

Imagine for a moment how you would function if you did not integrate looking and seeing. For example, if you are an *over-looker*—that is, a person who spends more time looking than seeing—you

---

[3]As a side note, the saying "looking good" fascinates me. Maintaining the image of "looking good" has become a cultural theme propagated by the clothes, fitness, and cosmetics industries. Is this simply a marketing ploy that preys on feelings of inadequacy? Or is it based on a genuine belief that we are not good enough unless we wear certain clothes, use a particular kind of makeup, have a body that's shaped a certain way, or drive a particular kind of vehicle? Is this a reason for the current trend to have refractive laser surgery to avoid wearing glasses? Think about how much your own self-image is influenced by external factors. We'll explore these questions in more detail later, in our discussion of the evolution of refractive eye problems.

rely more on foveal vision. The over-looker focuses his or her attention on developing a rational, logical, and analytical way of perceiving the world. *Looking* generally leads to a "doing" of one's life, with a focus on accomplishment and achievement—getting things done. You are busy with your perspective on life and the world around you organized around looking and everything associated with this way of seeing. This is a good quality to have while building a career or a house, when there are details that need focused attention. Precision, attention to detail, and the ability to concentrate are imperative under such circumstances. But what happens to your quality of life when looking and doing are exaggerated, that is, when you start living only as an over-looker?

Examine your life from these two perspectives. First, take your job or career and call this your professional life. Let the rest of your life represent your personal life. Assume that you are awake for about sixteen hours each day. Determine how many hours you devote to your professional life and how many you spend in your personal life. Then observe how much of your sixteen-hour day is spent in a *looking-doing* mode. How much of your life is spent looking rather than seeing? Here are some good indications that you are spending an inordinate amount of time as a looker:

You leap from bed at the last possible minute.
You find bathroom activities such as showering unpleasant because your mind is engaged in excessive thinking.
You eat breakfast on the run.
You meet with other people but feel an absence of a fulfilling connection.
Your work life and projects seem to be perpetually running through your mind.
You miss lunch, or eat quickly, because you are too busy.
At night you are exhausted and wish to escape by watching television or reading.
You escape into your computer.
Your body always seems tired.

You don't seem motivated to exercise, or you are excessively fanatical about physical fitness.

An over-looking lifestyle can also mean that you have given your professional life a higher priority than your personal life. You may be successful in your professional life while your personal life seems unfulfilled. The opposite can also be true. You can give so much focused attention to your personal life that your career and work life may lag behind.

In my case, my career and profession always took precedence over my personal life. I was definitely operating in the looking mode. It wasn't until I reached my mid-thirties, at the pinnacle of my doing and looking life as a successful doctor and university professor, that I realized I felt incomplete in my personal life. I had written many papers and published a book. But I lacked real presence in my role as a father. My marriage seemed tedious. I wasn't pursuing my love for photography. I was *doing* my life — looking too much at my career and not seeing or feeling inside myself. A *seer* I was definitely not. My vision was too narrowly and sharply focused as I struggled to gain a secure place in the world for my fragile self-esteem.

Once I became aware of the imbalance between looking and seeing, I began to take steps to change things, to move toward seeing, that is, toward the sensing, intuitive, and creative. I then began to notice the neglected places inside myself. To my amazement I discovered many areas within me that needed at least as much attention as I had been giving to my outer life. I began to look more attentively at my personal life. I spent more time with my children. I set aside moments to visually connect with my partner. I practiced talking about my feelings and getting to know them. I began to notice myself observing, being, and seeing rather than always being caught up in my doing life.

To *see too much* would imply a lack of focus. If you are an *over-seer* rather than an over-looker you might find it difficult to pay attention to one task at a time, to finish reading a book or balance your bank statement, for example. Seeing is being. In our seeing-being mode we move about, taking it all in, and thus we tend to occupy a broader area in space than we did as a looker. If you spend too much time in your seeing mode you may appear a little forgetful or "spacey." Seeing is creative and involves being. There are many people, myself included, who have excellent eyesight, who feel overwhelmed by how much they see. To be overwhelmed is to be unable to focus on one thing long enough to accomplish all but the simplest of tasks.

Many children cannot read effectively because they are seers, who have difficulty harnessing their ability to look. Instead, they use their ability to see almost exclusively. Their attention is scattered everywhere rather than focused on the written page or on their teacher. Parents of these children often find it difficult to hold the youngsters' attention for more than a minute or two. Such children are also given Ritalin and diagnosed with Attention Deficit Disorder. As these children get older, they may have trouble completing projects they start. They may also have difficulty fitting in socially.

Our society tends to reward lookers for their special abilities of being able to focus sharply and follow through on tasks they start. This is the stuff of which high achievers are made. A visual style in which looking is dominant tends to be associated with accomplishment. In the business world, accomplishments usually translate into promotions, earning more money, and realizing more success. These are highly coveted rewards in our culture. By contrast, seeing is the domain of artists, musicians, and people who live on the fringe, those who are tolerated but who don't quite fit into our achievement-oriented society.

Seeing is an intuitive skill that can be very useful when combined with looking. Einstein, for example, was a person who could focus his attention very sharply and maintain that sharp focus for days and even weeks on end. But he was also a seer, one whose imagination, creativity, and intuition are still celebrated in the world of science. This balance between looking and seeing is the aim of conscious seeing—to integrate both components of vision. But, you may ask, if integrated vision is most desirable, why would anyone let looking become dominant over seeing? Why have we become a world culture of lookers? Why and where did this begin? These are important questions to ask since they lead to making new choices about how we live our lives.

Examine your own life. Do you have a vision problem that might indicate an imbalance in the direction of too much looking? Or are you equally balanced between looking and seeing? If you are out of balance, how can you find more time for seeing, that is, for simply being?

## Socialized Myopia (Nearsightedness): The Cultural Tendency toward "Over-Looking"

Robert Kellum, in his 1996 Ph.D. thesis for the University of New York in Binghamton, talks about "Capitalism and the Eye." He makes the point that humans have historically relied upon peripheral vision for their survival. They ventured out into the world to hunt for food or to grow it. This is an outer-directed viewpoint. "This social system was a structure of self-empowerment," writes Kellum. In visual science terms, this way of looking is *farsightedness*, that is, seeing distant objects more easily than objects close up. Kellum claims that over the course of the past 700 years there has been a shift in how we view the world, a movement from the outward, farsighted view to a decidedly inward-focused view. Paralleling this perceptual shift was a biological one. Kellum states, "As the viewpoint becomes inward directed toward the 'self' and the body, so nearsighted perceptions appear in the mind. The thinking becomes self-centered. One's body is now the limit of the 'outer' focus. The eyes begin to be used in near-centered tasks. This is the consciousness of nearsightedness, to see as if the world exists nearby." From this we can draw parallels between nearsightedness and our increasingly "me-centered" society, where we lose the perspective of the hunter-gatherer, for example, whose farsightedness included an understanding of his relationship to his family or tribe and his dependence on the resources, such as animals and plants, that nature provided.

38

The nearsighted way of perceiving began to appear when commerce developed and money was first used as a means of exchange for food and goods. No longer having to hunt—using our farsightedness—we now focused close at hand, for example, at the food and goods displayed on a table or on the ground right in front of us, on the person we were negotiating with to buy the items offered, or on the money passing from one hand to another. Prior to that time people's vision was geared toward growing or gathering food, or hunting for animals for food, thus being intimately involved with the environment, being part of a community, observing the seasons, and seeing the big picture, whether that meant the vast landscape before them or the social interactions that maintained a healthy community. Farsighted people were more connected to nature, more accustomed to flowing with the seasons. Seeing was a part of a lifestyle in which people worked hard and took time to appreciate the natural beauty of their surroundings. The family and community took precedence over achievement. Seeing gave people the chance to feel they were part of life on a large scale. Looking was in balance with seeing.

We begin to see, then, how the ways we use our eyes have consequences that extend quite beyond the matter of how clearly you can focus on the words you are reading on this page, for example. Our daily activities determine, in part, how we use our eyes: The hunter needs to have excellent farsightedness, while the physician or engineer requires excellent nearsightedness. Linked to this, an entire culture will organize their predominant lifestyle around activities that are nearsighted or farsighted, the use of the eyes literally helping to shape the consciousness of that society. As long as individuals adhere to that way of using their eyes, they also limit the development of their consciousness. But it is possible to both function well within the society and not allow those activities through which you are rewarded to limit your inner development. And that, of course, is the challenge of this book.

Let's explore these concepts and put them to the test. Back in the days when trading and commerce were first developing, this new way of life brought about a perceptual shift, promoting a "we-they" way of viewing the world. How exactly did this work? Think of there being two camps of people: "we" who were hungry, and "they" who had control of the food to satisfy our needs. Using money as a medium of exchange shifted the focus away from the large natural environment which everyone shared, away from the community, which provided mutual support and the big picture, which was a sense of how all the pieces of the world, including people, sky, and other planets, worked together and had to be honored. What developed was a more individual, self-oriented viewpoint, where individual competition took precedence over community, nature, and the big picture. As Kellum states, "This led to a restructuring of the brain and mind."

Prior to this time, people were living in "relatively isolated and loosely connected groups." As trade and mercantilism expanded, people from diverse regions were brought together. With this global integration we began to notice, in Kellum's words, a "greater reliance upon highly concentrated interconnected neural cells involving foveal vision." This was the beginning of the imbalanced emphasis away from seeing, with the focus now very much on looking.

With greater value placed on looking, the width of the picture people saw in their minds began to shrink. This perceptual constriction meant that people began to do less and less seeing. At the same time, the role of metaphysics and spiritual healing as cultural norms began to be replaced by physics and medicine of the physical realm, which are focused and concentrated on a very narrow field. The importance of intuition was eclipsed by cognitive reasoning. Suddenly, if an idea could not be proven scientifically it was thought to be worthy of little respect or value. Native witchcraft and ancient shamanic practices, which epitomized seeing, were deemed primitive and without merit. They depended on farsightedness, on seeing the big picture, whereas this new way of being was nearsighted and focused on a narrow field of vision directly in front of us.

With the emergence of this physical, cognitive orientation, doctors were trained to find only the physical reasons for eye problems.

If a person was naturally farsighted but needed to do nearsighted activities to make a living in his society, that person was fitted with prescription lenses to "correct" the "problem." The eye was treated as an isolated entity, separate from the whole person. No thought was given to the fact that how we see shapes our consciousness. One hundred years ago eye doctors still considered it likely that near-sightedness was related to eyestrain and improper use of the eyes. The ophthalmologic literature cites exercises that were prescribed by physicians to relax the tension in their patients' eyes. In fact, it was not at all fashionable to wear glasses in the beginning of the twenti-eth century. In those days, someone who wore eyeglasses was simply not "looking good."

Kellum, in his dissertation, reminds us that in 1936 the Better Vision Institute was formed with the help of frame and lens manu-facturers, wholesalers, dispensing opticians, and optometrists. He tells us:

> This organization was to promote how "cool" and conscious it was to wear glasses. The idea was to promote a program of "eye con-sciousness." Endorsements from celebrities, safety posters, cou-pled with radio broadcasts, helped the public get over the prejudice of wearing glasses. At the time a book called *Be Beautiful in Glasses* was written. As this indoctrination was estab-lished, the consumer became aligned with the association of the wearing of glasses as being seen as more intellectual.

Kellum's proposition holds that the social consciousness of the time we live in molds and shapes physiology and how our eyes func-tion. The way we think, and the way we operate in the world, will affect the way we see. Our perceptions determine how we structure our lives. Kellum suggests that

> the eye responds to how we live. Living in an asleep state creates a certain vibratory pattern. This "life" waveform first appears at the quantum level of space known as the mind. Communication of

the practiced thoughts and feelings instructs the brain to program
the body to behave in a predictable way. How conscious or unconscious we behave is directed from the mind.

The body, mind, and brain function as integrated parts of the whole
human being. The body expresses messages that originate in the mind
or in the brain, and in turn receives input from the outside world to
be interpreted by the brain and used by the mind. Consider the words
in this book. Through my body I was able to express in writing observations I'd received through my brain and mind. In turn, you read
the words, interpret them with your brain, and if we were to meet, the
two of us might then have a "meeting of the minds," sharing thoughts,
ideas, and feelings about this content. When there is conscious intent,
the mind can even instruct the body to alter the functioning of the
brain. The eyes are a direct entryway into the consciousness of
the brain and ultimately the mind. Information can be delivered
through the eyes and stored in the mind like new software; with it
we can change the way we think, the way we see, and the way we live.

As we examine centuries of social history we see a transition
from a seeing, outer-directed orientation toward one that emphasizes
looking, with its inward, close-up focus. As a result of this transition,
Kellum writes, "we lost something of consciousness. As we moved
more inward our bodies became the center of our focus. This led to
a disintegration of our seeing the relationship of ourselves to the
outer world."

As a result of this shift toward looking and its logical, cognitive
perspective, the medical profession became more physical and
pragmatic in dealing with medical issues, including eye problems.
The deeper "seeing consciousness," which held an intuitive understanding of the reasons for an increase in nearsightedness, was
replaced with a physiological explanation based on the refractive
capacities of the eye. This explanation made perfect sense from a
looking perspective.

Today there are more than 70 million nearsighted people in
North America. This rampant eye disease is forcing people to reex-

amine their habits with regard to vision and their excessive orientation toward looking. As a world culture we are adopting a myopic viewpoint and overemphasizing inward behavior, ever more acutely focused on the self. Are these adaptations an attempt to discover something from within, that is by looking inward rather than outward? By practicing conscious seeing, which requires us to pay attention and be aware of the big picture, we can begin to find the answer. Rather than remaining in an over-looking mode, we can attain fully integrated vision by practicing conscious seeing as part of our regular vision habits. We can learn to see what is visible as well as what is invisible. Paul Gauguin, the expressionistic painter, described it well when he said, "I close my eyes in order to see." As we change our vision habits, so, too, do we change our perceptions of our lives and the world around us. We become more aware, more conscious, and, at the same time, learn to integrate our thoughts with our feelings.

## Thoughts, Blur, and Unconsciousness:
## A State of Disintegration

A great deal of research has been done in an effort to understand the structures and processes that are necessary for vision. What is obvious is that each eye feeds specific information through the visual pathways to the two sides of the brain. The further the light impressions travel back into the layers of the brain, the more our visual perceptions become integrated with our understanding of ourselves and the world around us. Our visual anatomy and physiology are constructed in such a way as to facilitate this process of integration. The ability to fully integrate our awareness of our surroundings with an awareness of self is unquestionably a desired state. This integrative process is the basis for oneness, for wholeness, for a feeling of being connected to all the parts of one's self. In a state of integration we are able to reach beyond ourselves and connect consciously with the world through our senses. In the case of vision, we are better able to discern reality through the eyes. The more we know ourselves inside the more our eyes reveal the truth of what we perceive. You are able to discern the difference, for example, between the objective material you are receiving through your eyes and the thoughts and feelings you may be associating with that material through your mind.

The combination of looking and seeing is used to construct our vision of ourselves during our formative years. This also translates well to the way we see outside ourselves—to the formation of our individualized perceptions of the world. Light travels into each eye. As light travels into each eye, the visual system harmonizes the looking and seeing from each of our two eyes, allowing us to perceive that information as a unified image. In scientific terms we call this "fusion." The information from the left eye and the right eye fuses and blends. When this happens the result is greater than simply adding one piece of information to another. One plus one no longer adds up to two. More than likely, the end result of fusion is three or even five. Fusion provides our awareness of an image with a sense of wholeness, which is much bigger than the sum of its individual parts. The process of fusion is comparable to a good relationship. Two well-adjusted people get together and combine their talents and skills. The combination results in a state of being that is much richer than either person would have standing alone.

One of the assets of integration and fusion is stereoscopic depth perception, that is, seeing in three-dimensions rather than just seeing a flat surface. In purely physical terms, this is important for perceiving and judging distance, a way of seeing that is particularly obvious when you drive your car or participate in sports.

In conscious seeing we study this perception of depth from the inside; we explore the level at which it is occurring in our minds. Seeing with depth allows us to experience our own knowing and how that knowing is linked to everything outside us. This whole process of becoming aware of the inner workings of our minds and how it affects and is affected by the external world is what we generally refer to as "consciousness."

Let's return to our earlier question about why looking has become such an overused phenomenon in our culture. Usually when we exaggerate a behavior, such as looking, it is because we are lacking in some skill related to that behavior. My research reveals that over-looking is an attempt to compensate for a lack of seeing skills. What is lacking? If you cannot access your foveal vision, then your eyesight without eyeglasses—what I call naked vision—is unclear. The images you perceive are blurred. When your vision of the outside world is blurred, it may be that you have not focused accurately and clearly on one aspect of your inner nature. Let's explore this concept one step at a time: The blur you experience is not just a matter of the lens of the eye malfunctioning but is often found to be related to an unresolved emotional issue in your life. If you don't address the inner blur, then it's likely you will continue to mirror that blur in your view of the outside world. Your looking may be out of balance with your seeing. If you wear eyeglasses in an effort to correct the blur, the over emphasis on looking is likely to be even more exaggerated.

If you are over-looking visually, chances are quite good that you are also overlooking your feelings. When you block your feelings a part of you becomes unconscious. That part of you is an important element of your true nature that needs to wake up. Often this over-looked element is related to a part of your history in which you were emotionally wounded. At the time this early wounding occurred, you may not have been intellectually skilled enough or emotionally prepared to deal with the intensity of what was happening. As a result, you may have had to block those troubling events from your conscious awareness in order to go on with your life.

In his book *Of Two Minds*, Frederic Schiffer, a psychiatrist on the faculty of Harvard Medical School, describes how "each side of our brain possesses an autonomous, distinct personality with its own set of memories, motivations and behaviors." A troubling memory may be held in a small area of one hemisphere of the brain. In our everyday, nonfeeling state, the trauma may remain dormant and unseen, rather like the blur we discussed earlier. Schiffer helps his patients awaken and release the memories of these past traumas by using a special form of visual stimulation employing goggles with various forms of patching while the eyes remain partially covered. As a result, the patients often experience a greater sense of well-being.

Some time ago I conducted a study of nearsighted patients who were accustomed to wearing corrective eyeglasses. I measured the degree of fusion ("integration") between the two eyes while the patients were wearing their prescription lenses. The lenses that gave them excellent visual acuity, as measured on the eye chart, actually interfered with the fusion. Compensating for the blur with a lens caused the two foveae to behave as an unhappy couple, "disintegrating" the partnership that might have otherwise allowed them to perceive stereoscopically. The lenses created a fight between the two foveae. Focusing the light sharply on each fovea actually seemed to prevent the two eyes from working together, inhibiting their natural tendency toward integration. Why? I didn't understand the reason until several years later.

When light enters a normal, healthy, naked eye, a portion of it is focused on the fovea while a more diffuse portion of it bathes the retina. However, when light enters the eye through eyeglasses, the artificial lenses focus it very sharply on the fovea—for looking—and dramatically reduce the amount of light that reaches the retina for seeing. As the sharply focused light stimulates the fovea, it also stimulates a particular part of the mind that is the home of thoughts—the content of your active daily life. But with little light reaching the retina, that part of the brain where feelings reside remains dormant. In the presence of eyeglass-focused light, retinal stimulation is suppressed, feelings are kept buried, and thoughts reign supreme.

To be stuck in our thoughts, lacking feeling, or to blur our awareness of our feelings, is to live our lives unconsciously. Wearing eyeglass lenses creates a false clarity, covering over the blurs of our inner lives. Just as surely as a mask hides the true emotions expressed in the face of its wearer, so the lenses of the eyeglasses produce the illusion that the blurs of our inner lives are not present. As the blurred vision is "corrected" by the lenses, our minds accept the illusion of clarity. The end result in terms of our actual inner experience is the absence of feeling. Contrariwise, if we pay attention to the blur, the blur itself can guide us inward, so that we may at last see and know the unseen. Retinal seeing challenges us to acknowledge our potential for seeing into the spirit of matter. The spirit of life, the invisible forces of creation, spring into view when we liberate ourselves from the domination of looking.

Thoughts and foveal looking are like twin sisters who both love to question and "understand" everything. When we cannot extract information clearly from the world, we seek answers within, abandoning the big picture and our intuitive sense of the world. This is called thinking, which is an ideal way not to remember or see painful experiences that are harbored in the blurs of our consciousness. In the final analysis, foveal looking turns out to be something like standing on a high hill and peering through a telescope that has a very narrow field of vision; we sharply focus on a single crow perched on a tree branch in the distance and are awed by being able to see it so clearly that we could nearly count its feathers. Meanwhile, we fail to see all that surrounds the crow. The blur of villages, trees, animals grazing in the fields, the hills, housetops, and people working in the fields are all lost to us. We see only the crow and are tricked into believing that's all there is.

## Seeing, the Art of Feeling

Newborn babies see. They also feel. In fact, fetuses begin to experience emotions while still in the womb. The growing fetus is fully cognizant of the sounds of its mother's breathing. Even sounds from outside the mother's body reach the fetus, amplified by the amniotic fluids. Likewise, the capacity for sight is established in the first four months after conception. The open eyes of the developing baby can perceive diffused light. At birth the eyes open to a new world, and seeing continues. However, light is not at all focused when a child is in utero or even when first born. The infant's mind has to learn how to process the light signals as they enter the eye and travel to the brain. It takes a few years before foveal clarity develops and, along with it, stimulation of those portions of the brain related to cognitive activity. This all starts with the capacity for receiving light as diffuse retinal stimulation—that is, a seeing mode. Early on, this stimulation is experienced by the newly born as a "diffuse pleasure." If you have been around infants very much you may have recognized this in their response of delight and excitement when colorful or shiny objects are presented to them, or a colorful mobile is hung over their crib, just beyond their reach. With seeing comes deep feeling and sensing, out of which intuition is birthed.

Young children are so intuitive, able to know about things we adults can't see, because they are seeing. They have not eclipsed that ability, as most adults have, with looking. Perhaps as we mature we don't wish to acknowledge the presence of what isn't being looked at. To see like a child is to project ourselves into the invisible. When you see, objects—or your own, singular point of view—may not be clearly focused. Instead, you may experience a vague sense of "knowing" or, like the small child, sheer delight. You might call it a "gut feeling." To be able to see, to be aware of and open to your inner knowing, is a very valuable skill.

Because it involves our deepest inner life, seeing is a very private matter. Ansel Adams, famous for his wonderful nature photographs in the black and white style, was very clear about the uniqueness of his own inner vision. When interviewers asked him why he took a certain photo or what he wanted viewers to get from his work, he emphasized that what a person gets from his photos was one's own business. And he added, "What I see is my business." Seeing is a personal perspective that can be profoundly creative, even in an art form, as in Adams's case. The way you see is a representation of your feeling nature. Behavioral optometrist Antonio Orfield describes seeing in terms of perceiving space in this way: "Space world is a mental perception of 'how far is far' and 'how deep is deep' and 'how wide is wide.' We can all measure twenty feet the same, but we all see that measured space in our own way." In the presence of perfect eyesight, with seeing and looking fully integrated, each of us has a unique appreciation for what we see. Your perception of what you see is directly related to your personal consciousness.

Your feeling side is a representation of one part of your nature, one aspect of your sensing capacity. To feel is to practice the process of sensing what is going on inside you. Unfortunately, this is not always pleasant, so we sometimes develop ways to fool ourselves out of experiencing these difficult feelings. For example, if you have a tendency to be an over-looker, you might mistake thinking for feeling; that is, you think about your feelings and believe you are actually experiencing them. Thinking about your feelings is not necessarily a bad thing, of course. With careful attention, thinking can also be a way to help you access your feelings. I have found that to be the case in my own life.

For me to enter deeply into my feelings, I need to explore them first by thinking and talking about them. This is consistent with my tendency to stress looking over seeing. I need to be able to explain my feelings in a logical way before I feel safe "being" with what I feel. This is a very important discernment. I need the safety of understanding my feelings intellectually before I am ready to fully experience them. My looking helps me to see and feel the truth. This process of thinking into our feelings is one aspect of the integrative process.

To practice conscious seeing is to explore many levels of seeing, just as we can explore many levels of feeling. Feelings can be pure, emerging spontaneously from within. They may arise as a reaction to a particular event that occurs outside ourselves. Feelings seem to be friends with emotions, or what I call "charged feelings." At this level, what you feel—and what you see—may be connected to what I described in *The Power Behind Your Eyes* (In German, *Die Integrative Sehtherapie*) as a state of reaction. These emotions can be explosive, like an outburst of anger. When we tune in to our ability to see, we are better able to connect with our pure feelings. And yet, there is an element of seeing that is linked to our thoughts. This is why, as in my own case, our thoughts can sometimes help deepen our experience of our feelings as well as our seeing.

There's another aspect of seeing that we need to look at, and this has to do with the fact that as you turn more inward you might feel sad and depressed. Images and experiences from the past may surface that can lead to regrets and feelings of guilt. And yet, seeing at this level encourages further discernment. By being present with your self, that is, conscious of your actions, you can steer your behavior in the direction of integration. This involves facing your reactive states boldly and mastering the way to respond to life by embracing your full self. In the process you'll discover that reactive states of being are based on unresolved feelings. They can be traced to the traumas and wounds from the past that are still present in your consciousness. Responsive seeing, as distinguished from reactive seeing, is creative, moving outward toward wholeness. Responsive seeing means that you take responsibility for your feelings without pointing a blaming finger outside of yourself to others.

When you are in reaction you are relating from a part of your self that you can feel in your body, which is as it should be. Your body is meant to be felt. Becoming aware and gradually more tuned in with your body is a way to find your self. One of my patients stated it this way: "When I relate from my self I go beyond the body. I still feel the body and yet my presence is so strong that I am vibrating at a much higher level and my connection to myself and life is much stronger." This is an example of integrating looking and seeing. This is conscious seeing.

## When Self Becomes the Focus

Some people believe that to fully be with the self is to become lost in feelings and emotion. This may be true. The first step to being with the self involves seeing and feeling. Use looking to help explain what is happening to your feelings, as I have described above, but be careful that you don't mistake thinking for feeling.

You cannot lose your sense of self by having a strong awareness of your body. Imagine being intimately close to a lover. Feeling your own body in contact with his or her skin is intensely physical and wonderful. How different that is from greeting an acquaintance with a formal handshake! At the feeling level, a deeper place within you is touched by skin to skin intimacy and sensuality. You don't usually judge this form of closeness; you react spontaneously, experience it in the "here and now." Feeling through your sense of touch takes you to a deeper level of your being, to a connection with your heart that vibrates a big "Yes!" Your physical body becomes a means for you to reach home within yourself. Through physical intimacy you can find the window to your consciousness. You are being conscious.

When you enter the experience of conscious seeing, you remember everything you need to know—about yourself and about your experience of the world now and throughout your history. In that moment you are your truth. You are in the very essence of who you are, and you are connected with everything around you.

> *You cannot observe self. Self is the process of observing.*
> —RICARDO ROJAS, a Peruvian theoretical researcher
> of the neurosciences

## Enhancing Seeing Capacity

If you have recognized yourself as an over-looker, there are many ways to enhance your capacity to see. First, if you wear eyeglasses or contact lenses, consider taking steps to reduce your dependence on them and challenge your eyes to see more clearly on their own. You can do this by wearing your glasses or lenses less of the time, and by obtaining a pair of eyeglasses that are not as strong as your regular prescription.

Try the following: Determine how many of your waking hours you use your prescription lenses. If you normally use them more than 80 percent of your waking hours, try to spend more time using your "naked vision." If you usually wear contact lenses, try switching to eyeglasses so that you are able to remove them more easily. Do this in the comfort of your home, and certainly don't experiment while driving an automobile or operating potentially dangerous equipment.

Next, ask your optometrist for a pair of glasses that give you 30 percent less assistance with your eyesight. Most likely the prescription you already have was written to give you 100 percent clear eyesight. A weaker prescription will allow light to stimulate your fovea and retina in a more natural way, and at the same time encourage your eyes to reach for healthier vision on their own.

If you have been relying on corrective lenses for some time, using a weaker prescription or trying to navigate with your naked eyes can be a bit disconcerting at first. You may have any or all of the following experiences:

- You dislike the blur.
- You feel uncomfortable and restless.
- Most of your world appears unclear.
- You cannot "do" your life.
- You have to slow down, sit, and "be."
- You feel more.
- You can't wait to put on your glasses once again.
- Everything looks and feels soft.
- Your world appears impressionistic and this pleases you.
- You feel free.

By paying attention to how and what you perceive with your naked vision, you can prepare your brain and mind for conscious seeing. Each day, practice looking and seeing through your eyes with weaker lenses or with no lenses at all. Keep a journal of the things you notice about your vision, as well as what you feel in your body and in your heart during this practice. You will find that your eyes begin to send your brain and mind all kinds of new directives, such as seeing colors more brightly, perceiving in more dimensions, and having a wider field of view.

Under these conditions, the light that strikes the retina and fovea is more diffuse. Since the light is less focused in the foveal area, your retina is encouraged to participate more. When I prescribed weaker lenses for patients in the study mentioned on page 46, they reported some interesting side effects. First, at least 85 percent of them said they loved the softness they experienced in their vision and in their bodies when they wore the lenses. As I watched them put on their new glasses, I could see them immediately relax. I videotaped their faces, and invariably their brow and facial muscles were less tense. These therapeutic lenses acted as a relaxant. Since most of these people were nearsighted, the therapeutic effect was obtained by weakening the minus (concave) lenses. The overall effect was of adding plus (convex) lenses. In pharmacological terms, this effect is referred to as a parasympathetic stimulant, which translates to a deep relaxant.

What does it mean to be relaxed in the way I'm discussing here? First, the tendency to over-look is reduced. Retinal seeing increases. As a result, looking and seeing become more balanced. Over 80 percent of the subjects in the study demonstrated greater fusion and integration between their two eyes as a result of the weaker lens prescriptions. As integration progressed, conscious seeing became a reality. The increased fusion and integration were measured in the study, and it can be verified by how effective you are able to do the practices in the photographic sequences that follow in later chapters.

To see is to look softly. When you see, you think less about what is around you and you feel it more. In short, you are more fully engaged in the experience of looking through your eyes.

Seeing means becoming aware of the *possibility* of what is present without attaching a specific form to it. It also means that you become inspired in ways that direct you to go beyond your present limited way of perceiving. Think of this exercise as inviting yourself to be more conscious, to feel. To not see consciously puts you in danger of cementing yourself into a view of the world that is limited to the perceptions of your thinking mind.

## Begin Now

I have designed the photographic collage (photograph 4) on page 118 to help you enhance your conscious seeing. Remove your eyeglasses and look at the image with relaxed, naked vision. Imagine that the picture is the flame of a candle. There are other images inserted into the background to stimulate your seeing. Look directly at the flame in the center of the image. Keep looking at one point. Notice that you are more aware of the object you are looking at directly than of the images that surround it. This is because the light reflected off that central object enters your eye and strikes your fovea, that area in the center of your retina that provides the clearest image. Light reflected from the rest of the picture into your eye strikes the surrounding part of your retina and creates the image in your peripheral vision, which is less clear. This doesn't mean you can't see it. You can sense and feel what is in your peripheral vision, but your eyes don't provide you with a clearly defined image of it.

Breathe. Allow and notice. Let go of trying to see. Integrated vision happens without struggle. With practice, you will begin to perceive what is present both centrally and peripherally. Seeing in an integrated way is like entering a meditative state. Continue to focus your attention on the flame, but also observe what is in the collage around the flame. This is the first stage of seeing deeply. Have you noticed the two eyes looking at you? How does it feel to be seen? These are my eyes welcoming you to conscious seeing.

*If the doors of perception were cleansed, everything would*
*appear to man as it is, infinite. For man has closed himself up,*
*till he sees all things through narrow chinks of his cavern.*
—WILLIAM BLAKE, *The Marriage of Heaven and Hell*

## Reintegration

Viewing the photographic collage as you did in the above exercise is the first step toward developing conscious seeing. Use that experience to help you start to move through your life with an awareness of both your central and peripheral vision. This is part of the reintegration process. If you relax and allow it to, your life will become a playground for you to practice this integrated way of seeing at any time. You don't have to do any more focused exercises beyond the one I just shared.

Just pay attention to your ability to see with this new awareness at different moments — at home, at work, at play, at rest. The following anecdote provides a good example of the kinds of changes people have experienced when they have opened themselves up to the new way of seeing they acquired through this one exercise alone. After weeks of practicing looking at a candle flame, seeing the surroundings, and integrating his experiences, Matthew wrote the following in his journal:

> I feel the presence of waves of change in my vision. I no longer desire to focus on my world. I find it difficult to keep my eyes open. I want to feel the pleasure of realizing that I am in my body. I sense my posture tall and erect. My vision blurs now and I hear the voice of my loved one. At first I adjust to hear her, then I feel really present. She is moving toward me. I feel Jean, my girlfriend, moving into my skin. This delicious feeling of creating oneness would normally overwhelm me. In this moment of an open heart I welcome her whole presence into my total being. I spend long moments entering into her glistening eyes. I feel so much openness. I tell Jean how much I love her and want to be this close always. Jean's eyes transport me to a place of love I have never felt in my whole sleep state life. My chest feels like it has broadened beyond the width of my shoulders and I am transported to an Adam and Eve state of pure bliss and light.
>
> My loved one looks very young. She talks and I hear her without the usual editing system of my mind. I welcome her needs into my life because in this state I am one with her. Her needs are mine, and my desires are her gift to me. There is nothing in our way of being separate. All we can rejoice in, this moment, are the grinning smiles of our shining teeth. I feel my jaw hurting from incessant smiling. The gentleness and young look on her face take me back to the time we played as children. We were very happy friends and learned so much from each other. In this blissful state there is no reaction. I float on my feet as I walk away for a moment. I feel light and free. The burdens of my karma have left my flesh existence.

I am transported to ancient Greece where the pure love of the gods rains upon my being. I only know love and I only see light. My eyes don't know how to react or see judgment in this state of total letting go. I wish to lead my life so free and full of love. I remember this feeling. I haven't been able to always access it but it is always available for me to bring forth when I let go. That is the trick. Let go of the need to control and edit what I see through my clear eyes. I am willing to see only love and light.

My eyes reach out to the burning candle. It seems blurry and then I realize I am seeing the aura of the flame. A bright circular rainbow aura surrounds the orange-yellow flame. I look at other objects in the room and they all seem to be glowing with light. I see the life and love presence in everything in the room. Just like Jean, they are sharing their love with me as well. I sit back, entranced by what seems to be an illusion. I shout out to Jean that I am hallucinating and seeing auras. She laughs and joins me. Her eyes are now glowing with pure love, a translucent light of purity of a newborn child flows from her. I realize that I can see this way any time I wish. I remember love. I feel it in my muscles and sinews. I feel light present in my bones and every cell of my being. I feel light as I stand and walk. The heaviness of my burdens is gone. I see only love and light. I only hear Jean's words as love calls. I feel like a bird whistling my love calls to Jean.

This day we spend many hours not saying anything, just looking into the very souls of our beings. There is no resistance to Jean taking me into her spirit space. Her open heart laps up my essence and we continue dancing our eyes over each other's face. I feel totally loved. We smile and breathe together and enjoy this blissful transport to another dimension. Why have I been afraid of this immensely beautiful kind of seeing and being love? I recall it being present when I first met Jean, and then my mind became very busy with life and the survival state I see so many others operating from. Now I am reminded of the accident I don't ever wish to have happen to wake me up. I am awake. I am heart connected and outside the realm of the frightened ego. I am consciously seeing. I am again experiencing love. I will not easily forget this kind of vision. It is too powerful a memory to let slip into oblivion. I love you, world. I love life and am ecstatic to be alive.

Reintegration involves remembering your essence. The qualities of your true nature can be accessed through conscious seeing. I believe that is why we have eyes—to see the purity of what is!

As you begin to venture into the world of conscious seeing, keep these ideas in mind:

Talk from power rather than fear.

Do not give your power away to anyone else.

Let words describe the love that you are.

See the *what is* of every situation.

Be free of the *what is not*.

Focus on the *what is*.

Share *what is*.

*What is* is to move away from self-pity and a dysfunctional addiction to living in the past.

*What is* is to let go of a tendency to judge other people.

*What is* is the realization that you are already able to access a state of perfection here and now.

Cultivate the *what is* of every moment with all your heart and soul.

*What is* is that you are constantly guided and know your truth.

*What is* is that you are clear.

*What is* is that you are to solve your own riddles and not seek answers from others.

*What is* is bringing to everyone you meet the spirit of your highest consciousness.

# 4

## Genetics and the Development of Personality

### The Origin of Personality

Since it is through our personality that we express who we are, we often see it as the source of our individuality. But consider for a moment the possibility of your personality acting as your mask, as the protection you don for the world. Like performers, each of us presents ourselves as having certain personal characteristics. We may be aggressive or meek, loud or soft-spoken, dominating, loving, inquisitive, or good-natured. Your personality is reflected by how you behave, how you "show up," and how you reveal yourself. But how did you develop the personality that marks you as you?

Imagine a new baby. Soon after birth, it is clear that the infant has already established his own unique behavioral patterns. As with most infants, his cries mean one of three things: Feed me! Change me! or Hold me! His personality dictates that he will perform in a certain way to get his parents' attention. Some babies are loud, others are quiet. Some babies will move their hands, arms, or legs a lot while others are very still. They all have similar basic needs—food, dryness, and physical contact—but each has his own special way of expressing those needs. Because a child's personality can be observed at such an early age, it seems likely that genetics plays a role in how it develops.

## It Came from Mom and Dad

At conception you receive many qualities from your parents and others in your family tree. You receive this genetic programming whether you like it or not. It might appear in the form of a physical resemblance, such as body size, weight, or hair color. You may sound like one of your parents. Best or worst of all, you may even find yourself behaving like them. As we move toward conscious seeing, we will examine how the physical structure of your eyes, as well as your way of looking and seeing and your deepest perceptions, can all be molded by this genetic imprint.

Have you ever considered why you ended up with the parents you did? Have you wondered why you encounter bits and pieces of them every time you look in the mirror or hear yourself speak? Perhaps you are often frustrated to find that you share some of their shortcomings. Like them, you anger easily. Or you hold back your feelings. Or you don't fully express yourself. In all of these observations, you may realize that your life history bears some resemblance to that of your parents. Perhaps even your poor vision is like theirs.

In your frustration, you may have spent time being critical or disparaging of things your parents taught you. We often judge our parents and their points of view, vowing never to repeat their negative patterns with our own children. And yet, in spite of our best efforts, we often do.

I have been observing these patterns in my own life and in those of my patients for many years. It appears to me that the origin of personality has a very specific role to play in conscious seeing. It is worthwhile, therefore, to explore in some detail the early stages of personality development.

## I Was Born with It

Imagine your parents for a moment. Really see their faces. Hear their voices. Feel their hugs. Remember the snuggles in bed. Smell the odors from their bodies. As you reach back in memory to experience these moments with them again, consider this: Is it possible that it was no accident that those two people you call Father and

Mother were the ones who ended up being your parents? In the larger scheme of things, is it possible that you may have had some say in choosing your parents? For the sake of conscious seeing, pretend that you even helped them decide when to conceive you, in order for your spirit to arrive on planet Earth at a certain time. Just suppose that your parents each reached a certain level of consciousness, at which point you were ready to meet them. I realize this may be difficult to imagine, or simply too incredible to take seriously. For the sake of cultivating conscious seeing, stretch beyond the way you normally perceive things. As you reach into your imagination beyond your everyday way of understanding things, you may begin to feel that perhaps the consensual reality we so easily accept takes only the surface view of our lives into account. Conscious seeing demands that we look a little deeper.

If, in fact, it is possible that you did have a say in your choice of parents, and you even chose when to arrive, many other interesting possibilities emerge. For one thing, it may be that the elements of your parents' personalities that you received were needed for you to have a particular life experience. This could mean that their good as well as their faults are integral to your individual *human beingness*. Why? Is it possible that as a child you needed to experience both the positive and negative aspects in order to evolve? Let's take this line of inquiry one step further. Your parents also evolved from their parents, each of whom had their own unique blueprint to contribute to the evolutionary beingness. Open your mind up to these possibilities, if only for a moment, as we explore how all of these elements could come together in our understanding of the development of conscious seeing.

For many years I have been amused at how many conventional eye doctors believe it is impossible for vision to improve. Some point to genetically deformed eyeballs as the primary cause of vision problems. Functional and behavioral optometrists blame environmental factors. They say, for example, that reading requires the eyes to focus too much; poor lighting puts too great a strain on the eyes. In conscious seeing we will discover how all of these variables—from the spiritual, to the genetic, to the environmental—contribute to the way you see, with environmental factors often triggering genetic predispositions.

## The Flexible Personality

Personalities can be flexible or inflexible. In the family I grew up in, it seemed that strong personalities most often revealed themselves as inflexible. Strength of character was associated with anger, fear, and control. Only much later, when I began to see my parents in a more conscious way, did I realize that they were evolving just as I was. Evolution toward consciousness happens simultaneously in all generations, although at different rates. Your parents' generation may not evolve as quickly as yours, nor will your pace match that of your children. Each successive generation appears to travel faster in making adjustments in personality as a way to become more conscious.

In my case I found that I needed to modify a tendency to suppress my feelings. This was very difficult for me at first. What often happened was that I would sit on my feelings, denying them or simply being unconscious of them. When I finally did share what I was feeling, I often did so in a way that was laced with deep, covert anger. As I began to integrate intuition with intellect, being with doing, and seeing with looking, I found it easier to express my feelings without that undercurrent of anger, at least to family members.

Consistent with Schiffer's discoveries, which I discussed in chapter 2, my incomplete understanding during my childhood distorted my view of reality. Just as he pointed out, my perceptions of hurt were recorded somewhere in the deeper layers of my brain. I had to bring them forth, make them a part of my conscious life. Only then was I able to begin making peace with those memories and progressing toward living a more conscious life. I had to face the shut-down intuitive and expressive, deeply frightened parts of myself. When I did, I experienced a dramatic shift in the way I saw my world.

Meanwhile, my daughter honed her ability to bring her deepest feelings into her awareness even more than I. As a small child she projected her anger directly onto me in a rather unskillful way. As she grew older, with the help of her mother and others, she dealt with her personality imbalances and faced her fears. Then she could communicate with me from her true nature. She was able to tell me how she felt and be fully conscious and present with me. She evolved to this stage at a much younger age than my father or I had. What she accomplished by age twenty-one, I was just realizing at fifty-two, and my father at eighty-two. In my daughter's generation there was a thirty-year acceleration in the evolution of consciousness.

For much of my life I received and accepted many mixed messages about my personality. First, I believed that *I was* my personality. I thought my identity was rooted in how smart I appeared, my physical appearance, whether I met society's expectations of how I should behave, and how effective I was in my career.

Examine for a moment what perceptions you have about the relationship between your personality and *who you are*. Spend some time looking deeply into your life and your self. Do you gauge your magnificence based on material success or outward appearance? On what do you gauge yourself and your life?

Is it more important for you to acquire material things rather than explore pursuits that enhance your knowledge of yourself?

When you clearly look back into your life do you discover experiences that were left incomplete?

Are you attempting to prove your success to others?

Do you try to control others because you feel uncomfortable with parts of yourself?

At the end of the day do you feel like there is something missing even though you have all your physical needs met?

Do you see yourself as being inadequate compared to others, such as your work colleagues or family members?

Can you honestly say you love your body?

When you look into the mirror do you spend moments reflecting upon how much you enjoy and love seeing your essence in your eyes?

If you answered yes to all but the final two questions, see how you can vary your daily patterns to reach the point where you no longer agree with the questions. In conscious seeing the aim is to be able to be with yourself nonjudgmentally, fully embracing the many parts of yourself and striving to be aware of what feeds your essence.

The predominant materialistic, capitalistic lifestyle in our culture tends to cause us to evaluate ourselves primarily from its own perspectives and how we fit into that model. Look good. Drive the right car. Live in the best neighborhood. Make lots of money. I suggest that for many people these values may limit their level of consciousness. I find that many of my clients who have attained these materialistic goals are plagued with eye disorders. These eye conditions indicate an imbalance in their perceptions of themselves. Their personalities are doing battle with their authentic natures, each one vying for the dominant role in governing their lives. In a more ideal world, the authentic nature informs the personality to achieve greater harmony and balance between the cultural demands and the unique personality of the individual. If the effort to find harmony between the two is consciously pursued, it can lead to a deep integrative process that results in a more flexible and genuine personality. Conscious seeing can be a helpful start in this process.

Sonia's story helps to illustrate this point. Her vision was dominated by perceptions of being stuck in the personality of her career life. When she realized this it helped her create a new vision.

Sonia was successful in her career working in a large auction house in London, England. Her job was exciting and offered opportunities to travel, be challenged, and socialize with people from all walks of life. Her relationship to her vision was a simple morning and evening ritual of slipping her contact lenses in and out. Sonia never really considered that her eyes were a problem or that she needed to focus on them in any way.

She eventually fell in love with Godfrey and they were married with great pomp and style. Sonia felt so taken care of by Godfrey. He offered her security, a gorgeous home, and a future filled with excitement and possibility. She continued to work but cut back her hours to enjoy being at home. Sonia thought she had it all.

Godfrey began traveling abroad and Sonia was left at home for long periods during his absences. She began observing that she felt empty. She realized she was neglecting her former friends and hobbies. She became dissatisfied with her daily life patterns. At this time her contact lenses began giving her difficulties. Sonia had to radically cut back the wearing time and had to resort to using her backup glasses. She introduced the conscious seeing concept of spending time in her "naked" vision and patching her eyes. This is a therapeutic concept in which part or all of one eye is prevented from seeing by covering a lens or wearing a covering over the eye.

While patching her dominant "doing" right eye, (the eye generally associated with the influence of the father), feelings of abandonment surfaced. Sonia started making a distinction between her perceptions governed by her personality and those of her true needs. She went deeply into her feeling and emotional nature. She began to see that being stuck in her stunning home alone while her husband traveled promoted a feeling of loneliness. Her house seemed like a mausoleum in Godfrey's absence. Sonia permitted herself to deeply feel this emptiness. Her true heart nature was asking her to stop giving up her emotional power to her husband. Sonia's desire was to travel and pursue her interest in the spiritual life of other cultures.

Looking through lower-strength spectacle lenses, and wearing her contact lenses less, helped Sonia to focus on her buried feelings and reclaim her true natural way of seeing herself and life. She now travels with her husband half the time and visits other countries on her own. Sonia is connecting to her own friends again, which she finds promotes her inner balance and joyous feeling for living.

## The "Survival" Personality

In a fully conscious state, your personality harmonizes with your true essence. You might call this state your "soul presence." This is the very nature of being, of being human. Joseph, a long-term client, described it this way in his journal.

When I was very young I was able to see, in a physical way, the purity of another person's nature. This ability is part of my deep inner makeup. I love this way of seeing. It brings me an intense feeling of connection with my truest self. Spending time out in nature, near the ocean, trees, and mountains, helps me cultivate this part of my being.

As a youngster it puzzled me to find that often people behaved very differently from the way I was seeing them. My seeing revealed their soul nature. What I experienced in their personality was something else. I now understand some of the reasons why any one of us may at times act in ways that are not consistent with our true nature. In fact, as I struggle to become more conscious in my own life, I have learned to examine this kind of behavior in myself.

When I am fully present I am a very loving person who needs lots of nurturing touch and affection. I can literally feel this in my muscles and skin. I feel an openness in my heart simply from sharing this with you. We might say that my personality is that of a nurturing person, one who gives and receives gentleness and tenderness. It's true that somewhere deep inside me there is a place where this description is accurate. My problem was that I didn't behave in this way. Tenderness for me was a one-way street. I set up my life to give, that is to be a nurturing man. What I lacked was a capacity to receive nurturing. I craved it. I also pushed it away, except in one arena: sexuality. I developed a part of my personality that could manipulate women to give me what I wanted, but only in the form of sexual intimacy.

Joseph said he developed an addiction, not to caffeinated drinks or cigarettes, but to sex.

Closeness with a woman gave me the touch and affection I needed to stay alive. But too often it was like junk food to me, giving me a hit that would only sustain me for a while. I began to lead my life under the power of this addiction. I had a contract with myself that went something like this: I crave love; I receive love

**66**

when I am sexual; I will behave in ways that create sexual experiences. The more I practiced seeking women for intimate gratification, the more my personality began to identify with this way of behaving. Eventually I came to believe that this was who I was, that this was my true nature.

In the throes of this sexual addiction, I behaved in a way that women classify as the stereotypical male. I attracted women to me to find love—love within the limits of my capacities at that time. I developed a personality that was charming and pleasing. I made myself inviting to women in order to receive love. This worked for a while. Just like a drug addict, I would get my fix and feel better for a while. But when I allowed myself to feel what was really going on inside, I knew that I was seeking something richer and deeper, that I was not cultivating a connection. I became conscious of an emptiness inside, caused by limitations in my ability to be in my true nature.

I was like an alcoholic who catches himself pouring another drink but is unable to stop. The fixes themselves felt good, for as long as they lasted. However, deep in my heart I knew my behavior was not getting me what I was truly seeking, particularly when it led to infidelity in my first marriage. Why was I choosing this path? To break out of this cycle I had to look back at my early life. Was I modeling some childhood experience that mirrored this predisposition in my personality? Was there a part of my past I was not seeing? If this was true then perhaps it was time to see my life in a more conscious way. Which part of my being had I suppressed in order to survive? Why did I feel like a victim struggling to survive around my need for a nurturing fix? What did I still need to consciously see?

## Thank You, Mom and Dad
Joseph carefully examined the way his parents had led their lives.

I reviewed my early childhood, looking for insights into this troubling issue. Even though my parents were married for forty-five years, the family harmony was destroyed when one of them began having affairs. As a child, I saw the disharmony between my parents and sensed their unhappiness. What I was unable to deal with was my own deep emotional pain. I needed to survive, so I built a wall around those intense feelings.

As an adult, my life had at many levels come to replicate the lives of my parents. I was unfaithful. I lied. I had emotional outbursts. For me conscious seeing became a process of observing those patterns. Fortunately, I was discontented enough to be motivated to do whatever was necessary to achieve greater happiness in my life. I needed to become intellectually strong and develop that part of my nature related to looking. This was my lesson. I was moving from the blur and confusing hurt of my early life to a more focused and concentrated way of being.

It became obvious to me that my parents' *incompletions* and unconscious ways of seeing life gave me an opportunity to be different. They were the perfect parents in that they gave me a starting point for my own evolution. Witnessing their inflexible personalities taught me the importance of becoming flexible.

As I began to apply this information to my vision habits, as well as my everyday life, I discovered that my left eye was dominant. This eye is generally thought to reflect the influence of the mother. In my case, I needed to feel less intimidated toward powerful females and transform my anger. Later, when this part of my flexible personality blended with my nature, I was able to cultivate a healthy partnership with a strong woman whom I could meet on equal terms.

I also found that I either suppressed the vision in my right eye or experienced double vision. This suggested to me that the male side of my personality needed maturing. I saw evidence of this in my reactive personality. I easily became angry. Defensiveness was my middle name. I resisted authority. Only rarely was I able to openly receive my father's love.

At first I feared that I was doomed to live my life this way—not fitting in, rebelling against anything others might say. And yet I knew that all this behavior was rooted in my childhood efforts to avoid frightening emotions. As I faced my resistance it led me to experience deeper levels of integration. I became aware of the different kinds of consciousness that I accessed as a result of integrating the vision of my right and left eyes. As I realized that physical nurturing and emotional intimacy were available from loved ones, I was able to incorporate that knowledge into my actions. I opened up and accepted tenderness in situations beyond the sexual ones in my life. As a result, my personality became more reflective of my true nature.

I was fascinated to find that, just as I was evolving through many of my own incompletions, my parents were also making some dramatic changes in their lifestyles. They were divorced and began building new lives for themselves. They began to talk more honestly about their feelings, and even entered more into their conscious seeing. I was deeply gratified to see each of them find a new sense of inner peace.

Thank you, Mom and Dad. Like you, I have been judgmental and struggled with a fearful personality. Your behavior guided me to enter life seeing more consciously.

## The Iris, a Map of Your Personality and Consciousness

As you age, the unfolding of your personality is dependent on the mastery of a balanced blend of intellectual understanding and intuitive knowing. If either the intellect or intuition dominates, your behavior will reveal the lack of harmony in your personality and consciousness. As you evolve toward greater balance and integration, it is not unusual to begin to realize an enhanced level of consciousness. I propose that your evolving personality provides you with a way to access consciousness, and that your life patterns in these areas are all portrayed in the markings on your iris.

It is interesting to note that from the day of your birth, your iris contains a physical map of your personality. It contains an intricate array of markings that reveal a great deal of information about you, including potential restrictions and deviations from being conscious.

At birth the iris is comprised primarily of two types of structures. There are areas that are fairly smooth, like the surface of a pond or a sandy beach. There are also indentations in the surface that look like small holes, often shaped somewhat like flower petals. These two kinds of structures can be seen in photograph 5 on page 119. In the blue iris on the right, you can see a smooth, even surface. In the brown-colored iris at the top, there is an indentation shaped like an open flower in the ten o'clock position and smaller ones toward twelve o'clock. Structures of this type are usually present at birth and change very little as we age.

During the first seven years of life, a different type of structure than those I've just described often emerges. Small, rounded protrusions, often a different color than the iris, form on its surface. Most often these "iris bumps" appear to be raised above the surface of the iris, toward the cornea (the shiny outer covering of the eye). Look again at photograph 5. In the blue iris at the bottom left of the page, you can see an example of an iris bump. In this photo, it is distinctly brown in color. An iris bump often has a white, cloudy appearance in blue eyes and a darker brown color in hazel or brown eyes.

Each different type of structure on the iris is related to a particular personality trait. To explore how these structures relate to conscious seeing, we will consider three primary qualities: thoughts, feelings, and emotions.

Close your eyes for a moment and take a walk with me along a white, sandy beach. It is late afternoon and the sand is perfectly smooth, with no footprints. The sun is setting and you can hear the sound of the waves at low tide. The sand is firm in places, baked hard by the sun's rays. The weave of the sand particles is strong and you can walk on this surface without sinking down. If the sand is like the iris, this strong, smooth surface represents clear, firm feelings, ones that you know and can trust. Consider them to be helpful feelings.

In other places we walk, our naked feet make impressions in the softer sand. Our footprints are like hollow openings that sink below the surrounding area. To continue with our metaphor, when we come to the softer sand we sink down to a place of deeper sensing. Here, where our feelings stand separate from thoughts, our sensitivity is as delicate as a flower petal or as wild as a raging fire. This is emotion.

The depressions made by our footsteps can have many forms. They can be shallow or deep, large or small. When we translate our discussion of these images to the patterns on the iris, we find that the indentations may be large enough to cover a significant portion of the iris's surface area, or they may be so tiny that they measure less than a millimeter. They can also be fully enclosed with borders that are steep, or they may be open on one or more sides. These indentations allow us to see a slightly deeper layer of the iris, and their varied shapes and sizes point to the kinds of emotions we are likely to experience.

Finally, as we continue our walk along the beach, we find a rock in our way. It is hard and can hurt us if we stand on it with our bare feet. This protruding rock is like a mountain standing above the surrounding landscape. When a structure like this appears on your iris, it tells us about thought patterns that you are likely to experience. Those patterns, like the rock, predict hardness, rigidity, and pain.

For the purposes of developing conscious seeing, let's examine three distinct types of personality: the thinking type, the feeling type, and the emotional type. The thinker is the intellectual, logical and rational in the way he or she approaches problems. The feeler is sympathetic, in touch with his own feelings and able to understand those of others. The emotional type is the actor, one who likes being on show, the center of attention. In one of these three ways, most people find their inner ground to firmly stand on. Of course, most of us exhibit a combination of all three types of behavior. Still, more often than not one is predominant over the others. With a little thought, you can probably name people who clearly demonstrate each of the three personality types. Ask yourself which type is most prevalent in your own personality. Do you operate most often with thoughts, feelings, or emotions?

It's very common to have an inaccurate view of our own dominant behavior. For example, I believed that I was a feeling-emotional type, but when I looked at my iris I noticed many protruding, rock-like structures that I knew represented a reliance on thought. In my own eyes, these were more pronounced around the pupil margin. This was an indication that I use thoughts to work things out and only then do I allow myself to acknowledge feelings and emotions. At the time, my experience of myself was the opposite. I described myself as being too focused on feelings, with uncontrolled emotions. I was amazed to see that my iris indicated I had an innate, genetic tendency toward intellectual processing. Some time later, as I evolved into a greater integration of my true nature and my personality, the traits mapped out in my iris emerged as well.

The first step in realizing your true nature is to get to know your innate personality based on your genetics. By examining the structure of your iris, you can discover those traits passed on to you from your parents, some of which may come as a surprise to you. The knowledge you gain may help you to become more aware of hidden aspects of your personality, and to ultimately become more present to your own true nature.

Since I am not sitting there beside you at the moment, I cannot look into your iris and give you individual feedback. So, let me help you discover your true personality traits with an exercise. Below, on the left side, is a list of personality traits that can be predicted from looking at the iris. The corresponding statements on the right side are what a person might feel at a conscious or unconscious level. Typically, if I mention one of the left-column comments to a person, it will trigger a memory much like that which appears in the right column as it relates back to certain experiences from his or her life.

| | |
|---|---|
| Fear of attack | I don't like the way my father screams at me. |
| Uncertainty of nurturing | I am not sure when my father loves me. |
| Suppression (of emotion) | My mother talks so much from her head. |

Deeper suppression ...... My mother complains to me.
　　of feelings

Low self-worth ......... My brother is smarter than me.

Fear of physical abuse. .... My father hits me.

Lack of nurturing ....... My father loves my brother
　　　　　　　　　　　　more than me.

Distrust of self ......... My parents don't think
　　　　　　　　　　　　I am smart enough.

Blocked listening. ........ I don't listen when
　　　　　　　　　　　　my parents speak.

Blocked communication ... I can't really share
　　　　　　　　　　　　what I am feeling.

False, exaggerated ....... I tell lies to get attention.
　　expression

Consider the behaviors on the right side to be how a particular person feels in a given interaction with one or both parents. When they feel the significance of the phrase inside their mind, they need to find a peaceful place in order to survive what is happening to them, as they exist outside their parents.

The level of integration or disintegration of the parent's personality will determine how they relate to a child. If their child needs to protect herself from distance she feels from her parents or any harmful perceptions or actions they project onto her, she develops a survival strategy. The intensity of this mechanism will be determined by the depth or lack of depth of consciousness of her parent's interaction with her. That is, the parent's degree of personality flexibility and survival will influence the daughter's perceptions. This in turn affects whether the child's seeing will be constructed as a brain-dominant survival function or whether it will evolve to include deeper levels of integration in the mind. In the case of survival, a child's primary channel for seeing will be directed through the brain's specific pathways in a way that will help her to cope. For example, the autonomic nervous system is known to be one of the coping mechanisms for distress. The eyes are affected by this distress. On the other hand, when the personality of the parent is flexible, a child's deeper integrative pathways of the mind are accessed. Her thoughts and feelings merge. When this happens, a daughter welcomes perceptions through her eyes that are pure and related to being. Her eyes are the windows that consciousness has a chance to peep out of.

To illustrate how all of this works, let me relate the case of a patient of mine, whom I will call June. I asked June to reflect on her childhood and then pick out how one of the above statements referred to it. Her response was, "My brother is smarter than me." She recalled an event in which she watched her parents enthusiastically praise her brother for his excellent school grades. On the same occasion, June's parents said nothing about her own work; in fact, she received very little attention of any kind. Later, she was reprimanded for being lazy and not smart enough. It's easy to understand why June's recollection of these events triggered feelings of inadequacy.

In June's view, her parents were excessively critical of her and favored her brother. Through this favoritism they acted out an incomplete aspect of themselves. Their daughter activates the memory of an incompletion within themselves, which they project onto her. This is a less-integrated way of being. The parents are being less conscious than they could be.

June feels that she is different from her brother and her peers. Her perception of how her parents treated her has led her to question her own value, her own capabilities. "How capable am I really?" she may ask. If she is in a survival mode, then the reflex circuitry in her brain is stimulated to handle future situations in the same manner. She reacts on the level of pure survival and goes no deeper into her thoughts or feelings. She is not yet aware enough in her developing mind and consciousness to realize that she could take this feedback another way.

As June and I worked together, I encouraged her to engage in a logical examination of how capable she really is. She searched inside to discover ways she was proficient. At last, with a huge smile spreading across her face, she said, "I am gifted in my own, unique ways!" June felt the wisdom of what she said, which took her feelings deeper. The deeper she went, the more her perceptions of herself improved.

As an exercise, reflect upon your childhood life and consider those qualities of your parents that you disliked or found uncomfortable. Imagine that you are back at that time in your life, reliving experiences where you felt uncomfortable. Write them down. Stop reading and take ten minutes to contemplate this question. Let me share an example of this from my own experience.

I remember a time when I did not like my father's breath or I found my mother fat. Then, use these remembered reactions to construct phrases like those on the left side in the preceding example. For example, I would create from my qualities the statements "I don't like it when you drink" and "I despise fat women." Examine what each of these remembered reactions brings you now. How did it help you then? For myself, I associated alcohol with my father screaming at me. Also, I was able to protect myself from being smothered by a big or fat woman. I found that it became easier for me to let go of my judgments and fears by using the sentence statements.

I propose that these inner interpretations are the way perceptions are constructed into either disintegrated personality states or conscious seeing. Stimulate your memory. This is a process for being conscious.

## DNA and Perceptions

In psychological terms, June was dealing with low self-esteem. There is a particular location on the iris associated with this issue. For the right eye, it is located inwards toward the nose at the bottom, near the six o'clock position, at about five-thirty. It is opposite for the left eye—still toward the nose but at six-thirty.

Denny Ray Johnson, author of *What Your Eye Reveals* and a highly intuitive, spiritual man and inspirational teacher, looked at the markings, shapes, and patterns of many eyes. He also interviewed the people behind the eyes to find out about their lives. He then correlated what they told him about themselves and what he saw in their irises. Over a few years he saw repeated themes and realized that the iris holds information on how the personality is constructed. He originated the names "jewel" for thoughts, "stream" for feelings, and "flower" for emotions. He proposed that the iris is the genetic representation of the DNA transmission at conception, a point upon which I will elaborate later. He also noted that the way a child is treated by parents and caregivers will have a bearing on the development of his thought patterns and, in turn, on his iris, during his first seven years of life.

Johnson made an iris map of his research and began sharing this with clinicians from varied backgrounds. There were osteopathic and medical physicians, healing practitioners, eye doctors (Johnson himself was not a doctor), nurses, and other therapists. He stated that he was not aware of other methods of reading the iris, such as iridology. I was fortunate to be one of the practitioners who met with Johnson in the early nineties, and thereafter attended regular meetings with him. All of those physicians who met with him agreed to begin photographing the irises of our patients to test the reliability of the map that Johnson had created.

As a trained clinician and scientist, I was skeptical as I began looking into my patients' eyes using the Johnson map. But I was surprised to find that his descriptors were true and reliable at least 80 percent of the time. Looking at the iris from this perspective became a marvelous tool for me to help my patients in a much deeper way. I began correlating the iris markings with my patients' perceptions of themselves, other people, and their life stories. Later, I linked these findings to their lens prescriptions. The power of the lenses I prescribed each patient was another external representation of the inner perceptions of their minds. When I measured their eyes, it was as if I were recording the way their individual mind perceived. I began to modify the iris map as I found deeper connections between the iris markings and a way to reach higher levels of conscious seeing.

Without my teaching a whole course on reading irises, which is not the intention of this book, I wish to share with you information that will be directly helpful as you progress along your path to conscious seeing. The proposition to date is that at conception your parents' DNA is genetically passed down as the blueprint for your personality development. Their flexible and/or survival personalities become part of the imprint for your brain development.

Through your interactions with your parents, you have the opportunity to test your DNA blueprint for accuracy. Where your parents have not mastered survival behavior, you have the ability to transform your perceptions and perhaps even theirs. In the areas where their personality is flexible, you can even evolve further. The iris information can provide us with a glimpse into the potential "quicksand" of those who operate by the dictates of the survival nature. We can contrast this with the flexible personality, where you can find "monkey ropes" to swing away to freedom. The iris tells you how to deepen and broaden your life experience beyond survival—and this provides the polarity that frees you from a state of duality; that is, it allows you to direct your life in a more conscious, integrated manner.

In June's case, I looked at the iris of each eye, and without asking her any questions, I made the following comments, which match the left column in the list on pages 72–73:

June, it appears that you have fear of being hurt, even of physical abuse. You might have compensated by holding in your feelings. You may not have felt sufficient nurturing from your parents. This could have increased the intensity of a low sense of self-worth. This would lead to mistrust, being rebellious, and falsely exaggerating the way you talk about yourself to get attention.

I then asked her this question: "Is this true?" And she answered, "Yes." You can imagine how powerful this was for her, to be given such feedback. It was as if I had looked inside of her and read her mind. Of course I hadn't. I was like a logger who can say how old a tree is by counting the number of rings in a cross section of its trunk.

The insight I shared with June illustrates how the information from the iris can guide a person into deeper levels of self-perception. I told her about herself without knowing much about her history. As she listened to me talk, it activated the memories in her mind. In this way she was able to link what I was saying to her deepest inner perceptions.

I talk with June about her low sense of self-worth. In her mind, she responds with a thought, a feeling, and/or an emotion. The mind takes what I say and organizes the content of what she perceives, now in relationship to her past perceptions. As she thinks, feels, and experiences emotion, June's mind also matches this information with the genetic DNA-coded memory of what her parents passed down to her. In this case, her mother had a similar low self-worth perception of herself. June was able to accept this survival aspect of personality from her mother once she changed her perceptions about her feelings and emotions in present time. June became aware of a deeper part of herself, the place inside where she could "truly be" with her self. The change in perception was that she no longer identified herself as being the person with low self-esteem. The poor self-image was part of her experience but not really her essence.

June needed to access deeper levels of her own mind, where she discovered how this restricted part of her nature was hindering her being herself. Once this happened, she changed her perception of being a reflection of her mother's personality and became more flexible within herself. She no longer needed her survival thoughts to judge and construct negative perceptions to hide this memory. At about the same time, her clearing eyesight reflected the changed perception. What this means is that she witnessed her eyesight becoming clearer even in the presence of her nearsighted diopters being the same. The changes in perception of the mind's eye happen faster than the structural changes in diopters of the camera eye.

Changing seeing is changing consciousness. Being conscious reveals the part of your personality that is either evolving or is staying in a disintegrated state.

## Seeing, Space, and Consciousness

Bruce Lipton, who has a Ph.D. in biology and is a former researcher from Stanford University, has developed an interesting perspective on DNA. Drawing on his review of basic research from his own lab and the work of other investigators, Lipton has stated that there is a possibility that when we change our perception we have the ability to modify the code of our DNA.

This is quite a concept. Altering the way we see can influence the genetic programming we receive from our family tree! This seems like a tall order. Future research will need to validate the truth of this. One way will be to monitor the changes in the iris of the eye. It is already possible to photograph the iris of children and observe that a certain structure present in the parent is less pronounced in the child. This means that what may have been a survival personality trait for the parent will have less of an influence on the child. To be able to see this in the eye can have deep implications for the psychotherapeutic community. One can then question whether change in the iris reflects a DNA change.

If we alter perceptions in one generation, that is, develop conscious seeing, is it possible that genetically coded eye conditions, such as nearsightedness, may have less tendency to be passed down? It's an interesting proposition. This means that if parents deal with the underlying perceptions related to their survival personality and the resultant eye condition, their child may not have to recreate the eye condition in order to survive or evolve.

The implications of this possibility upon human consciousness are deep. Even within the conservative discipline of visual science, an outgrowth known as "behavioral optometry" has occurred in the past thirty years. The behavioral optometrists took a bold step forward in 1994 when, in their publication *Journal of Behavioral Optometry*, they published an article entitled, "Seeing Space: Undergoing Brain Reprogramming to Reduce Myopia."

The title of the paper, by optometrist Antonia Orfield, is enough to get your attention. The reference to "brain reprogramming" implies that the way we process our seeing (in our mind) can shift and modify the way the brain handles visual data.

In turn, this change alters the dioptric refractive measurement in the eye. The paper does not present a controlled study but an in-depth discourse of how the author undertook many lifestyle changes as well as vision therapy. In the process, the dioptric measurements of the eye reduced by nearly four diopters. Recall that diopters refers to the slower-changing refracting power of the camera eye, whereas increased eyesight reflects the faster-acting changes of the mind's eye. In this case, the change in diopters implicates larger changes in eyesight. Interestingly, Orfield studied to be an eye doctor after she had these excellent results from her vision therapy program.

Dr. Orfield begins the paper with a profoundly gallant statement, "Functional myopia is not just an embedded (accommodative—focusing) spasm and it is not just an enlargement of eyeballs. It is a reflection of the shrinking of the brain's space world by closure of the periphery, first by stress, then by errors in spatial judgment induced by minus lenses."

Here is the link to the survival personality. It is in the word "stress." Secondly, in the comment, "shrinking of the brain's space world by closure of the periphery," Orfield suggests that mismanaged stress can induce a non–genetic-related but functional variety of nearsightedness. The mechanism that comes first is the shrinking of the periphery, and it may be caused by nothing other than how we respond to the world around us.

Recall that I talked about this phenomenon in chapters 1 and 2. I mentioned that it is the suppression of retinal function, which Orfield refers to as the periphery. I added that the retina is related to feeling. If you cannot manage interacting with your visual world, the easiest solution is to suppress the retina, not feel, and thus shrink your space world.

The fact that the mind can cause a suppression of peripheral function without there being a change of the structural measurement of such information in the eye is very important information. It correlates very well with my published research study on children's visual fields, that is, how much access children had to their peripheral seeing. I conducted a study for the College of Syntonic Optometry (see reference to my 1983 paper under "Suggested Reading," on page 256) of twenty-two children, nine of whom were reading at a level two grades below where they should have been. For all intents and purposes the structural visual fields were normal. But when I measured color visual fields (how much peripheral vision was possible with colored as opposed to white targets), their functional visual fields were reduced from forty to as small as ten degrees. These kids could kick a ball and not bump into things but had problems reading. The distress of not being able to function well in school, particularly with reading, leads to a reduction of peripheral awareness. After using color before the eyes, the functional visual fields were statistically larger.

My findings also support the notion that when there is a structural measurement in the eye of a condition like nearsightedness, then this is a representation of a genetic influence of a survival personality of one or both of the parents. This can be the primary influence. Then follows the life stressors. If both the genetic factor and the life factors are present, then the measured eye condition will tend to be more severe.

Orfield speaks strongly about the distortions in perception of space through minus lenses that are conventionally used to compensate for nearsightedness. When a person reduces their looking ability, resulting in unclear eyesight in the distance, this is called nearsightedness. The lens treatment is a minus lens. The wearing of this lens further shrinks the perception of space. This means that the person has less mobility. The wearing of minus lenses causes more looking, with less seeing and less feeling. This in turn leads to having less access to one's own consciousness.

Orfield states, "Lens reduction is truly brain reprogramming.... Each minus lens has its own virtual world that is achieved by the interaction of the individual and the optics of the lens, and once one adjusts to that lens, one is looking into that world and has learned a new brain perception of spatial perception. The compressed view then continues one's need for the lens."

The inference from this is that reducing minus lenses affects how the brain responds to incoming light. This is the brain's reprogramming process. Weaker lenses promote more seeing and less looking. The outcome is that your mind has to reorganize and more elegantly integrate perceptions. New meaning has to be constructed for old points of view. Former belief structures have to be dismantled. In the process of letting go, parts of the mind are liberated as you flow effortlessly into conscious seeing.

## Structuring Personality with Lens Prescriptions

In the fields of optometry and ophthalmology, corrective lenses are used in much the same way as medications are used in allopathic medicine. A patient comes in with an eye problem and walks out with a prescription for eyeglasses—no different from a prescription for medication. The correlation is unfortunate. In both cases there is a risk of simply putting a Band-Aid on a bullet wound. Why? Because both treat the symptoms and ignore the underlying problems. Unclear eyesight is like a headache. It is a symptom of a deeper problem. Mainstream medicine, like vision care, is a symptom-based profession. Give the patient an aspirin and the headache will go away. The lens makes the blur go away as well. The patient is happy. Most people wear the lenses and even believe the doctor's assurance that "this will correct your problem."

My own experience, and that of thousands of behavioral optometrists, suggests that the opposite is true. The wearing of most prescribed lenses suppresses the deep, inner cause of the condition, which actually makes the symptom worse. This is why most eyeglass wearers return for stronger lenses within a year or two. The symptom goes away for a while but the real problem is never dealt with and therefore is never corrected.

One of vision science's greatest secrets is that the potential of altering a conventional lens prescription can have a therapeutic effect on the retina, fovea, brain, and mind. I have been researching such design parameters for thirty years. The evidence suggests that therapeutic lenses may emerge as a powerful form of medicine for visual and other healing. (See chapters 4, 7, 8, and 9 for more thorough discussions of therapeutic lenses.)

## A Flexible Personality Practice

Granted, if all this is true, you may still be asking the question, "How do I apply it in my own life?" If you wear glasses, begin taking them off as you go about your daily activities. Begin to see. Speak to the blur. Embrace the blur. See your parents bringing you the gift of their presence. Repeat the earlier review practice, where you considered things about your parents that you didn't like. This time, think about the qualities you do like.

Here is an example from my own memories.

*I love my father when he smells of pipe smoke.* My father was generally in a loving mood when he smoked his pipe. *My mother listens when I share my feelings.* I felt love when my mother listened to how I felt. These are positive perceptions of my parents that I treasure. I feel nurtured by these memories. In their presence I easily let go of my perceptions of a lack of love. I feel joyous that I had a father and mother who were really present for me in spite of their inadequacies. I realize now that they too were growing up as I was.

I invite you to spend time looking and seeing photograph 6 on page 120. This practice is a form of visual contemplation. First, concentrate on the flame as you did in chapter 3. Then let your eyes wander around, allowing the less visible elements in the photograph to come into your awareness. You may find yourself reliving memories of experiences with people in your extended family. The images of the iris help promote flexibility in your personality. By looking at the pictures, you begin to see your physical self as reflected through your eyes, as one part of your total self. The flexibility is accessing the part of your self called your "being."

To really perceive what is in the material world is to see the underlying light patterns in it. This light is made up of geometric forms. They are like waves. Music to the eyes. Conscious seeing is allowing yourself to stop long enough to notice these patterns, to be aware of the invisible. Becoming aware of what you are not looking at allows you to feel and see more deeply into other aspects of existence.

By being with photograph 6 for ten- to fifteen-minute practice sessions, you will find yourself being liberated from your past. It may at first bring up issues. Be patient. Write your discoveries down, keeping a journal record as you progress into conscious seeing.

# 5

## *A Personal History of Looking and Seeing*

### Who Am I, Really?

The most significant external influences on our lives usually come from our parents. Their personalities, and the way they interact with each other and with us, play a role in our personal evolution that extends into our own adulthood. In this chapter we will examine our parents' impact—good and bad—on who we are today. We'll explore ways to use that information to help us become more fully integrated human beings and, at the same time, take an important step toward achieving conscious seeing.

Just the other day, in a moment of exasperation, one of my children said to me, "I wish I had a different parent!" You may remember saying something similar to your mother or father. I believe I said it many times in my growing-up years, mostly when I felt confused about who I was and how I fit in. When I heard the comment from my son, I reminded him that he does have another parent—his mother. This was a reminder to me that the parenting we receive may be synergistic; that is, the product of our early interactions with one or both parents plus other caregivers who have taken part in our parenting.

Even the most loving, well-intentioned parents can sometimes leave us with childhood memories that are painful. Our minds might try to protect us from those painful memories, obscuring feelings even when we are intellectually aware of them and of the issues they bring up for us. But the more we can be open to all of the experiences that molded our early development—especially the emotions related to these experiences—the more we are able to make choices about how those experiences still influence our lives today.

There are numerous ways of accessing memories, and different personality types require different approaches. For example, thinkers like myself tend to be visual. I can see what happened in July of 1979 almost as if it were a movie before my eyes. On the other hand, emotional personality types are generally good listeners and may relive memories best and most vividly by hearing sounds. Sometimes conversations from years gone by will come to mind with what seems like word-for-word precision. The feeler, on the other hand, is kinesthetic. They process and remember experiences best through touch and movement, sometimes at a deep, visceral level—that is, "gut feelings." How do you remember? Take a moment to get in touch with your own medium for accessing your memories. What do you remember most vividly—sights, sounds, or touch? Spend some time thinking about the specific form your most vibrant memories take. A conscious awareness of how you relive old experiences will help you clarify what your memories have to tell you.

The only images I have of my life before age eight come from either photographs I have seen or stories I have heard my family talk about. While preparing material for a biography of my life, I came upon an exercise I found very revealing. I would like to share this with you because it had such an impact on my ability to uncover the roots of my personality and accept those parts of myself that I received genetically.

Take a blank piece of paper and, on the left side, write down your age in years starting from the earliest time you can remember. Begin with the year you can recall your first image or sound or feeling from an experience of your life as a young child. On the right side of the paper, jot down a few words about an event that you remember and, most important, the feeling that it brings up for you now. Write

86

down the very first event that comes to mind for each year, and stay with that memory until feelings or emotions come to the surface. Examine your present feelings as they relate to what was going on in your family at that time. Continue with the exercise year by year, all the way up to the time you no longer lived in your parents' home.

Here are some examples of the memories that came up for me when I did this exercise:

| Age in years | Event and Accompanying Feeling |
|---|---|
| 4 | I have a feeling of being abandoned when my mother's love is directed toward my younger brother. |
| 7 | A very traumatic time when I began attending school. I can't relate. I feel pushed to excel. |
| 8 | I am with my father who is carrying me. We are with our dog, walking across a hot, sandy beach. I feel so loved. |
| 9 | I am being reprimanded for not wanting to do swimming laps. I am despising my father, not wishing to be near him. |
| 12 | I remember my parents not understanding me. I feel different and lost. |
| 13 | School is challenging. I feel dumb, unloved, controlled. |
| 14 | I remember being physically hit because of my curiosity about sexuality. I close my heart. |
| 16 | I am sensing my parents' unhappiness. Why don't they do something? I will help. I feel frustrated and determined. |
| 17 | My parents are pushing me into a career choice. I will please them. |

Your parents and the events of your life with them are part of your history for a good reason. All of these experiences helped to shape who you are today—your genetic, emotional, thinking, and feeling parts all needed to be constructed, and it is largely through our parents that this is accomplished. Even the most difficult experiences will ultimately help you develop your strength and discover valuable information about yourself that you might otherwise have missed. It can be helpful to think that you probably needed these experiences to allow the many facets of your personality to emerge and integrate. Use this exercise to help you find clarity about the emotionally charged times in your life and how you feel about them now. As you do, try to identify the parts of your personality that are still in survival; that is, the places where you have avoided experiencing difficult or frightening emotions. This awareness will help you access conscious seeing.

The life story of Juliana will illustrate how our childhood experiences play an intimate role in the evolution of the many parts of ourselves. Her words will help you understand just how much our looking and seeing mechanisms can be influenced by these experiences.

My heritage is Italian. My father's family was from Sicily. We lived a very simple life. I felt my mother's unhappiness. Having five children to take care of was traumatic for her. My father was a fisherman until an accident left him disabled. He was put on permanent sick leave. He seemed lost at home. I felt his discontent.

My mother wore glasses. I got mine when I was eight, to correct nearsightedness and astigmatism. There was never enough food for seven of us. Being the eldest I was last in receiving gifts and love. I felt rebellious from an early age. My mother ran a little canteen from our home. I used to steal sweets and drinks. The family spoke Italian. I went to an English-speaking Catholic school. I learned to speak English, so well, in fact, that unlike my family I was able to lose my Italian accent.

My father had a problem with intimacy. He flirted around with other women. I knew about this. So did my other siblings and my mother. She never said anything. This infuriated me. Why does she just let him do whatever he wants? She was afraid to confront him. I felt angry. I wanted to fight. Later, I discovered he was touching my younger sisters. Once he tried to touch me. I thought allowing a man to touch me was a way of being loved.

From Juliana's story so far, we begin to get a sense that even as a child, her life—just like yours and mine—had a design quality to it. The playing out of the dysfunctional side of our parents' personalities becomes the impetus for us to evolve. At first you may choose a *reactive* approach and adopt a rebellious behavior pattern. This is one part of the maturing process. Later, your reactive behavior may begin to evolve into another possibility: *responding*. Keep in mind, as you read, that when I use the term "reactive," I am referring to experiencing an event from your own presuppositions; that is, surrounded by whatever emotional charges you bring to the experience. By contrast, "responsive" would mean experiencing the event more nearly as a new experience. In the reactive approach we may be defensive; in the responsive one we can be more open.

The shift from reactive to responsive requires a shift in perception. This is a part of the healing process. If your parents, like Juliana's, were unconscious in their behavior, you can use the knowledge you now have about their actions to help you become a more conscious person now. This requires adopting a new perception of your genetic self and your history, which in turn helps you become more conscious of how you think and feel about yourself and the manner in which you express emotion.

Start becoming aware of your deep inner desires to be all of who you are. To do this, allow yourself to be more fully aware of your dreams and aspirations, of the person you'd most like to be in your life. Step beyond your restricted past. Find the parts of yourself that are waiting for an opportunity to come forth, whether it be in a relationship, in a creative venture, or in some other area of life that you feel would bring you a sense of greater fulfillment. This is a way to bring about a change in the restrictive patterns of your genetics. My own experience directs me to accept nothing less than my own vision of who I want to be. I am on this planet to evolve. When I resist my own process of becoming whole, the universe sends me another version of an earlier experience. Our reflections about what our lives can be shake us out of our genetic slumbers. Start to consciously see what behaviors and patterns exist in your life and the lives of your parents and you can start to change your life.

## The Thinking Self

Juliana continues:

> As a young girl I learned that the safest way to exist was to bury my feelings. I ate sweets and when I was old enough I began to smoke cigarettes. I carried so much anger toward my family that at fourteen years of age I ran away from home. In hindsight, I realize that I wasn't really seeing reality. I developed my thinking part of myself to protect me from the hurt and pain of my family's *asleepness*. I read books and wanted to travel. I found a man who took me away at fourteen. I was introduced to sexuality early. This man took advantage of me, a theme I played out into my adult life. I gave my body to be loved.
>
> I excelled at thinking activities. I learned about computers when they first came out. I traveled for years around the world to escape my family. Now I can see that I was escaping that part of myself. I was running away from my fear of dealing with my hurt and pain. My boyfriend and I kept traveling and I was able to find work as a word processor. I had learned to be very quick with my *thinking* mind.
>
> Before I reached the age of twenty I was using drugs to further suppress my feelings. This was a good way for me to disconnect from the emotional pain of my genetic family life. The deeper feelings of my emotional body were dormant. I was shocked when my girlfriend talked about how she could vaginally orgasm. I never could. This feeling part of myself was like dead. There were aspects of myself related to my earlier life I wasn't yet

ready to see. My contact lenses were part of my addictive, protective personality hiding what I was not ready to see.

In Juliana's case she effectively harnessed the thinking part of her personality to protect the feeling and emotional side. This demonstrates the disintegration process we discussed in chapter 2. Until she became aware of the separation between her thinking, feeling, and emotional selves, Juliana would continue to act out her unhappy past and feel discontented. As her story continues, we'll see how life ultimately brought her the experiences she needed to wake up from her drugged state. It's fascinating to see how her vision — the way she looked through her eyes — would play a key role in that process:

I kept attracting men who would abandon me. They would run off with another woman about the time I was ready to settle down. I believe I never really opened my heart to a man until I married. Prior to my marriage I started practices to develop conscious seeing. I read *The Power Behind Your Eyes* and gave up wearing contact lenses. I recall the day I was walking in Pardova wearing my old glasses. My eyes began to ache. I had to stop and cover them with the palms of my hands. My boyfriend had to hold me, the pain was so excruciating. I had been storing tension and anger in my eye muscles all those years.

I dearly loved my husband-to-be. I felt his commitment to me and had no fear he was going to leave me. My vision was clearing. My growing belly brought many deep feelings to the surface. I gave birth to a son. I loved this baby with my whole being. I wasn't prepared for what was to surface from my past.

Georgio was a beautiful child. His long curly hair and bright eyes made me look more deeply into life. The first experience that started changing my perception happened in the kitchen one morning. Georgio was about fifteen months old. The kitchen had a tile floor. I reached into the storage cupboard to fetch a glass bottle of juice. Just as I was reaching back to the counter, the bottle dropped onto the tile floor and exploded into millions of little pieces. Even though Georgio was far enough away from being hurt, my feelings and emotions went into automatic panic. The blast that followed was louder and more intense than the glass breaking. I screamed out to protect my baby son. I panicked. I shook all over. My body and mind reacted even though none of the glass had touched Georgio. Frederico, my husband, grabbed our son and took him away. I continued to behave like a mad-woman for the next minute or two.

This experience made me realize that I had much emotion and feelings deeply buried inside of me. My reactivity went beyond my actions. I looked through my eyes with the same emotion. I needed to examine my looking perceptions. My vision was not complete. Was my overthinking keeping me from feeling? Did my thinking prevent me from fully seeing? Was my lack of fun and cre-ative expression blocked by this survival mechanism? Could I ever have a more fulfilling sexual experience in my body? Did my previ-ous substance addiction affect my capacity to access my feel-ings? I knew my tenderhearted husband was to be the catalyst for my discovering more power within myself. What would happen if I harnessed the energy of this power that screamed out of my being? I wondered, Is this a hidden form of passion?

As Juliana wore weaker and weaker lenses, she accessed a more accurate vision that allowed her to be less reactive and more respon-sive. This was a gradual process, and her son and husband, with their love and support, played an important role in it. When Georgio was three, Juliana wore her first therapeutic lens prescription to help overcome her astigmatism. The lens design helped to focus the light onto the parts of herself that had been astigmatically distorted: her denial of her deep sexual feelings, the roaring anger waiting to be released, and her passionate, dancing body waiting for a chance to express itself. When she wore these glasses, her perceptions of her outer world were unclear. Juliana had to use her retinal seeing. This is what brought the suppressed feelings and emotions to the surface. The lens altered the light coming into the periphery of her eye, whereby the retinal fibers carried the message to those blurred, buried feelings and memories that still held a charge of fear, anger, and bewilderment for her. The modified incoming light helped direct her awareness to her consciousness, allowing her to become increasingly aware of the painful past so that the heavy charges of emotion were able to be healed and finally dissipated. Her expanding vision allowed her to move beyond the genetic and historical limitations that had been smoldering in her mind. This new way of seeing made her conscious of the parts of herself that she hadn't seen before.

The technique of using therapeutic lens prescriptions to bring awareness to suppressed parts of ourselves was replicated in the work of Frederick Schiffer. He called his approach "dual brain therapy." Rather than using lenses, Schiffer designed patching goggles. While wearing these devices the patient receives light stimulation to a particular area of the retina of one or both eyes. The light activates one hemisphere of the brain. Schiffer writes: "The goal of dual brain therapy is the care and nurturance and education of the mind of the more troubled hemisphere. The troubled side is often like a traumatized person. The trauma can remain covertly present because the mind on the troubled side fails to notice or trust the improvement."

## The Emotional Self

Continuing with Juliana's story, we get a dramatic picture of how therapeutic lenses can affect conscious awareness.

My new glasses were intense. In the past I was unaware of which eye I was looking through. With these glasses I felt all the energy directed toward my right eye. This was a strange experience given that I am usually left-eye dominant. Each day I increased the wearing time of these glasses by a few minutes. I started at twenty minutes and worked my way up to a few hours. At the point of reaching the third hour, I felt a power surge through me. This feeling was unlike anything I had ever witnessed before. The energy moved from within me. The feeling was soft, but stronger

than anything I had felt before. This was the power of me responding to life rather than reacting. I was observing. I felt myself being
consciously present. I was seeing more than I had ever looked at
in my life.

Shortly thereafter, I had two additional "wake-up" calls.
I entered into deep awareness of my inner self. One day I
screamed at my beloved husband, Frederico. I am normally quite
passive. This most amazing anger came out of me like a volcano.
I behaved in an unreasonable way. I was like a little girl bellowing
out my unhappiness. In the middle of my theatrical episode I
flashed onto my father. I didn't really feel anger toward my husband. I was projecting the anger I felt for my father onto Frederico.
The glasses were activating this hidden part of myself. In the middle of the anger performance, I stopped and stayed with this revelation. I glanced out the window and my eyesight was perfectly
clear through the therapeutic glasses. [*Recall that these glasses
usually make things sufficiently blurry that you would easily
observe changes.*] I can remember the feeling. My body vibrated
in the joy of such presence.

Emotion is like a stormy ocean. If you are in a small boat you
need to go with the motion of the waves until the storm stops. This
was Juliana's experience as she began to deal with the powerful feelings she discovered as she explored her relationship to her family.
This was a critical step in her process of growing up emotionally.

Juliana's experience illustrates another interesting phenomenon. In the development of conscious seeing, I have discovered that
each person's life revolves around twenty-year cycles. Beyond the
age of twenty, we experience a *current age of consciousness* that corresponds to our chronological age twenty years earlier. In other
words, at the age of twenty-five your current age of consciousness
would be five, and you would be in a position to revisit the emotional events you experienced at that young age. In Juliana's case,
her age at the time she revisited her difficult childhood emotions
corresponded to her age when she first experienced the events that

triggered them. For example, Georgio was born when she was thirty-five. In conscious seeing terms, Juliana's age would have been fifteen. This cycle continues. At fifty-five Juliana would revisit the age of fifteen for the third time.

Why is this significant? I predict that each time you revisit a particular age you become more conscious of how the experiential content of the earlier time has affected your present way of seeing. I have tracked this with patients and in my own life, and the correlation is remarkably accurate. For Juliana, the anger and teenage rebellion she first experienced between the ages of fourteen and seventeen returned when she was thirty-five. Fortunately, she had made a commitment to evolve toward greater consciousness and stop the pattern of reactivity and blaming others for her unhappiness. Juliana was determined to free herself from her self-destructive survival personality. Although she didn't realize it, Juliana was freeing her family as well. Our personal evolution energetically transfers to the family members who are open. We see this in Juliana's story, as she continues:

> Fredrico's business required doing lots of paper work, and I helped. It gave me something to do. I had so much love for this man, I wanted to support him. We could save money by not hiring someone. I was not really meant to work at computers and do numbers. I found my passion was moving my body, like in belly dancing, or moving my hands on a drum. One day, while wearing the therapeutic glasses, I had a vision. I could also hear music. Like in a movie, I watched myself in a band hitting an African drum with my hands. Then I was dancing, moving my hips. The vision helped me remove an imaginary veil from in front of my eyes to what I hadn't been seeing. My "doing" work for my husband was certainly supporting the family, but not me. I was giving up a part of myself. I did this in the name of love and the marriage. But what about me? Georgio was old enough to be in preschool and I had time for me. I needed to access the deep creativity locked in the prison I had built for myself.

Life sometimes has its own surprises. Frederico reacted by becoming withdrawn, feeling abandoned and depressed about my departure from helping him. I met a woman who became a very close friend. This happened about the time my way of seeing demanded that I face my womanhood and my blocked sexual feelings. Frederico was a wonderful, patient lover. But I needed to explore a deeper part of myself. I knew my friend was a lesbian. This didn't bother me. One day while having a sauna, we began to touch each other. I knew this was risky. But, to me it felt totally right. I spoke to Frederico about this, since we were very open in our discussions. As I expected, he wanted the best for me. My husband loved our sexuality before this experience. If this was going to help open me up to being more of myself, he was very interested. During this love affair I felt my pelvic area in a deep way. The vaginal feelings were like emotional explosions. Childhood memories rushed through me. My eyesight fluctuated. I felt like I was being born. For days I could walk down the street without glasses and have perfect, sharp vision. Other times I was wearing three or four diopters less. [*This meant that Juliana's eyesight was significantly sharper and her camera eye was recording these changes.*]

## The Feeling Self

By this stage of Juliana's journey into conscious seeing, she and Fredrico had been trying unsuccessfully to conceive a second child. I believe there was an obstruction within their joint evolution that kept this new baby and spirit away. As you may recall, I have proposed that we might have a say in when our parents are able to conceive. Perhaps in Juliana's and her husband's case they needed to see and deal with an issue to which they had been blind. Their inability to conceive may have been a gentle indication that they needed to look a little deeper. Juliana related it this way:

One of my personality traits was to never really say what I wanted. I had difficulty making calm decisions. If I was pushed, then I would move really fast. In survival, I could organize a banquet in Tuscany in a few days. In a moment of clear sight, I realized that I had been letting my husband make the decisions, just like I did with my father. I falsely believed that he had the power and I was to follow. Only afterwards, when I felt frustration and resentment, would I say what my needs were. This was a very important step for Frederico and me. We needed to meet each other heart to heart and to each be in our own power. We did this.

One night we met in this way. Georgio was away with a friend. Frederico was gentle. I was strong and passionate. I saw my man as my equal. There was no need to fight this man I loved. We played quiet music, took a sauna, ate delicious pasta, lit a candle, and gazed into each other's eyes with long moments of silence. This was being. I saw Frederico with new eyes. It was as if this was the first time I could really see his beauty without my filtering through my past. Many memories returned. My will had clashed with my parents. I carried this pattern into my relationships with men. Now I was living it with my husband and son. I realized that until I faced this feeling of being put down by men, I would not open to my true potential. As I was reminiscing on this point I noticed Fredrico's eyes coming into perfect focus. I was in my naked vision, no glasses. I felt so much love in that moment. I reached toward him and we embraced the love between us. I allowed a feeling of letting in this love. I opened my heart and my eyes to see and feel. The longer I stayed with the feelings the more I felt the rich nurturing of my soul. Something inside of me came alive. I became conscious of myself.

The way Juliana closed off parts of her self was reflected in her nearsightedness and astigmatism. Her suppressed seeing mirrored her closed-off and suppressed feelings and thus protected her emotions. It was with considerable difficulty that she began to express her truth, ask passionately for what she wanted, and step into her power. When she did, she at last found herself excelling in a career of her own choosing.

Juliana's stifled creativity was another example of the way her blocked emotions and restricted sexuality limited her ability to express herself. Juliana started to practice being more open to feeling while having sexual intercourse. With time, she began to experience new and exciting sensations. She faced the reality of her history and discussed her childhood with her father; with her sisters she discussed the issues of sexual abuse and brought the feelings associated with these early feelings out into the open. All of this facilitated a powerful healing process that restored Juliana's feelings of power. As she began to live with greater consciousness, she more freely expressed her will with less and less anger. Her personality became more integrated. This helped the flow of emotion. In turn it promoted her creativity. She became interested in African drumming, singing, sewing, and Middle Eastern belly dancing.

In time, Juliana discovered that the most important feeling of love she felt was the love she found for herself. This is the source of all love. As a result of her long process along her path to conscious seeing, Juliana now has more to share.

## Bringing the Lessons Home

The feeling self deserves recognition. Feeling is nurturing. To feel is to stop, be open, and see with eyes of innocence. Like Juliana, we all need to see life with eyes focused from the heart of consciousness. Here are a few exercises to help you reconnect with your history in a way that integrates the different parts of your personality and deepens your conscious seeing.

If you have photographs of your grandparents, put them in a conspicuous place, such as around your mirror in your bathroom. Each day get close to the images and gaze at them for three to five minutes. Do this for at least twenty-one days. Repeat the same process with photographs of your parents and of yourself. If you are in a relationship, use pictures of your partner as well. Record any thoughts, feelings, and emotions that come to the surface while you gaze at the pictures.

I recently did this exercise with a photograph of my maternal grandfather. It was an exhilarating and emotional experience. He was a powerful man, and very spiritually inclined. He knew what he wanted and usually accomplished his goals. Even though he left this earth many years ago, as I gazed at his photo I felt his presence guiding me. On one occasion I felt a shiver pass through my body. My youngest son's face appeared in front of me. I sensed a strong connection between my son, myself, and my grandfather. It was as if we were united. This guided me into a new awareness of my purpose both professionally and as a father. I became aware. I reached a deep level of my mind that helped open up the consciousness that I had been mentoring my son with the help of my grandfather. I discovered a new source of strength inside myself. I became inspired.

Lastly, looking at photograph 7 on page 121 will help you integrate the different parts of your own iris structures. Spend three to five minutes per day being with this image.

As you look at the iris pictures on that page, realize that you contain inside of your being the complete universe of your family tree; it is contained within your genetic personality. Imagine conscious seeing being available to you now as you fully integrate your flexible personality with your soul. Familiarize yourself with the different iris structures, that is, thoughts, feelings, and emotions. Permit those parts of yourself to awaken. Let them integrate. Let the light rays that join the three iris structures metaphorically link the different parts of yourself.

Write down any experiences you have.

# 6

## Perceptions and the Revealing Eye

*The content is not relevant. You are relevant.*

—RICARDO ROJAS

### The Evolving Human Eye

In chapter 1 I introduced the concept of the camera versus the human eye. The eye structure itself can be considered to function like a camera. This I called the camera eye. Behind the retina is the human who operates from their brain and mind. I described this latter arrangement as the human eye.

I have illustrated the potential design of the mind existing in various degrees of depth. Each deeper stage of the mind is set up to mingle the foveally guided thoughts with the peripheral retinal elements of seeing. This process of integration is joining the doing and being parts of our consciousness in preparation for a deeper vision of our life. In the science of vision the integration of the left and right eye perceptions is physically designed to create three dimensionality. From a conscious seeing perspective, the integration goes much deeper.

My experience is that we human beings have the capacity for what is known as fourth-dimensional vision. In the shamanic trainings of the ancient Dur Bon tradition of Tibet this type of seeing is called "auspicious" vision. One is able to see into the invisible depths of physical matter. This may take the form of seeing energy waves or light colorations. Those who attain auspicious vision see more than what appears on the surface. Auspicious vision calls for a high level of observation, similar to what Sara was experiencing in the cave in chapter 1.

## The Mind's Eye

Conscious seeing can lead to perceiving the world around us in a much deeper way. To go deeper, it is necessary to break down the functions of the human eye into two parts. When light leaves the camera eye it is first processed in the brain. Then the mind is used to construct meaning of the light sensations. I call this part of the human eye the mind's eye. This is where thoughts, feelings, and emotions are woven together to construct the meaning we give to what we see.

In the mind's eye we form impressions and construct a perceptual reality of how we see. Many of us believe that the reality we see from the mind's eye is the one and only truth. I propose that the mind's eye may be partly or fully composed of perceptions related to our survival personality. This means that what we perceive from the mind's eye usually is seen through filters of fears, anger, and other emotions we've accumulated from our varied states of woundedness. Once these perceptions have been firmly established into the matrix of our mind's eye, then their software messages, so to speak, can be programmed back to the camera eye. This is our physical eyes relaying our pasts to us through the symptoms and eye conditions that each of us possesses.

Also, in the mind's eye we are still under the influence of our usual way of dealing with the concepts of space and time. When our view, our sense of space inside and outside ourselves, is "mentally" distorted, this can result in refractive conditions like astigmatism. Over time this mind's eye state will be mirrored in the camera, or physical, eye. In other words, what starts on the level of thought and feeling can be transformed into a physical manifestation in the physical structure of the camera eye. We are in a time frame where we see life in terms of yesterday, today, and tomorrow. In conscious seeing you can use the information from the camera eye to become more fully aware of the software programming of the mind's eye.

## The Eye of *Vivencia*

You can enter into a level of your mind where you know that you are "being" versus "doing" something. This sense of being is at a deep level of the mind called the *ground*. Consider the ground of being to be a nonmeasurable quantum space, a place where there is no reference point for measuring time. If you go even deeper—that is, underground—you can reach the place of total consciousness itself.

There are different levels of the mind above the ground, where the thoughts and feelings derived from foveal and retinal inputs through the eye are processed. In order for thoughts and feelings to fully integrate, you have to be present to your own consciousness. To see this deeply is to transcend understanding and enter *vivencia*. Vivencia is the place where you are not your personality, your thoughts, your feelings, or even your emotions. Vivencia is where you are aligned with your true nature. No mask is worn. You are your authentic self.

> *Dismantle the control of the thinking mind and time melts away.*
> *Be with a lover and days feel like hours.*
> —THE AUTHOR

This means that to see from the eye of vivencia is to perceive from pure consciousness. This is the point of observation where you are present with what is. You are unaffected by fleeting perceptions, which are like moving clouds. In this way your vision can no longer be contaminated by survival perceptions. You let them move through you. You stay in observation of what is. Because the influences of the mind's eye are sufficiently known to you, you can enter into the eye of vivencia.

We all have had exceptional moments like this, of being so into a hobby, work, or being in love that we lose ourselves. Time flies by and our sense of space vanishes. This is conscious seeing. In this state, you have the ability to know how to differentiate between perceptions that are survival oriented and levels of awareness that arise from pure consciousness, because you are becoming visually aware of reality rather than being highly influenced by states of illusion.

When you see from a state of illusion, you are projecting some need, like a thin curtain, over what you are looking at. You may see only what you want to see rather that what is! This happens very often in relationships where one partner sees the other person the way he or she wants rather than the way the partner actually is.

## Exploring the Space of the Mind's Eye

At the level of the mind's eye, your seeing makes use of the normal understanding of the space-time paradigm. You notice variations of unclearness and whether objects appear smaller, bigger, closer, or further away. It is important to accurately use what you perceive through the camera eye to skillfully reprogram the mind's eye. Conscious seeing requires you to make physical observations about your perceptions of reality or illusion.

In this chapter you will gain new awareness of how breathing and using your eyes to gaze in a certain way helps refine these perceptual discernments. You have already been preparing for this with the practices from the first four chapters. This method of gazing includes

- Receiving and programming light that enters your eyes
- Knowing that the iris of your eye holds messages from your genetic past
- Observing the different ways in which you see through your left and right eyes
- Knowing how different lenses before your eyes impact your perceptions
- Being in your naked vision and keeping a journal of your experiences

The more accurate you become at perceiving equally through each eye separately, and then speedily integrating that information, the deeper you will enter into three-dimensional perceiving. All of this practice prepares you for reaching the fourth dimension of seeing.

In this chapter, you will learn what camera eye conditions like the refractive errors of nearsightedness and farsightedness, astigmatism, and eye diseases reveal about your survival perceptions. The descriptions of these conditions will point you toward questions to ask yourself that will help you to better understand your individual way of seeing. This in turn gives you experience and knowledge that will help you travel to the eye of vivencia.

## Seeing Yourself More Deeply

Stop reading and look into a magnifying mirror and catch a glimpse of your eyes. Bring the experience from viewing photographs one through seven to this moment. In this way you can consciously appreciate your eyes. They are really very beautiful. The colors and the markings are a visual feast of dynamic, pulsating energy. The reflection of the light off the cornea, the outer covering of your eye, is much like the light of the sun reflected off the atmosphere covering Mother Earth. While looking at your eyes, imagine floating in outer space. You see the planets of the solar system.

This practice prepares you to expand your sense of space beyond the way we usually look at the physical world around us. What you observe outside yourself is representative of your own nature, the recorded history of time; in other words, your perceptions carry a historical message, like a voice-mail recording, that can influence how you currently see. Your past perceptions may mask your present seeing.

What is outside of you influences your earthly presence, just as the sun affects all living matter. Look at your eyes and consider how they hold the genetic mystery of your family tree. Ponder the thought that the outer world is like the inner space of your eye. Continue to gaze into your eyes as you hold these ideas in your mind.

Let each marking, opening, or raised mountainlike structure speak loudly of how you might see yourself in a new light. This opens your mind up to the possibility of different perceptions of yourself and is the first step in incorporating them into your outer view. As you look at the colorations, let your iris pattern talk to you about the influences of the past that keep you from your potential for conscious seeing. Consider how your structures have modified their shape from your parents' generation to yours. What incompletions in your parents' generation have possibly been exaggerated in you and any siblings?

After a two-minute session of looking at and seeing your eyes, consider responding to the following questions:

- How do you feel when you closely look into your eyes?
- Are you resistant to looking at certain places in your eyes? What past experiences does this resistance remind you of?
- Do your eyes remind you more of one of your parents than another, and how does this make you feel?
- Are you able to reach a point while looking at your eyes that allows you to appreciate the beauty of what you see, and feel love for yourself? Can you bring this feeling of love to others? What does this experience reveal to you?

After you have answered these questions, consider the twenty-year cycles of time (from chapter 4) as they correspond to your current age of consciousness, and use them to backtrack to specific events in your life that relate to your eye condition. Consider choosing an exercise from chapters 1 through 4 to focus on. For example, you choose to wear your glasses less; improve your naked vision eyesight; explore your own survival perceptions; forgive one or both of your parents, siblings, or a teacher; or reintegrate the male and female sides of the way you see yourself. Each time you revisit the past, try to see beyond the survival way you saw your life and world around you in the past. Remember to see from the now perspective. Use this opportunity to refine being conscious.

## Universal Space

The ability to see through the eye of vivencia requires observing yourself "being conscious"; in other words, through your eyes you have to experience presence. You can reach a state of presence by staying long enough in three-dimensional vision that you suddenly find yourself extending your perceptions beyond the way you normally look. Something else pops into your awareness that you haven't previously seen. There are certain ingredients, like a recipe, that are useful for you to reach this advanced state of being and seeing.

Breathing: Begin with breathing. The goal here is to use breathing to lessen your thinking. Breathing activates a flow of energy. From within, you become the source of inspiration for seeing. Concentrating on listening and feeling yourself breathe will help bring your attention to your body, where your feelings are most deeply experienced. Conscious breathing slows down bodily functions; this deep relaxation permits you then to enter more deeply into your mind. The key to breathing consciously is to lengthen the out-breath with each successive in-breath. Then let the pause between the out-breath and the next in-breath lengthen as well.

Gazing: Once you have mastered slowing down the busyness of your thinking mind with your relaxed breath and closed eyes, then you can open your eyes and begin a gazing practice. In chapter 2, I asked you to imagine a candle flame in photograph 4. For this gazing exercise, use a real candle. Continue breathing and let your attention softly focus on the flame. Use your naked vision — no spectacles or contact lenses. The flame doesn't need to be perfectly in focus. Notice everything around the flame. Where in space is the candle positioned? What is behind, to the sides, and in front of the candle? Don't think about what you see; be in the experience of what you are bringing to the candle through your eyes.

In the practice of gazing you can transcend controlling your eyes from your brain. Perceiving the candle in this manner will help you to remember to see through your eyes. In your gazing practice, you will begin to transcend the restrictions within your mind's eye. Conscious seeing evolves by viewing from your eye of vivencia in a self-inspired way. You are inspired by the sensations received by your eyes. As you embrace this form of seeing, it may feel like you are moving back into your head or self, much like Sara did in chapter 1.

You can reinforce this practice by using photograph 7 on page 121. It is a compilation of the many aspects of outer and inner space. Let the iris remind you of your genetic self. View the three iris images from the eye of vivencia. Let yourself feel and let go of your survival personality as much as you can. Stand above and behind your life history. Envision your past slipping into the darkness of outer space. Imagine receiving the light beams from the sun and uniting universal consciousness with your personal consciousness. Let the background image be the planet Jupiter, reminding you that your conscious seeing is infinite.

Stay with the photograph a little longer. Go deeper. Imagine Jupiter looks like the back of your retina. Acknowledge that you are simultaneously experiencing inner and outer space. You are connected to everything. It is this oneness that is being perfected while gazing. You are mastering the art of being in a quantum space of the eye of vivencia. Practice gazing on this image, alternating back and forth between the different aspects of space for a few minutes each day. Over time, your inner and outer space will melt together and new dimensions of perceiving will open for you.

## Survival Perceptions of the Mind's Eye

I notice that my clients' eye conditions correlate to specific stories about their lives. My case histories reveal that each eye condition suggests a survival theme, a representation of the mind's eye.

Each one of us is on this planet in order to evolve into being conscious. The eye conditions speak to me of a pathway to reach conscious seeing. First, you must understand your survival perceptions and diminish their control over how you see the world. Your ability to do this will give you the edge you need to recognize when your mind's eye tries to seduce you into believing that what you are seeing is reality. When you see from the eye of vivencia, you are able to discern which of your perceptions spring from a survival nature and which arise from pure consciousness itself. Conscious seeing is the freedom from perceiving yourself as a mere victim of circumstance.

Mario had many survival perceptions to deal with in his life. Even as an adult his mind's eye presented images of the past like haunting video replays. One of these perceptions was an experience that he had when he was eight years old. He was visiting a distant female cousin who was five years older than he. He adored this cousin Gina. During his stay, she engaged him in childhood sex play. It was a pleasurable experience for Mario. His adoration for Gina turned into infatuation, though this was the only time he expressed his feelings for her. Mario, being farsighted, kept this love for Gina going inside of himself for many years as he matured. His inner perception of love was shattered years later when Gina flatly denied that this early sexual event ever happened. It was clear to Mario when he brought the incident up that Gina didn't even want to talk to him and certainly not about that experience.

In Mario's mind's eye, he kept trying to replicate this early sexual experience when seeking solace with a woman. He even fell in love with women whose physical characteristics reminded him of Gina. Mario's way of approaching sexuality was by attempting to create a replay of that earliest sexual encounter. In other words, his survival perceptions of that time with Gina continued to control his present and his future.

During a short period of counseling, Mario was guided back into the experience with Gina. He was told that what had happened is called sexual abuse, and from a psychotherapeutic point of view, this was a problem that had to be remedied. The outcome of this therapy was devastating for Mario. It was during this time that Mario noticed more disintegration between his left and right eyes, when he had moments of double vision as well as loss of concentration. A deeper split occurred between his male and female parts. A new survival perception, that he had been sexually abused, had been unskillfully planted into his mind's eye. He had difficulty centering in on his personal needs. Mario was more scattered in his life, didn't manage his affairs well, and couldn't finish projects or maintain long-term relationships.

Meanwhile, Mario kept attracting women with whom he could play out his perceptions of his past. This was done in an innocent way in which Mario had no conscious awareness of any buried emotion. Once the idea of sexual abuse came into his experience, however, he began to realize deep emotion. The difference now was that his anger toward women surfaced. He chose women who were emotionally suppressed and would enjoy his sexual attentiveness. In addition, during intercourse he could act out his anger toward women. This is a perfect example of how buried genetic patterns and life experiences can influence our projected vision from the mind's eye. Any love Mario would feel for the woman he was with was predicated upon a sexual union filtered through the unskillfully handled emotions of anger and his continuing need to recreate the past. Mario didn't actually perceive his lovers in the now moment; he continued to try to see Gina. Later in this chapter, Mario's story will continue, with his journey to Peru, where he experienced entering seeing that separated the mind's eye view from the eye of vivencia.

## The Mind's Eye Recorded in the Camera Eye

In the sections that follow are a discussion of various eye conditions that I encounter in my practice, and how I believe these conditions are related to the survival perceptions of the mind's eye. I have included at least one question or observation for you to make regarding each condition that you may suffer from. These questions will help you immediately begin to use your eye condition to explore your survival perceptions more deeply. See if you can convert the usually rigid survival perceptions into more flexible perceptions that expand your perceived potential in sight and in life in general.

## Nearsightedness

People with this condition have difficulty identifying small print and objects at a distance. For them, the visual world is inwardly projected. Their sense of self is closer than the perception of the outer world. Their visual style is to be logical. Good thinkers, those who are nearsighted prefer reading. They love to talk about intellectual matters. They can behave as if they don't notice what is happening outside their sphere of influence. Nearsighted behavior can be considered an "over-looking" form of personality. The goal of experience for many nearsighted people is to understand everything, seek explanations, and talk about what they see. This outlook is revealed as a lesser "looking ability" in eyesight. Their identity in their mind is constructed by figuring the world out in their head. If you are nearsighted, you will find it helpful to examine where you still experience fear in general, and fear in seeing. Nearsightedness is covered in more detail in chapter 8.

*Question:* Where do I still feel fear?

## Astigmatism

This is a distorted form of eyesight. To people with astigmatism, objects appear warped, unclear, or are seen as double through one eye. Astigmatism is a mechanism by which a person's mind's eye avoids certain content that it is storing—that is, unconscious material. The eyesight is pulled and twisted in order to warp the reality of what is seen. This condition may be accompanied by unusual head and neck postures. Exaggerated near- or farsighted conditions may exist in conjunction with astigmatism.

The time of onset of astigmatism is a clue to when certain awkward life situations that are related to suppressed feelings and emotions occurred. For instance, the development of astigmatism can be related to unresolved issues involving sexuality, particularly very early sexuality, as in Mario's case. Astigmatism is further discussed in chapter 10.

*Questions:* What areas of my life have I distorted? Is any part of my body warped or turned in an unusual posture?

## Farsightedness

This is a condition that particularly affects a person's close viewing activities. Eyesight at far distances can also be affected. The farsighted visual world is a projection outwards. A person with this condition senses himself or herself as being further away than the point of observation. It takes effort for the farsighted person to stay present in what is happening in their immediate visual world. They often dream beyond the present moment. They have difficulty staying with what is here and now long enough to forecast future outcomes. Farsightedness may be associated with a predictive form of genius; in other words, farsighted individuals may be able to intuitively know, in a highly evolved way, what is to come in the future. The farsighted person seeks to evolve toward being grounded in the here and now, which requires her or him to learn patience. Farsightedness is further discussed in chapter 9.

*Question:* Where do I hold resentment and unresolved anger?

## Farsightedness after Forty

After age forty, many people experience a loss of lens flexibility and muscular focus, resulting in small details appearing unclear. The condition is known as presbyopia. This farsightedness often occurs in people who are seeking to claim independence. This is a time in life when people begin to free themselves from their parental upbringing and finalize their lives according to their own, independent values. Past beliefs and opinions, such as those regarding religion or career, are now less important than living according to the individual's own truth and vivencia. Chapter 9 discusses presbyopia in more detail.

*Questions:* Where in my life can I focus with more precision and clarity? How can I invite more intimacy? How do I feel about reading less each day? How would I make use of this time?

## Strabismus

For people with this condition, their two eyes do not work together as a team. One eye appears to wander in or out. Some people have strabismus that alternates between one eye and the other. There are two types of strabismus:

### 1. Walleyed: Outward Looking

For those with walleyed strabismus, one eye appears to move out in relation to its mate, which signifies a divergent way of seeing life. Outward strabismus can be related to a desire to push some over-whelming perception away from one's existence. Postural distortions, like a twisting of the spine, can accompany the condition. Recall how I explained in chapter 3 that the right eye is the father's side and the left the mother's.

*Questions:* Is there a link between the eye that deviates and the parent associated with that side? Or is the link actually between my strabismus and the quality of parent I myself am?

### 2. Crossed Eyes: Inward Looking

In this condition, the eye appears to move inward. This may occur some of the time or all of the time. When it only occurs occasionally, the survival mind causing it may be traced to only a small perceptual conflict. A constantly inward-turning eye suggests that survival decisions made at the level of the mind's eye are more complicated. Often, in a constant eye-turning condition, one parent is physically or emotionally absent from the child's experience.

*Questions:* Is there a link between the eye that deviates and the parent associated with that side? For example, is there a correlation between the absence of the father and the right eye, or the absence of the mother and the left eye? Or is it a quality of the parent in myself? What could have been my survival perceptions?

## Lazy Eye

This seeing impairment is known as *amblyopia*, where, no matter what lens is placed before the person's eye, full, 100 percent vision does not result. The person suffering from it may not look very much through one eye, causing it to drift. Often the capacity to see out of the eye that drifts is intact. Inner conflict with the parent of the corresponding eye can be a good starting point from which to examine this tendency. The term lazy eye is unfortunate: it should be thought of instead as a *special* eye because it is the focus of a lot of attention.

*Questions:* Is it too painful to look at specific aspects of my life? Is one side of my personality underdeveloped?

## Floaters

People who have floaters complain that objects or shapes appear to be floating around inside their eye, blocking part of their visual field. Floaters can occur in one or both eyes. They may take the form of branchlike matter, dots, or solid forms. Doctors usually view this condition as physiologically normal unless the number and frequency of floaters increase suddenly.

*Questions:* What is floating around in my life that is incomplete? Is there an aspect of my life that is returning for me to reevaluate?

## Cataracts

Individuals suffering from cataracts experience a starlike cloudy formation in the lens of the eye that leads to a progressive loss of sharp eyesight. Cataracts have been likened to a waterfall obscuring seeing. They can occur in an otherwise healthy eye. I have found that cataracts develop in people who have a survival need to not see certain aspects of their life experience. Their eye of vivencia cannot accurately perceive. There is a clouding of reality. This keeps illusion alive.

*Questions:* What is blocking my view of my inner nature, my true self, maybe even my soul? Is there something in my life that needs to be cleaned up—a family conflict or even an unkempt house?

## Glaucoma

This condition is characterized by a buildup of pressure within the eye, leading to a reduced drainage of the aqueous fluid from the front of the eye.

*Questions:* How do I put myself under undue pressure? Where do I feel excess pressure? Do I sabotage myself by working too hard? Am I eating foods that are counterproductive to maintaining good

**See your eye. Let the light focus on the fovea. You and the way you see are connected to the universe. Look and see.**

The images that follow can be used to develop your conscious seeing. The photographs are sequenced according to the chapters in the book. It is wise to practice the looking, seeing, and fusion phases in sequence in order to achieve mastery at each level.

Consider re-reading each chapter prior to proceeding to the next photographic collage.

Remember to breathe while viewing the photographs. If your eyes become tired consider palming them.

Enjoy.

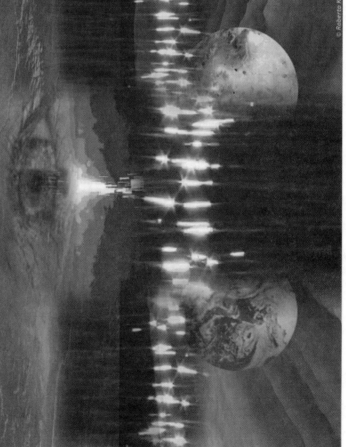

© Roberta Kaplan

**Anatomy of Light and the Eye**

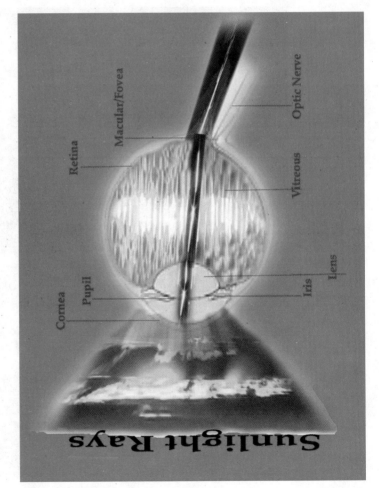

# Photograph 3

**Experience light in your eye and around you.**

Imagine you are inside your eye and it is like a dark cave. There is a small opening in the front where you can see light entering. The walls of the cave hold the eternal history of time. You become the light. You are being filled with universal consciousness.

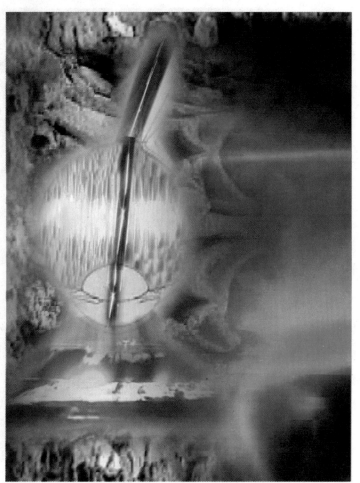

## Photograph 4

**Look at the flame in the center of the picture.**

Notice the images that surround the point of your looking. What is in your peripheral vision is less clear. You can sense and feel what is in the present. Breathe. Notice what you see in the surround of the flame. Have you noticed the two eyes looking at you? How does it feel to be seen?

118

# Photograph 5

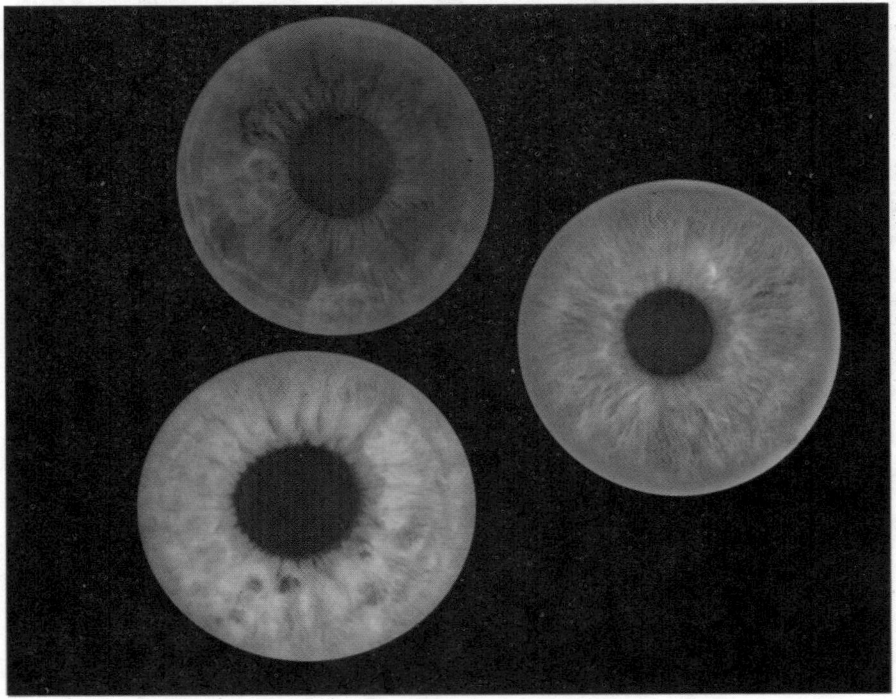

## The Iris Structure

See the smooth surface of a pond or sandy beach. Observe flower-petal-like shapes. Notice the floating clouds. Look for the bumps, like mountains.

## Visual Contemplation

Look at the flame between the top two iris pictures. Let your eyes wander around the less visible elements. See the underlying light patterns. Light is made up of geometric shapes and forms. Do you see faces? How do you feel?

## Visual Link to Consciousness

Inside of your being is the complete universe. Let the light rays metaphorically link the various parts of your personality and family tree. Feel your flexible personality self integrating with your unique consciousness.

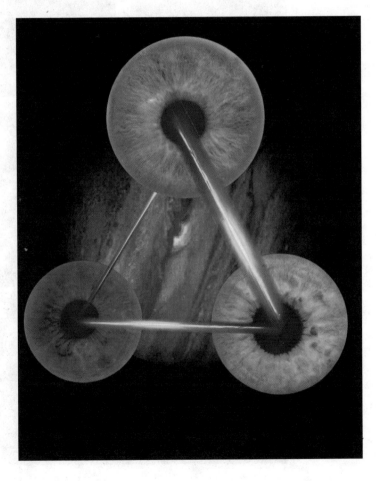

# Photograph 8

Look at the different parts of the image. Notice you can look at one place and see many elements at the same time. Maintain your stillness. Hold your sense of space.

Uncrossing

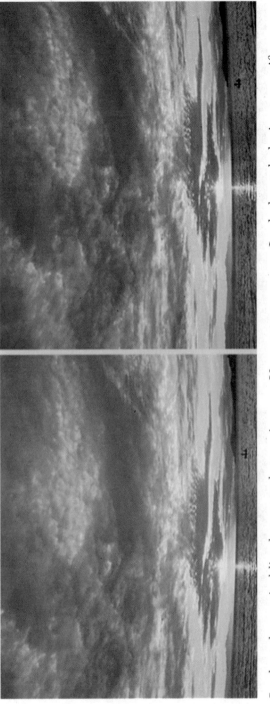

Look at the vertical line between the two images. Uncross your eyes — Look through the images as if you are looking behind and past the page. See two lines. Keep uncrossing your eyes while the two lines separate more until you see three pictures. Breathe, relax, and explore the middle image.

**Eye Crossing**

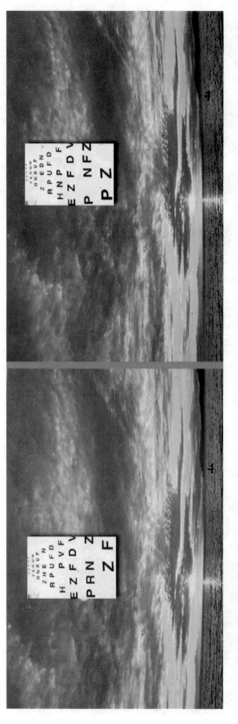

Cross your eyes—look and watch the vertical colored bars separate into two. Keep crossing your eyes while the two lines separate to the point where you see three pictures. Breathe, relax, and explore the middle image. Notice how the eye chart jumps off the page toward you.

# Photograph 11

See the iris patterns of throughts, feelings, and emotions.

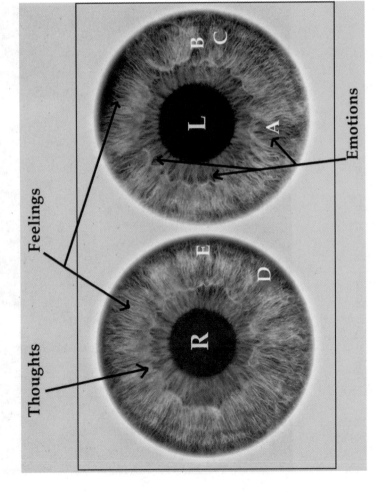

Natalie's Iris

Thoughts

Feelings

Emotions

125

**Nearsightedness—Uncrossing and Expanding**

Uncross your eyes—look through the images as if you are looking behind and past the page. See three or four eye charts. Keep uncrossing your eyes until there are three stable eye charts. Notice all the letters. Breathe, relax, and explore the depth of the middle image. Notice what you see in your side vision.

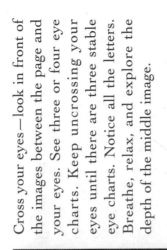

# Photograph 13

## Farsightedness—Eye Crossing and Focusing

Cross your eyes—look in front of the images between the page and your eyes. See three or four eye charts. Keep uncrossing your eyes until there are three stable eye charts. Notice all the letters. Breathe, relax, and explore the depth of the middle image.

## Farsightedness after Forty

Slightly cross your eyes until you have four black dots. Hold your eyes in this crossed position. Observe that the middle column of print has no black dot. Notice whether you can read the second and fourth column of words and see right through the black dot. Cross your eyes further until you have three black dots and seven columns of words. Notice how far the middle black dot stands out. Zoom your focus to the letters on the wall and back again.

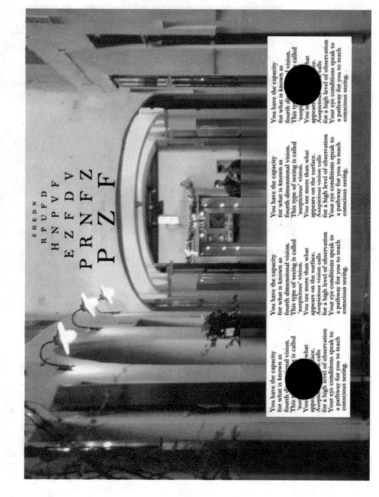

## Astigmatism—Integration of Vertical and Horizontal

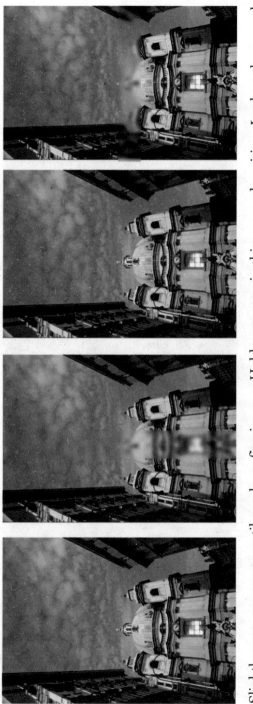

Slightly cross your eyes until you have five images. Hold your eyes in this crossed position. Look at the second image and attempt to clearly see all parts of the image. Notice whether it is more difficult to see the vertical section. While keeping your eyes crossed look at the fourth image and again attempt to clearly see all parts of the image. Notice whether it is more difficult to see the horizontal section.

Astigmatism—Oblique Distortion

## Astigmatism—Diagonal Distortion

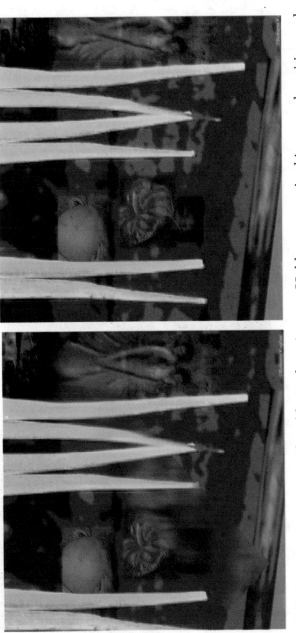

Slightly cross your eyes until you have three images. Hold your eyes in this crossed position and attempt to clearly see all parts of the middle image of, first, the upper and, then, the lower photographs. What else do you see in the middle images?

**Eye Diseases—Wake Up and See!**

Look deeply into this image. Let your feelings and emotions come to the surface. Let the pain of the past now float away. What else do you feel while looking at this Photograph collage?

The Eye of Vivencia

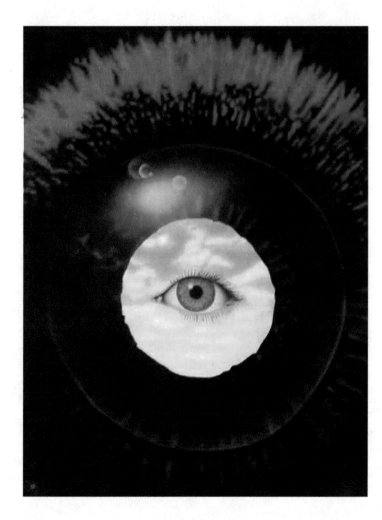

health? Am I not getting enough physical exercise? Am I in a job I don't really like? Am I in a relationship where the fire is gone and I feel stuck? Am I in denial about my life?

## Macular Degeneration

As the name implies, this condition involves a loss of sharp vision in the macular region of the retina, leading to an inability to focus clearly. The macular region is a valleylike structure in the eye, directly in the line of sight. At the center of the macula is the fovea centralis, the point of sharpest eyesight. If you suffer from macular degeneration, and if you are like many of the patients I have seen with this condition, you may be approaching the most exciting time of your life, retirement, and you are afraid of facing loneliness. The central point of your life—your work life—is degenerating. Facing the end of working life may terrify you.

*Questions:* Can I face the fact that I am getting older? Do I spend too much time looking at and trying to understand my life? Does my soul seek more evolvement? Do I pay enough attention to my feelings and how I *see*?

## Iris Conditions

Iris conditions involve an irritation of the iris structure. Persons with iris conditions feel pain, have redness, and an annoying and uncomfortable feeling in the eye. From a Chinese medical perspective, there is probably too much heat in the individual's metabolism. This imbalance can be controlled by eating cooler foods, such as fresh vegetables and seasonal fruits.

*Questions:* Is there anger I haven't expressed? Am I carrying resentment? Is there an aspect of my family life that is irritating me?

## Corneal Conditions

The cornea holds most of the refracting power for the optical focusing capacities of the eye. Corneal conditions often accompany a power struggle the person is having within himself or herself, struggling between what they think and what they feel.

*Questions:* Am I in emotional survival? Am I pushing and expressing too forcefully in the world? Is there something special I am attempting to bring into existence?

## Retinal Detachments
This sight impairment involves the retina separating from the surrounding layers of tissue within the eye. The word "detachment" is important. The retina metaphorically speaks of feelings and seeing. So, if the detachment is in one eye, examine which eye the retinal condition presents itself in.

*Questions:* Am I detaching myself from a particular part of my life? Have I cut off feelings about a certain situation? Do I need to become unattached to an aspect of my existence?

## Optic Nerve Conditions
The optic nerve facilitates flow and integration among the eye, the brain, and the mind. Impulses carrying the sensations of light from the eye flow through the optic nerve to create eyesight in the brain and vision in the mind.

*Questions:* Am I blocking the natural flow of situations? Do I try to work things out with understanding?

## Perceiving Reality versus Illusion

Now that you have had a brief introduction to the common ways in which issues we struggle with can affect our sight, let us return to the story of Mario and his trip to Peru. His friend Rosa had invited him to go there on a sacred journey into the world of shamanism. Unbeknownst to Mario, Rosa had been apprenticing with a shaman, a teacher and guide of ancient healing and spiritual practices. Although it is not usual to invite outside people into a blessed site of a shaman, Mario was chosen. The shaman had recognized the evolutionary work of healing that Mario was involved in. Upon hearing of this honor, Mario told the shaman that his wish was to master the ability to discern between reality and illusion. With this in mind, the shaman devised a week of preparation for Mario. For seven days, Mario consumed only water and juice, steamed vegetables, and fruit.

"Stay away from drugs and sex for the week," instructed Rosa. Mario was to learn how desire and need affect the perceptions of his mind's eye.

After the week was over, the meeting took place on a warm winter night in a lush garden in Lima. The shaman from the jungle arrived at eight o'clock with a cellular phone strapped to his belt. He directed the group of eight people to lie down on mattresses on the grass.

The shaman had brought with him a jungle concoction he had prepared from a vine. Rosa whispered in Mario's ear that the green drink was called *ayahuasca*. The shaman counseled them that, after they drank the ayahuasca, they were to not get caught up in their thoughts, and to "let the feelings and images move through them like a cloud passing above."

"Stay present with who you really are behind your thoughts and the content of your mind," continued the shaman. He lay a blanket down for himself. Then there was silence. The evening sounds made themselves heard. From a Coca-Cola bottle the shaman poured a half glass of the green potion. He gestured to the first person to come and drink.

Rosa whispered to Mario that the shaman knew exactly how much drink to offer each person. He scanned each one's body and spirit with discriminating eyes. Mario's turn came and slightly less than half a glass was handed to him in a spiritual offering. He cautiously drank it and, after bowing to the shaman, returned to his reserved place on the grass. Rosa's turn was next. This was the 100th time in her spiritual apprenticeship that she had ingested ayahuasca. Rosa spoke quietly to Mario about what happens in the body and brain after consuming the green potion.

She explained that ayahuasca has a natural chemical ability to negate the limbic physiological mechanism that determines neocortical and cognitive processes. In other words, the means we use to protect ourselves in survival are dismantled. Those who drink ayahuasca can no longer use their brain and thinking mind to keep from seeing the contents of their mind. They become aware of what is content and what is them. The effect of the drink allows one to discern between what is really taking place through the senses versus what is imagined. One might see an animal and really think it is an animal, and yet it turns out to be a bush. Ayahuasca eliminates the capacity to use muscles to armor and protect oneself.

When hearing this, Mario felt excited to visit the content of his life, especially those places of unfinished business, like his episode with Gina. Rosa again whispered into his ear, "Be ready to see from your eye of vivencia, the place where you stand naked without your mask."

Now Mario understood why the shaman had said, "Don't get involved with the content of your mind. Go to the experience behind." He was telling Mario to go to the vivential space of fully realized potential, the place of the possibility of enlightenment. To be full of light. Mario knew this experience was the stepping-stone to being and conscious seeing.

Mario lay down, closing his eyes. A feeling of relaxation began to move through him. He lost touch with the activity outside of his own experience. He curled up into a fetal position. Images began to appear. Swirling, colorful kaleidoscope pictures came into his awareness. They became stronger. At first Mario felt swept away by the intensity of the images. He remembered to let go. He remembered the instructions not to hang on to any content. In that moment the swirling patterns of light images disappeared. It was as if Mario had stepped into a garden. The bushes took on the appearance of animals from nature. Mario was greeted like an old friend.

Then he heard a voice saying, "This is not possible." In that precise moment the glowing, flowing images, like an ongoing fireworks display, returned, this time more intensely. Mario felt swept out of control. He then smelled what seemed like cigarette smoke. He heard faint bells and a chant. Was that the shaman? With eyes closed he felt the presence of a spirit being. He opened his eyes to verify the truth of his experience. Mario saw the shaman lying down in his place. He remembered Rosa saying that during the ayahuasca journey the spirit can travel without the body. Mario had witnessed this phenomenon. He thought the shaman was actually at his side, and yet it was really his spirit, because the shaman was still lying on his blanket some meters away. There were more waves of images and body sensations. He had the urge to vomit and urinate. In his mind Mario could rationalize that this should not be real because he had eaten or drunk very little in days.

Mario's body felt otherwise. It was this discrepancy that let Mario go deeply into himself. He forced himself to ask very specific questions: When do we believe what our mind's eye dictates? When do we really listen to our bodies speak? When does the eye of vivencia begin? Which of these mechanisms are real? Where is the illusion? In the experience of ayahuasca Mario learned how to discern between his true vivential experience, his own nature talking, and that of perceptions from his survival mind's eye. His inner perceiving from consciousness dictated how his physical eyes saw clearly. Conscious seeing became an exploration for him to enter his mind and reintegrate in a way that produced a higher vibratory state of awareness. Via conscious seeing, you can—within your mind—master knowing what is real by being your self in life versus imagined perceiving from fear or expectation. For Mario, perceptions of fear could no longer be blinded by avoidance. The mind's eye perceptions surfaced from memory and association. Through conscious seeing each memory acted as a stepping-stone to increase the friendliness and supremacy he had with his flexible personality.

Mario lay on his back, stretched out, more at peace and relaxed. He again opened his eyes. Mindful seeing became a metaphor for consciousness. He realized that to have full seeing and clear vision was to access his own personal consciousness. He found the bridge between consciousness and seeing. This way of seeing is the entry point into living a life that is of a soulful nature.

Through this experience, Mario realized that conscious seeing looks at the variables in the genetic, personal, and experiential life. It provides a glimpse into how we have survived through our brains.

This means that our perceptions are processed through pathways that are designed for quick action. When you are in survival you access nerve pathways in the brain in order to quickly move your body to escape. An example would be if you were walking in a forest and saw a bear. In that moment, seeing through the eye of vivencia and saying what a nice, furry bear it was would not be a very conscious way of perceiving. You would need to mobilize your emergency reflexes and get away as quickly as possible. You use the reflex pathways of your brain to accomplish this and not your mind's eye. To see and live in survival creates a disintegrated state for the mind's eye. When this happens there is a lack of wholeness. We identify with the content of our lives. In the above example, it is necessary to look at the bear so it becomes the content. In other survival situations, like encountering a boss that you are unhappy with or a dissatisfied partner, you may find yourself behaving in the same way; that is, you treat them like content that you have to run away from or face and fight. In the case of your boss or partner, in conscious seeing it would be useful to view these situations from the eye of vivencia.

It became clear to Mario that in these moments he was more than his thoughts and ideas. Behind this veil of pretending and being fearful was another being. Within him, something like a second personality existed that was more authentic. Mario became determined to practice living in a state of being conscious. He would pay attention to what is really seen versus illusions created from perspectives of survival and fear.

In the early morning hours Mario felt the full effects of the green drink wearing off. He was present and his heart was wide open. Was it a vision of reality or his survival brain that dictated the need to go to the toilet? In his survival brain he felt the urge to go, yet he consciously knew that there was very little food that he had ingested during the past days. Was this fear? This was a strong urge. He left his warm blanket and moved toward a little outhouse. It felt so good to sit down, and he listened to the rumblings of his bowels. As he had a movement he felt like a large part of himself was leaving forever to enter the Lima sewage system.

As he was sitting, he became aware of fear. Mario imagined that the cistern was filling up and would soon be touching his backside. He quickly stood up and looked down into the relatively empty bowl. He realized that he was hallucinating in fear. Since he was still under the influence of the ayahuasca, the experience taught him the distinction between reality and illusion. Next time, he would not need to react to fear. He would see when it is happening and realize that it is just fear. This experience showed him the power that fear can exert—it produces false perceptions. Do I live my life this way, thought Mario? This was a frightening confrontation to be able to discern reality from illusion.

Mario returned to his place on the grass and glanced toward Rosa. She was smiling. Mario considered that she already knew what had happened. The amazing discoveries through ayahuasca were not new to her.

Mario was drawn into Rosa's eyes and transported back to his university studies, to the dissertation writings of Robert Kellum:

The self remains the realization that one is the center of consciousness. The capability of holding onto this awareness while letting oneself go into experience is the capability of centrally fixating one's core. In our focus amongst these variables lies the point of our self-identification. The self freed from the various personages of its essential experience, the self able to dis-identify from the contents and flow through the succession of various psychological states while realizing itself as the center of consciousness in its social constellation of its being. One that is capable of multiple focusing with the clarity of its central fixation not atrophied into a blur by the dominance of a restricted being.

Mario traveled further into Rosa's eyes. As he did, he thought, "I am at the center of consciousness." He reflected further, "This is my consciousness and this is connected to the consciousness around me." At that precise moment, Rosa's face came perfectly into focus. Mario could see every detail of her olive skin. The brown freckles shone brightly in the early morning sun. This was contrary to his forty-nine-year-old experience of looking at small details this close to his eyes.

Words came from Rosa's mouth. "Mario, realize that you are a shaman. You produce magic by your presence. We all have shamanic qualities. Your shamanic quality is your heart. To be conscious is to be aware of the possibilities of your sensory experiences. To see is to sense, through your eyes, what is possible in the invisible of that which you are looking at."

Rosa continued:

Conscious seeing is living through your physical body, sensing the possibilities of what is around, inside and past the physical reality of what you are looking at. It is a misconception to believe that we have to develop our consciousness or seeing. We are all in a process of becoming aware that we are conscious. Go home and teach others that they have the potential to be conscious. When we are conscious we are seeing. Our physical reality around us already offers the possibility for conscious seeing. It is something in us that wakes up and aligns itself with what is already present. There is nothing wrong with us. There are no problems. It is tuning in to why in this reality did we shut down our visual sensing capacity to be aware.

Rosa brushed his cheek with her hand. Mario went off to rest.

He had a dream. Or was it reality? Gina came to visit him. She smiled with the same look he saw in her face at age eight. After connecting through the eyes, Gina talked to Mario, "I do remember what happened those many years ago. The experience wasn't as big a deal for me as it was for you. I love you dearly and I wish you to see that at that time this was my way of playing out this love. Now, you can see differently. See me and everything around you as it is now. See what is."

Mario let Gina's words enter into his being. Like an automobile going through a car wash, he felt his soul being cleansed of past misperceptions. He suddenly surfaced from his sleep to hear the cars of Lima racing around like fire trucks trying to find the burning building.

Mario had engaged with the spirit of the shaman and animals. This had not been accomplished in the normal way of seeing with his eyes. His seeing occurred from the deeper layers of his eye of vivencia. Here he was able to examine his perceptions and discern reality from illusion. Through Mario's experience with ayahuasca, he refined seeing from the eye of vivencia and reclaimed the love he had for Gina. Except that love was now centered from spirit rather than from the physical flesh. Once he mastered integrating his camera eye perceptions, he was able to travel beyond the limiting vision of his survival mind's eye. He no longer needed to falsely project a sexual need onto others. Mario consciously began to see women for who they were. He physically connected with the actual reality of the human being he was with rather than projecting who he needed in the past.

Mario had taken part in a shamanic ritual that included the use of hallucinogenic plants, and his insights came to him during this time. However, even without the special rituals that Mario experienced, you can structure your daily living and conscious seeing, and reach to life through the eyes of vivencia. You can reap the same benefits of Mario's ritualistic experience without using ancient medicinal plants. By staying present to "what is," Mario showed how to enter into an observational state—the state that is the precursor of conscious seeing.

# 7

## Being Conscious:
## Integrating Thoughts and Feelings

### Personality and Identity

We have been exploring the many factors that contribute to the development of your personality. We discussed the thinking, feeling, and emotional aspects of your personality and took a look at the traits you acquire as a result of your parents' influence. We used all of that information to gain an understanding of how your personality is related to your vision. We have discovered a relationship between thinking and looking, and learned that feeling and seeing can guide you to a deeper understanding of your emotional self. With all of this information in hand, you have taken the first steps toward the integration of your personality with your true nature, which is a vital step toward conscious seeing. As you grow toward consciousness you develop a sense of who you are — your identity. Ideally, your identity is the result of an understanding and acceptance of your inherent nature and all your life experiences, including your emotional history. A healthy, well-integrated personality accurately portrays this identity and enables you to move around within yourself and interact with the world in a way that is free and effortless. You relate to others in a clear and integrated way. This translates to an ability to see in a conscious way through your eyes.

On the other hand, when there are gaps in your ability to integrate your experiences into your identity, you may find yourself operating in an unconscious way. You may have trouble focusing on a career or staying in a relationship for more than a few months. You may simply find that your life is unfulfilling, with a lack of intimate friendships or meaningful work.

Interestingly enough, when many of us encounter the disharmony I refer to above, we often find ourselves in circumstances that require us to revisit emotions that we may have been reluctant to face in the past. For example, if your relationship with your mother was stormy when you were young, as an adult you may enter into a relationship with someone who behaves much like your mother did. The emotions you experience in response may be similar to the emotions that were too difficult for you to accept at a young age. Now you find yourself with another opportunity to explore those feelings from a new perspective.

Patients who have embarked on the road to conscious seeing often find these kinds of events emerging in their lives. As they work toward improving their vision they discover opportunities to gain clarity about their inner lives as well. It's as though, when you enter into conscious seeing, you are aligned with a deeper, universal consciousness that is wiser and more vast than your own. It provides guidance in the form of events that help you increase your awareness of your true nature. In this state of alignment, your journey through life brings the exact reflections and messages you need to gain the clarity and the freedom you deserve.

When your personal consciousness is aligned with universal consciousness, you enter another level and awareness. Here your beingness vibrates in such a way that you step into an experience of not being your identity, or being much more than you might believe is your identity. You no longer feel comfortable relating to your mental idea of who you think you are. Sara entered into a part of this seeing in the cave in chapter 1; Matthew had this experience looking at a candle and being with his lover in chapter 3; Juliana used drugs to discover this kind of vision until life showed her how to accomplish it without drugs, contacts, or glasses, as I described in chapter 4. Through his ayahuasca experience, Mario was able to replicate and observe his mind, and master being conscious and seeing from his own nature, as revealed in chapter 5.

As you become increasingly aware of consciousness, you are able to create your life from the wisdom of your truest nature. This means that you are integrating your own nature with that which is congruent with universal nature. Your being is based on your personal needs and is harmonious with those of the earth. This enables you to manifest what you choose as your true intention. You are literally "authoring your life."

The opposite can also be true, of course. When you are aligned with your ego or you are attempting to manifest your identity with fear or anger, you become a "false author," or what Rojas sometimes refers to as a "fauthor." In this case your creative vision is usually limited. This is why so many teachers say, "If you don't at first succeed, try again." Also, "Take what comes to you as feedback and don't take it personally." Feedback from life is showing you your false vision of reality. Most times false seeing is a form of "blindness" we have when attempting to understand ourselves. In unconscious seeing you become a "fauthor" rather than an author.

## Stillness

From a practical perspective, conscious authorship of your life begins with stillness. In the following exercise we will use the breathing and gazing techniques to help you quiet your mind and help you relax into a state of awareness and observation.

Sit in a comfortable position with a lighted candle in front of you, directly in line with your eyes. Begin by looking softly at the candle and becoming aware of your breath. Your breathing will be divided into three phases: (1) The in-breath is the beginning, where you are drawing in life, inviting universal consciousness to enter into you; (2) the next phase is the out-breath, which is then followed by (3) a new in-breath, completing the cycle. In this exercise, let the out-breath be slower and more deliberate than the in-breath. As you breathe, let undesirable thoughts and feelings leave you with each out-breath. Once you are comfortable maintaining this awareness, then let there be a pause at the end of the out-breath. Each time, increase the length of the pause. Enjoy the experience of the "nothingness" in this pause. With practice and awareness, it will become a point of stillness. Your thoughts and feelings will be replaced with an inner calmness.

## Thoughts and Feelings

Quiet your thoughts while you breathe in, breathe out, pause, then breathe in again. Begin to use the pause as a moment to be aware of your feelings. This can be a way to help you integrate your thoughts and feelings. The candle will help you make a visual connection to this process, as the light stimulates both the retina and fovea of your eyes. Remember that foveal looking is related to your thoughts, while retinal seeing is related to feelings.

As you gaze at the candle, enter a state of simple observation. Allow your quiet mind to be aware of everything that your eyes perceive. Allow your out-breath to neutralize the thinking activity of your mind. The in-breath will help oxygenate your blood, stimulating your ability to observe. During the pause, let go and allow yourself to feel. Notice whether the stillness alters the way you look and see. You may find that what you observe through your eyes begins to change. In an observational mode your retinas and foveae integrate light in a way that may heighten your ability to enter your emotions and experience all your senses. The emotions you experience in this state are those that emerge from the deeper levels of your being.

## Presence

Practice the above exercise at least once a day, six days a week. As you do, you will begin to master your ability to observe. Look and see in an integrated way. *Be*, and learn to distinguish between thoughts and feelings.

Enter into a state of integration, where you find yourself in a space of fusion, that is, seeing in a way that is fully integrated and clear. Integrating space in this fused way leads you to the next level of being: presence. Here, in a state of presence, you no longer make a distinction between what is you and what is not you. There is no assurance that being present will last more than a few seconds, minutes, or hours. In visual terms, being present is like having a flash of clarity when you are in your naked vision, without your glasses. You are not paying attention, then suddenly your visual world pops into focus, as clear as if you were wearing your glasses. And then the clarity is gone just as quickly as it appeared.

Since my eyesight is sharp for far-off (distant) looking, my experience of presence is different than a flash of clearness. I have a glimmer of insight. What I mean is that an idea or message is revealed to me, and it appears to be inside my head. When I stay present, I can keep that insight alive; if I start thinking too much, it goes away.

There is a specific mechanism behind the loss of presence. It has to do with reaching the part of the mind where emotion resides. When this emotion is unresolved, as in the examples demonstrated in the stories from earlier chapters, the mind holds it as a state of woundedness or unresolved emotions. In my experience, as I acquire presence I enter into the state of "fused space" through my eyes. I am being present in such a way that my looking and seeing merge. Note that space involves infinite depths, a sense of being where no boundaries exist. I venture forth into a space that is both visible and invisible. Then, emotions I need to deal with reveal themselves to me. This reminds me of being in relationship. The deeper I permit myself to feel and be love, the more my fear of intimacy forces its way into my awareness.

What happens is that your life circumstances, your aches and pains, and your eye conditions all reveal the subtle, fresh way you need to look at past situations now. Being present is a way to restructure your fused way of looking and seeing. Something about your past that needs completion is then revealed.

Presence gives you the space to find out how to maneuver within yourself and create a new perspective of the past situation. In this way you manage what you are seeing right now with a point of view I call "being conscious." Being present, your perception is accurate and you consciously see a solution that is not simply a reactive expression projected from your former wounded state. This does not mean that the feelings of the past go away or even that you have to get rid of them. Rather, you change your perception by being present with your thoughts, feelings, and the state of integration.

Francina had such an experience in her life. This is how she describes her breakthrough:

I grew up in a small town in Chile. My father had emigrated from Germany and married my English-born mother. He was a businessman. He was very successful. He had built a beautiful home. It was my castle up to the time I was ten years old. I had a governess who spent time with me when my father was busy working. My parents' lives were centered around the image and the prestige of their successful business and large home. I adored my father. I was the youngest child. He was the king of the castle and he would always take care of me. This was my perception. This is how I saw men.

My eyesight has always been good, with my left eye the dominant one. I remember, as a child, being in touch with another world. I played imaginary games and had vivid visions. My imagination took me beyond the walls of my castle home, where I played with make-believe characters who became my dearest friends. I loved getting lost in the stories I read.

I recall times in the evening when my father would interact with me. He was an affectionate man who loved me. He listened and talked. I fantasized that I was his queen. He was a firm man, as well. He knew how he wanted his children to behave. I had to develop a side of myself that was strong and assertive.

My world changed at age eleven. My father's business collapsed and he became ill. My mother protected me from this reality. Our "castle" was managed like in the old days. Everything seemed just fine. Maintaining our image was the most important consideration. Keep everything on the surface looking just the same. At first I even believed that nothing was changing. But I soon learned that you cannot ignore feelings and deep emotions. I felt my father's pain. There was a different energy present. I could feel and see into this space. My father's presence was disappearing. I moved inward. I chose to stay in my room more and create a new imaginary world inside of me. Fortunately, my eyesight stayed clear.

My father died within a few years and my mother and I had to move from the castle. It was being sold. The prestige was gone. The "king" was no longer taking care of me. When I was old enough, I left for the city and worked, and began my journey to become my own person. I married a man who I thought would take care of me as my father had. I was mistaken.

It was around this time that I became aware that my right eye was blocked, and my left eye dominated my view of the world. I learned that my right eye was related to my father, and that I needed to access that part of my nature. For my evolution, I was to discover the power of my father in me. That power was in my ability to plan the story of my own life. I couldn't again give my power away to a man, in this case my husband. However, it took years of much anguish, pain, and suffering before I understood this.

Forty-five years later I divorced my husband and emigrated to Greece, where I lived in a lovely cottage on a small hill. In my eighties, I found my peace. I could sit on my balcony, watching the colorful flowers. I reflected on my past. My addiction to cigarettes and sleeping pills and my alcoholic, unfaithful husband were far away. I could look through both eyes and be present in my vision through my left eye as well as my right. I have macular degeneration now. The distortion in my left macula shows me the distortions of my past. I patch my right eye each day to have the experience of the stored emotion. I retreat further and further from my family. I find myself not wanting to be reminded of the past.

With time, I allow my children to get closer than I ever did before. I deal with the pain. I enter into conscious seeing in these last years of my life. My earlier life is behind me. Now I can see in a more integrated way. I love myself. I feel so much peace when I see my flowers. I remember my childhood days, playing imaginary games, jumping over the flowers of the castle. Today, my life is my castle. My inner desire, the male side of my being, directs me to the future. I will one day see my father. For now I have found my home again, inside myself.

## Eyes, Enhancing Thoughts and Feelings

In my model I call "good" emotion "emotionality," meaning that it is energetically a calmer variety of emotion. This emotionality occurs at a deeper level of the mind, known as the ground of being. You might consider this place in the mind—the ground of being—to be where your truest nature takes center stage. It is here that your vivential nature takes precedence over the fragile, restricted places of your woundedness. The ground of being is the place you enter after you let go of who you think you are. You are simply being, observing that consciousness exists, then being aware that you can enter consciousness. Finally, in stillness, you observe yourself being conscious. You are aware that this is a particular state of being and you have entered it. Your being conscious is at the same time allowing conscious seeing.

Once you have gotten this far, stay present with the candle practice. Keep observing. Try to remain conscious. Keep your conscious seeing alive. Continue your breathing and further enter into an area of your inner space, deeper and deeper into your ground of being. Empower this part of your real self, your vivential nature, and encourage it to come to the surface. If you do this, you will sense deep joy, love, and happiness filling your presence. This is a form of discernment.

Stay present and see from this place of stillness. As you discern more deeply you will become aware of another space. Here you can see that all realities coexist at the same time. You may have first noticed this while looking at photograph 6 on page 120. Your attention, your

152

looking, is on the candle flame. Yet you can simultaneously experience another reality of what is happening in the surrounding area. As you further let go you can attend to both sets of experiences at the same time. This ability to see and allow both of these experiences to coexist is a very important observation in conscious seeing.

At the beginning of this chapter you practiced breathing and gazing at the flame of a candle while allowing your eyes to perceive foveally and peripherally at the same time. In the stillness between breaths, you explored integrating your looking and thinking with the seeing and feeling parts of your mind. In a similar way, it is possible to become aware of two sets of realities existing simultaneously in your life. That is what happened to Francina.

She was living what seemed to be a happy life by society's standards. Her world appeared to be orderly and satisfying. What was less obvious to her or anyone else was that she was married to a philandering husband, felt overwhelmed by the demands of three children, and was barely managing to make ends meet. The lack of integration in Francina's life showed up in her addiction to cigarettes and sleeping pills, in her disgust with her overweight body, and in her willingness to be treated disrespectfully by her husband. Inside, she knew that there must be more meaning to her life, and she began at last to take steps to find it.

By practicing visual observation and discernment, and by overcoming the suppression of that part of her nature associated with her right eye, Francina was able to recognize those parts of her past that she had denied for so many years. As she learned to effectively stay present with both her thoughts and her feelings, she allowed the deeper realities of her life to enter into her consciousness.

Francina continues with her story:

As a young mother I felt that the proper thing for me to do was to look after the children first. My maternal side said to me that when my children were older the time would come when I could take care of my own life. My false, dominating male side usually led me to overreact through my right eye. I was overbearing.

I controlled through anger. Somewhere inside of myself I believed that my life would begin when I retired.

This lack of integration between my male and female sides revealed itself in how I suppressed my true needs from my vivential nature. I behaved as the dutiful mother and loyal wife, while my husband was being an irresponsible adolescent. At the time I couldn't consciously see this. This denial was similar to the way the fantasy world of my childhood separated me from the reality of what was happening in my father's life. So many years later I still hadn't consciously united these two parts of myself. My adult life view lacked the same integration as my childhood view. I convinced myself that I was a happy wife and mother, just as I had as a child seen my father as a successful man protecting me in our castle. I wanted my "king" back. I needed to be taken care of.

Things have changed now. I am alone. I am my own king and queen. I have my dream. I am integrating the reality of "what is" with the way I want things to be. I comfortably enter into my vivential nature. I face the emotions and experiences that I used to deny. This is the job of integration. I am able to *be* in both realities of thinking and feeling, looking and seeing. I am conscious of all the parts of my self.

## Steps for Seeing

Following are the specific sequences that Francina and many of my patients have used to gradually see consciously:

1. **Stillness.** Start finding opportunities throughout the day when you can stop and quiet your mind. Challenge yourself to see how often during your day you can stop and take a deep breath. Find a peaceful moment at a stoplight in your car, while sitting on a bus, going to the bathroom, standing at the front door, or while starting the car—all are good times to remember to go inside to your place of stillness.

2. **Observation.** Be aware of what you are doing any time you begin slipping into a reactive state. This is when you behave in a reflex emotional way, like screaming in anger or becoming very subdued, feeling depressed or lonely. Observe yourself from a distance. Chuckle to yourself. If you are with someone, say, "I am noticing myself going into reaction. This is not the way I wish to behave." Become aware of an alternative to your reactivity. Choose instead to be responsive by stopping your reaction and being still for a moment. Take a breath. Practice the following: Take responsibility for how you feel at that moment by saying to yourself, "What I am feeling in this moment is ____." (Fill in the blank with the first honest feeling you can identify.)

3. **Presence.** Once you are able to accurately identify and stay with your feelings, then you are present and can remain present. Deepen your experience of where your feelings take you. This opens up your conscious awareness. Presence is an extension of stillness with observation. Through presence, you can deepen your awareness of your own nature.

4. **Discernment.** This is the process of integrated looking and seeing. You are able to more accurately focus on reality by recognizing what is you and separating it from what is not you. While you are in the process of being present, your observational ability deepens. In stillness, space expands. You step past your personality and step into your ground of being, into your true self. You speak in an accountable way, taking responsibility for what is you and recognizing that this is not the same as what is outside of yourself. You leave your victim identity behind, no longer experiencing the distortion of your woundedness. The intention of discernment is to be aware and present.

5. **Action.** By now you are in your vivential nature in observation. You might have an awareness that something more than your self is present; that is, you are guided by a purpose quite beyond any motivations like those of your woundedness or

your lack of awareness of your woundedness. Consciousness hugs you like a gust of warm air.

Conscious seeing is knowing where you are in space. You can discern where are you looking and what you are seeing. There is very little thinking in this state. That is, there is no separation between your thoughts and your beingness. Accomplishing all of this in a reflex manner takes practice. There are steps to accomplish this, which I present in the following.

## The Practice of Seeing

Obtain a piece of colorful string about three meters in length. Mount a large photo (size A4 for European readers, 8″ × 10″ for U.S.) of yourself onto a stiff piece of cardboard. Using a knife or scissors, make a small, round hole in the photo, on the bridge of your nose halfway between your eyebrows and the tip of your nose. Thread the string through the hole and tie a knot on the back side of the board so that the string is well anchored and will not pull through. You might want to put a spot of glue or tape on the back of the cardboard to help secure the knot.

Firmly mount the board to the wall or another secure fixture. Pull the string tight and hold the loose end of it with your index finger, pressing it against a point on the bridge of your nose halfway between the tip and the line of your eyebrows. Look down along the taut string to the other end. Focus on the image of your nose. Practice this exercise with or without your glasses. Vary your distance from the photograph by shortening the length of the string.

As you gaze at the photograph at the far end of the string, go through the steps outlined above, finding a sense of stillness, observation, presence, and discernment. When your vision is fully integrated, when you are using both eyes equally, you will observe two strings as if they are coming out of each one of your eyes. The two strings will be in the shape of a reversed letter *V.*

Stay present and notice whether or not both strings are visible and at the same level at all times. Do any parts of the string disappear? If so, determine which part of the string goes away. This will direct you to which part of your inner space is suppressed. To identify where the suppressed area is, imagine each of your family members one by one. As you do, notice if you lose sight of one or both of the strings. If you are able to see only one of the strings, you may be deeply suppressing the perception in one eye. In this case, you will benefit from patching the other, dominant eye so that the other eye will be encouraged to awaken. If you have any doubts about patching, please consult your eye doctor to obtain professional advice prior to beginning patching practices. Also see chapters 7, 8, and 9 for more detailed ways to train the awareness of both perceptions through each eye.

Next, observe that if you look at the string at a point between your own face and the photograph, the V turns into an X. Wherever you are looking becomes the center of the X. Move your focal point gradually along the string from the photograph toward yourself, and observe how the center of the X moves toward you. This practice is called eye crossing. It is not dangerous. Your eyes will not get stuck. On the contrary, this practice is helpful in guiding you into a conscious way of being more present with your self, your feelings, and perceptions.

Remember, the goal of the eye-crossing exercise is to maintain a perfect X with no parts of the string disappearing. When you are able to maintain your view of the perfect X, you will then be perceiving all aspects of your own space. This will help you in looking into your vivential nature.

## Integrated Vision Therapy

Vision therapy is an established branch of the profession of optometry. The use of therapeutic exercises for the treatment of vision problems is practiced in England under the name "orthoptics." In that country, children with crossed or wandering eyes were given pictures to look at through an instrument. By positioning the instrument, known as a "synoptophore," an image could be aligned in front of each eye. Simultaneously, the brain was encouraged to become aware of the images received by both eyes. In many cases the person was able to learn how to fuse these images without the aid of the synoptophore. Using this technique as a starting point, a dedicated group of optometrists in the United States developed a series of "non-instrument" therapies to treat patients with fusion problems. Today, these practices are used successfully by vision therapists all over the world. You can locate a vision therapy practitioner by consulting the Web sites referenced at the back of the book.

In my earlier book, *The Power Behind Your Eyes*, I introduced the concept of integrated vision therapy. In this process, I used the preceding vision principles to explore and expand the deeper emotional and spiritual sides of vision. In my practice as an eye doctor I had found that while training a person's vision the changes that occurred impacted them as a whole person. From this I deduced that integrated vision therapy was a fast way to open up a direct pathway to the self and to a more conscious way of being.

The past practices and those that follow I've designed to engage you in a sequenced approach to deepen your sense of self and become conscious of your own consciousness.

## Extension of the String

Return to the string practice described previously, except this time use a piece of clear, sticky tape to attach one end of the string to a clear windowpane. Be sure you have a broad and long view through the window. Sit or stand comfortably, and place the loose end of the string on the middle of your nose, just as you did before. Now position yourself close enough to the window so that you can make out some of the details beyond the window—your backyard, the city skyline, a natural landscape, whatever it happens to be—without your glasses.

Begin by looking at the sticky tape on the window. Observe the V created by the image of the "two" strings. Make sure that "both" strings are at the same level horizontally. If not, adjust your head by tipping it to the left or right until you find the balanced position where the "strings" appear to be at the same height.

Next, let your focus move past the end of the string, through the window to the world beyond your window. Feel your eyes spreading outward. In visual science we call this *diverging*; I refer to it as "uncrossing." This is the opposite of converging, which is like "eye crossing." Converging is an important skill to have when you read a book and your eyes turn inward to focus on a point close by. Diverging is a skill that helps you better focus on distant points.

As your eyes diverge, you will begin to see that the strings no longer appear to meet at the window. Notice that the strings seem to be furthest apart where they are closest to your eyes, and closest together at the point most distant from your eyes. Pay attention to that slight separation that appears between the strings at the window. The more your eyes diverge, the further you can separate the strings in the distance—but there is a limit, so don't push yourself too hard. Breathe and relax, and see if you can see the strings moving toward a parallel position. If your eyes feel strained or tired while doing this exercise, cover them with your palms and rest.

Next, to help your eyes relax, look at the string between the window and your nose by crossing your eyes slightly. Also, include lots of rest breaks. Observe that as you move your focal point closer to your nose, the strings make an X, with the center of the X moving closer as well.

Once you are able to do all the phases as described above and feel relaxed and inspired, you will have reached a beginning level of mastery. Then add an additional step to gain flexibility and strengthen the muscles that move your eyes. As you inhale, uncross your eyes and look back through the window. Then exhale while you cross your eyes until you find the exact point where you were looking before, and see the X. Repeat this back and forth movement for ten breaths and then rest by "palming"—placing the palms of your hands over your eyes.

## Eye Crossing, Uncrossing, and Consciousness

The practice of crossing and uncrossing your eyes is a vital step for opening up a space for consciousness to manifest itself to you. To see the surrounding space of the string and what is outside the window, while looking at one point, opens you up to an awareness of space. When you increase your eye crossing and uncrossing toward the end of the exercise, your perception of the space around you may appear disorganized and double.

The challenge in this practice is for you to let go when a lot of activity or even visual chaos is going on peripherally. Can you maintain your focus—that is, your looking presence—while your seeing is haphazard or open to distraction? This practice replicates the disturbances around conscious seeing that many of us have to face in our daily lives. When you begin these practices, you may find yourself feeling a little dizzy or disoriented. Deep feelings and emotions come quickly to the surface during this exercise. Your goal should be to stay with the experience. When you feel ready to stop, take a moment to ask yourself if you are resisting the consciousness-expanding process or if your eyes really need a break. Take a moment to jot down a few notes about your discoveries, from two perspectives: First, what do you perceive about what is going on? Second, what is happening inside of you?

The longer you can stay present in your looking and seeing, and in crossing and uncrossing your eyes, the more you will become flexible in your seeing. In consciousness terms, this is called "mobility." The goal with an exercise like this is to gain more flexibility within your inner ground of being. Mobility allows you to move away from the influence of restrictions from the past. The farther you can advance away from those limitations, the more often you will observe yourself as being conscious. Then you are seeing from consciousness. This exercise helps you to approach an integration of your thoughts and the feeling part of your mind's identity. For many of my patients, and perhaps for you, this ability to be mobile is a step beyond what you have probably mastered in the past.

## Extension of Candle Practice

Let's return to the exercise in which you practiced looking at a candle flame and seeing everything around it. Here, I would like you to allow your attention to rest right on the flame. As long as you continue to focus directly on the candle, you will see only one flame. Now, look beyond the flame. Observe what happens. Does there suddenly appear to be two flames? For most, this is the case.

Now, bring your focus back directly onto the candle. This time pretend there is a string, just like in the previous exercise, stretching from your nose to the candle. Imagine that you can see the string form the letter *V* at the candle. Try to cross your eyes. Focus on a point on the string closer to your nose until you begin to see two flames. As you draw your focal point closer, you will see one flame moving to the left and the other to the right. Notice whether or not both move at the same speed. If one flame appears to move slower or disappear, it may indicate that one of your eyes is not participating or is being suppressed. If this happens, blink and breathe until you see both flames and they move equally fast to the right and left.

Crossing your eyes is a way of becoming more centered, or more focused, within yourself. Remember, one of your goals in conscious seeing is to build balance between the two eyes. The more they participate as a team, the higher the probability is that you will attain a deep state of oneness with yourself and with your universe. You can accomplish this by using the nose-crossing and candle practice.

## Increasing Depth of Seeing

Look at photograph 8 on page 122. Practice shifting your gaze from the front to the back parts of the image. One after another, bring different elements of the photograph into your awareness. Integrate your foveal and peripheral vision so that you can look at one part of the photo while still noticing all of its other elements. If thoughts creep into your practice, observe how you lose stillness and discernment. Realize how peaceful you can become when you steady your gaze and yourself in the moment. When you do this exercise after your practice with the candle and string, it will improve your ability to deal with the parts of your inner world that keep you from seeing through your eyes in a conscious fashion.

The goal with these exercises is to fully embody the experience and familiarize your eyes with the actions they entail so that when you use your eyes in your day-to-day routine, you will do so in a way that is similar to what you did with the candle, string, and photograph. In other words, you will be better able to hold your sense of space while focusing on what needs to be accomplished.

## Ways to *Be* Conscious

Look at photograph 9 on page 123. Position the page in front of you at arm's length. Let yourself relax, just like you did when you looked through the window in previous exercises. Focus your eyes at some point in the distance, beyond the page. Notice that when you do this there appear to be either three or four photos present. Relax, breathe, and adjust your looking until you can hold three distinct photographs in sight. You will be looking off into the distance, uncrossing your eyes and seeing three images. Since this is a high-level and often challenging way of seeing, please be patient with yourself if you are unable to see this way or hold such a sight in your view for any length of time. You may also find it helpful to skip ahead in this book and choose a chapter that deals with your particular eye condition, whether that is nearsightedness, farsightedness, or astigmatism. The information in those chapters will help you practice the skills you need to master this exercise.

Next, go to photograph 10 on page 124 and cross your eyes and again perceive three photos. Do you notice a change in the size of the middle picture, between the uncrossed and crossed modes? Observe that there is a sense of depth, or a three-dimensional quality, within the middle picture. Spend some time "wandering" around the center picture while feeling what is happening inside your eyes, your body, and your being. Are the letters on the chart clear?

Here are some questions to consider while you continue to practice this exercise:

- Are you able to stay present in the here and now, even when your perceptions of the image are changing?

- What enters into your awareness while you hold the image of the third photograph?
- While remaining in this fused and integrated state of seeing and being, picture each of your parents, one at a time. Do your perceptions change?
- Think about some changes that you have wished to make in your life, like changing your job, your career, your partner, or your home. Do you see the image of the photo in front of you differently now?

Go back to any major discoveries you made about your emotions, your family, or your identity as you read the earlier chapters in this book. Consider each one. Are you able to keep the three pictures? Change from eye crossing to uncrossing and reevaluate your response.

## Looking Back, Moving Forward

In this chapter you have explored letting your personality take a place in your life that is secondary to your true self. In this way you start to become aware of your own consciousness that is reflected in the very essence of your being. Ideally you should bring these practices into your daily life as rituals, like bathing and eating. Let go of any false notions that you are fixing or repairing your eyes. Think instead that you are cultivating being conscious and seeing.

The goal you are moving toward with these exercises is a simple one. With enough practice, no matter what you are contemplating, your vision will become solid. Rather than outer circumstances dictating how you see, you master your personal consciousness, maximizing the clarity of perception that your eyes can provide.

# 8

## Nearsightedness: Expanding and Focus

### Rational Thinking

Each eye condition offers a metaphor of your personality. The lens prescription for your nearsightedness, like a map, reflects the kind of outward behavior you are likely to present. From interviews of tens of thousands of nearsighted patients, I've been able to catalog patterns of personalities and their potential behaviors that can present clues to direct you into a deeper self-understanding, helping you to know who you are behind the illusionary perceptions and beliefs of your present way of seeing.

In this chapter, through the story of Natalie, you will be able to examine your own nearsightedness, if that is the eye condition you have. You will deepen your experience of how your genetic influences, your life experiences, and your wearing of strong contact lenses or glasses have helped mold your personality and behavior. Then, by moving deeper into your feelings and emotions, you can further discover how to dissolve residual fears from your childhood or earlier in your life. With fears dissolved, conscious seeing can develop.

Rational thinking is useful and is encouraged throughout the modern world. By being logical, you can minimize feelings, stay focused, get the job done, and be rewarded. The payoff is usually a promotion in your work or material rewards.

It is interesting to note that nearsightedness is the eye condition most widely treated with corrective lenses as well as surgery. Nearly half of all North Americans are nearsighted. In Europe, statistics are similar. Clinical records show a strong correlation between nearsightedness and analytical and intellectual activities. This correlation is not surprising since our world culture for at least the past 800 years has moved toward a nearsighted way of life, wherein we construct our perceptions around intellectual and analytical paradigms.

In light of these cultural biases, we need not look far to find reasons for our nearsightedness beyond the normal explanation that the "eyeball is too long," or "I inherited it from my parents." A nearsighted way of perceiving is inner directed, an overfocusing on the "me" content of one's life. Nearsightedness is a fear-based, survival way of looking that supports logical and linear forms within the personality. Vision therapy–oriented optometrists often see the behavior of nearsightedness in an individual before it structurally reveals itself in the eye.

Nearsighted people, for example, lean forward to see. They are avid readers, and tend to hold a book very close to their eyes. There is a characteristic frown, a visual sign of the struggle to identify with anything or anyone outside of the self. Nearsighted people prefer staying indoors to going out. They may suddenly move from an extroverted to introverted way of behaving. This is quite common between the ages of eleven and fifteen, corresponding to the onset of puberty.

Kellum writes:

Myopia is a constricted behavior of consciousness. The person's thinking dominates. Feelings are protected. The brain corresponds by setting up fear directives. The individual develops a way of seeing that is fearful and protected. They lose some of their integrative capacity because of a dominating survival posturing. This is authored from the mind and written into the pages and hardware of the brain. Directives are issued to the musculature and nerve control of the eyes: protect; be cautious. New consciousness is cemented into the person's behavior.

Kellum proposed that the over-fovealization process—that is, when perception is constructed around intellect without being moderated by feeling or intuition—began in the thirteenth century. This "over-looking" gained momentum over the centuries as cultures became less agrarian and more concerned with mechanization and intellectual pursuits. By the twentieth century eye doctors themselves were looking at the world in this "myopic" (nearsighted) way.

Kellum writes that this logical worldview resulted in doctors focusing on a physical and more pragmatic approach to dealing with eyes. The goal was simple: find the physical reason that is causing the eye problem and treat the symptoms. Nearsightedness was explained as being an eyeball that became too long or that had too much refractive power. A very logical explanation.

There is a reason why rational thinking becomes a useful strategy for those with nearsightedness and other refractive conditions. It deepens the thinking process and, as Kellum points out, it protects feelings. The difficulty with this strategy is that the mechanism of armoring keeps the person from engaging their vivential nature. Nearsightedness is a perfect way of looking into the world and quantifying it—but it keeps consciousness in a dark, mysterious cave.

Fortunately, consciousness is like vision: alive, dynamic, and just waiting for a moment to reveal itself. I believe we are on this planet to evolve by being conscious and seeing our truth. Nearsightedness is a temporary interlude in the vast scheme of the space-time paradigm in which our lives take place. At any moment of being conscious you can shift to a farsighted way of being. Bruce Lipton, whose ideas were discussed in chapter 4, gave you the remedy: Change your perception and you can modify your DNA. Modifying your nearsighted "thinking" opens you up to farsighted perceptions. The antidote to nearsighted vision and nearsighted behavior therefore is to refocus and expand outward into your true self.

The following story of Natalie will take you deeper into the mechanisms and nature of nearsightedness and how it can change. Natalie began wearing glasses at age twelve. Consistent with what most eye doctors would advise, she was to wear her lenses all the time. In the beginning, her right eye lens prescription was nearly three times stronger than the left. This meant that, without her glasses, Natalie saw much further in the distance through her left eye than her right.

A discussion of lens prescriptions is useful here. Lens prescriptions are measured in diopters. Each diopter can be further divided into quarters. The smallest lens power measurement that we consider is 0.25. In nearsightedness, a minus lens is used to compensate for the refractive eye condition. This means that when you see a lens prescription number with a minus sign in front of it, the compensation is for nearsightedness. A plus sign is for farsightedness. In Natalie's case, her first right-eye lens prescription was –4.50 and that for her left lens was –1.50. Another way of explaining this is to say that through her right eye, Natalie is three times more constricted than through her left eye.

Imagine twelve-year-old Natalie putting on her new glasses. Everything pops into clear focus. She is elated and overcome with relief that her vision is clear. She believes that these glasses are going to correct the problem of her eyes. Does this remind you of your own eye history?

I will let Natalie share her point of view:

I thought I looked ugly in glasses. I thought my eyes would get better. They got worse. By the time I was twenty-two, my right eye was measured at –7.00 and my left eye at –3.00. I couldn't stand glasses anymore. I got some soft contact lenses and the diopters stayed the same for many years. My life was normal. I didn't know that eyesight could be improved. During a six-month trip to Tibet I learned meditative practices. The experience was so deep that I felt I had found love and a God presence. My eyeglasses then seemed too strong. My eyesight got significantly better on its own. The prescription that was measured on my return to Poland was right eye –4.50 and left eye –1.50. With these glasses I noticed that I would use my right eye more of the time. I felt more whole.

Natalie's description brings up two aspects of vision that we need to revisit from earlier chapters. One way to measure the eye is with diopters. The other measure is the level of vision the person experiences. Recall that these two visual findings do not necessarily correlate. In other words, a person's vision can improve even though the diopter measurements stay the same. Or the diopters can change for the better, with a corresponding vision improvement.

The main point is that eyesight is related to perceptions of the mind. The diopters simply address the structure of the eye. And while logic would tell us there would be an exact correlation between the two, this is definitely not always the case.

The important lesson in Natalie's story is that her eyesight improved unexpectedly after she immersed herself in a mind-relaxing practice of meditation. Not only did her eyesight improve but when she had the doctor check her eyes, it was discovered that there was also a reduction of the diopters. This lowering of the diopters is not common, though it is common for those who have followed the system of eyesight improvement I describe in this book. I like to cite Natalie's example because it shows us what is possible.

Consider how Natalie saw through her right eye and how this affected her behavior. Her right-eye view of the world was constrictive. Did this result in her exaggerating the rational side? Was her nearsightedness passed down from her parents? Were her siblings nearsighted? Would there be markings on the iris that would give us a clue of her moving into an over-rational way of behaving in her life? Would this behavior affect her perceptions of men? The answers are found in Natalie's continued story.

## Genetic Myopia

The degree of Natalie's nearsightedness would be deemed genetic by most eye-care professionals. This was not the case. Her parents both had good eyesight. However, what makes Natalie's story particularly fascinating is that she had a twin brother, Rolf, who received his first glasses when he was six. His most recent lens prescription was right eye −12.00, left eye −6.00. Like Natalie, his right eye was more near-sighted. What profession would you expect Rolf to be in? Remember, nearsightedness provides an excellent way of looking with details, facts, and rational thinking. It allows you to be inside your head and work out the smallest of details in a logical and organized manner. Rolf was an attorney.

Natalie continues her story:

> After my trip to Tibet, I began to wonder where my nearsighted-ness came from. A vision teacher guided me to search for these answers. Relaxation practices for my eyes became a daily ritual. I stepped out of contact lenses and have never since used them. Walking in known places gave me the practice of using the blurri-ness as a way to open up parts of my sleepy self.

Natalie was able to remember more about her early life after her irises were interpreted. You can see her irises in photograph 11 on page 125. The right eye is represented by the letter *R* and the left eye by the letter *L*. It is not my intention to teach you how to interpret the iris. The photograph has been included to illustrate how much information about a person's genetic history can be determined by examining the eyes. Also, the irises are tools to open up to consciousness. Natalie was able to remember more of her life experiences and what factors at different ages deeply impacted her being. Then Natalie could be guided to the restrictive places where new perceptions could be constructed. This in turn more permanently altered the way she was using her eyes. Later these modifications were recorded as additional decreases in diopters and remarkable sharpening of her eyesight. Orient yourself by identifying the patterns on the iris that represent thoughts, feelings, and emotions. The black arrows point to the respective markings.

In a session with Natalie I guided her into her mind through the following dialogue. The comments in parentheses and letter codes will help you locate and understand the information in the iris pictures.

*RK:* Natalie, it appears that your mother had an enormous impact upon you in your first seven years. [Brown coloration of "thinking" laid down like a template between birth and age seven.] I would suspect that your mother valued thoughts, discussions, and may have been a mentally controlling person?

*N:* You can tell that from the iris? Yes, my mother was a very important figure. She ruled my life. [Thought patterns tend to be survival. In Natalie's case the orange coloration is heavily around the pupil, guarding her self-expression.]

*RK:* Did you find yourself holding back self-expression?

*N:* I had to learn to keep myself constrained. I felt like a prisoner, controlled by my mother's pattern of living to survive.

*RK:* Would you say your mother had a stronger influence on your childhood than your father did?

*N:* Definitely, my father was away a lot. [The patterns and markings in the left eye seem more pronounced. In this case, the consciousness from the mother's side of the family is more necessary for the laying down of personality at the stage of Natalie's life between birth and age seven or eight.]

*RK:* Imagine for a moment that you needed to learn certain things from your mother. Let her be present with you now. [I am beginning to assist her in realigning her perceptions. Can Natalie go deeper into her feelings and emotions to remember and discover? Much of her emotion is at the edge of her thought borders, as seen in her iris. This means that she had probably practiced using thoughts to protect her emotions. With a little assistance, Natalie could express her feelings and deeper emotion. In this way she would begin freeing her restrictive places.]

Is it possible that your need to be closer to your mother might explain why your right-eye vision was so much lower than your left? [I wait a moment for Natalie to consider this point. She nods.] Pretend for a moment that you needed your mother's qualities to show you how to have a good self-image and find yourself worthy—is that possible? [I wait for a response or maybe even a reaction.]

*N:* No way, my mother couldn't show me that. [I let her feel and be with her reaction. We talk about her perceptions for a while. I point out that her reaction is part of her survival personality. With a stronger parental influence on one side, in Natalie's case her mother, she may tend to suppress the less dominant side until she enters the age sequence of birth to seven, in the second (age twenty to twenty-seven) or third cycle (age forty to forty-seven) of consciousness. The region marked with a letter *A* indicates open emotion within the aspect of personality known as self-esteem. Observe how on the pupil side of the flower petal–like pattern there is a steep ridge to the orange coloration, the thought part. There is an orange coloration on the outside part of the iris as well.]

*RK:* Do you find that you use your thoughts to protect you from feeling emotions?

*N:* That's me.

*RK:* Do you trust yourself?

*N:* Not always. [See area B, the region of the iris associated with trust.]

*RK:* Is it easy for you to make commitments?

*N:* This is very difficult for me. [See location C, the area of commitment.]

*RK:* Do you easily become resentful and angry?

*N:* (Laughs, somewhat nervously.) It seems like you really know me. Are you getting all this from the iris of my eyes? [I nod my head yes. See below C. The iris structure in B and C indicates that emotion is present and thoughts protect Natalie from feeling them.]

As Natalie integrated this experience, she shared more:

I am back in my childhood. My brother seems more important than I am to my parents. I never feel like number one. My parents don't understand me. I feel pressured into doing things in my life. I would say I have a difficult time in this phase of my childhood. I don't remember much before age twelve. I get my first glasses.

My mother tells me she has breast cancer. I clean the house. I feel rebellious. My own breasts and backside are fully developed. I am only twelve. I am confused. My body is of a woman but I am still a child. Where is my father? He is emotionally and spiritually absent. I feel like I am just trying to survive. I am in survival. In my imagination I wanted my parents to die.

## Myopia and Personality

Natalie later revealed that these deep feelings in her imagination saved her from her family. She retreated further into her own inner, nearsighted world. Intellect, thoughts, and understanding were what she strove for in order to protect her sensitive emotionality. Her escape from the family dynamic saved her from dealing with her outer-directed survival perceptions.

After further inner exploration Natalie shared it this way:

I became a woman. I overexaggerated my expression through my masculine side. I protected myself by being intellectual. I would ask lots of questions. I wanted to understand. In this way I avoided my feelings and emotions. I could keep people and my resentments at a distance. As a teenager, I was able to keep men away as well. I didn't have to look and see this part of my life. This makes sense now when I remember how I see out of my right eye. My world seems inward. The aspects of my father's side, my masculine characteristics are less familiar to me. I structure my life around this way of perceiving.

My left eye is clearer and preferred. I cannot cross my eyes and integrate what is close to me. However, I manage my life well. I am professionally a great teacher. In my personal life I keep people away. At age forty-five, I am still without a man to whom I can spiritually connect. I wish to live my life in partnership with a man.

Here is more of my session with Natalie:

*RK:* To be with a man means to connect to your masculine side. Go into your emotional, spiritual nature [see region E] that is present when you consider being with a man. Feel how your body talks to you and guides you to the sensual side of your nature. Feel how you like to be touched. [Area D; I wait for Natalie to integrate this.] To be in partnership means to integrate your male and female parts. Feel the qualities from your mother's side integrating with your true masculinity. Discern what qualities from your father's side you replicate. Which are genetic qualities? Which are your true self? This can only happen when you integrate the strengths of your feminine nature with the true aspects of your male nature.

As Natalie listens, I continue:

*RK:* Your genetic self reflects that you can accomplish your goals by feeling more. Step down from the attic of your mind and your thoughts, into your emotional body. Begin wearing a patch over your left eye. Sit quietly. Be with yourself. Find your sensual nature. [I wait for an answer. The right iris, region D, indicates that Natalie may be protecting her male-sided sensual nature. There is emotion and it is heavily guarded by thought patterns. Feeling practices will help Natalie discover her own sensual nature.]

When you have your left eye covered, speak on the phone, converse with your friends, and practice speaking your truth that comes from deep within you. [In region E lies the mystery of Natalie's male-sided expression through speech. The deeper aspects of her spiritual nature are also here. This can explain why meditation and stillness provided the eyesight improvement.] Consider that your interest in meditation and being still is a doorway to your integrating your male and female sides.

The overreliance upon thinking was genetically programmed into Natalie's embryonic self. Her life with her parents helped launch this way of perceiving reality. Her protection of feeling and emotion by using thoughts and understanding manifested itself in nearsightedness. The greater diopters in the right eye gave her additional feedback to address the male side of her projected personality. By patching her left eye, Natalie began making the necessary discernment of her various selves.

She observed when she was projecting thoughts through her right eye. Natalie mastered how to direct a softer feeling into her right eye and consciously stay present in her feelings. She was able to transcend the conditioning of her genetics and childhood. Natalie more successfully entered into feeling before she talked. Her resentment toward male authority shifted to a perception that a man in her life could be a sacred union. Integration of her many parts became the focus. The information from Natalie's iris guided her to access her true nature. She was able to leave behind the quicksand of her parents' conditioning.

## Fear of Seeing

Information from the iris helps identify genetic influences that might predispose patterns of fear. Nearsightedness can be related to a fear of seeing. Quite often this fear is related to an uncertainty about the future. One might presume it is of seeing the outside. But this fear could also be fear of seeing something about yourself. It might be a fear of believing that how you see might be a part of your personality.

Natalie's iris revealed some fears. By understanding that below fears exists another polarity, like nurturing, inspiration, or self-expression, Natalie was able to shift her perception and connect with what I call the "opposite polarity," that is, a quality or way of seeing that is just the opposite of our present one. For example, a fear of loss of love can be discovered to be a capacity to intensely love. Some fears Natalie faced were fear of invasion or attack, fear of being criticized or reprimanded, fear of being controlled, fear of intimacy, trust, and commitment.

She continued talking about her discoveries:

I am at a point where my teaching career cannot go any farther. I am seeing my personal life in a fresh way. I chase people away.

I project so much overbearing energy. I stop. I feel my fear of being close. I want intimacy and I protect. While patching my left eye I had a flash of clear eyesight. I realized in that moment my fear had turned into excitement. I took the patch off. Everything was brilliantly clear. I am sure my eyesight was 100 percent. I did yoga. I looked at three-dimensional fusion photographs [like photographs 12 and 13]. As I integrate the perceptions of my left and right eyes, special experiences happen. I enter a different perceiving. I am stunned. To fuse my female and male realities does not require perfectly clear eyesight. I am aware of what is peripheral to my normal, central understanding focus of my looking. I integrate my thinking with feeling. Then it happens. An energy moves through me. I sense through my physical nature a wonderful aliveness. I know I must go into that world I'm seeing now and be myself.

Natalie did this. Her diopters kept peeling away. She reached a point where her left eyesight was almost good enough for driving without glasses. Her work was not yet over. There were more fears to face through her right eye. Natalie's next step for entering the new world she was beginning to see was to extend her acknowledgment of her spirituality and bring it through her teaching into the world. Her challenge now was to extend herself a little beyond the comfort zone of her survival personality.

## Feeling What You See!

As Natalie entered more into her feelings, childhood memories surfaced. She was now able to view her childhood perceptions from the vantage point of her current awareness. Bringing her presence and discernment to this new view, Natalie was able to cultivate her conscious seeing. She had withdrawn from her parents' nonfeeling approach to parenting. Once again, looking at Natalie's iris pictures, it is apparent that the right-eye image has more orange coloration in the upper portion than the left eye. This means that Natalie carried more thought-controlling perceptions through her right eye. Once she crossed the "mountain range" and reached the outer part of the iris, there was much feeling and calmness. Natalie accomplished this in the following visual sequence. You can replicate these practices in your case of nearsightedness.

## Visual Steps for Nearsightedness:
## Reduced Lens Prescription

Whenever possible, wear a weaker nearsighted lens prescription. Reducing the diopters resulting in a 50 percent level of eyesight is acceptable for driving in most cases. In North America, the acceptable eyesight for driving is 20/40. The best situation would be to have two pairs of glasses: one full-strength set for driving on rainy or cloudy days and at night, and a second pair of reduced strength for everyday wear when you wish to practice sharpening your looking. Spend more indoor time in your naked vision. You will find that you move much more slowly than when everything is finely focused. This is the exact setup for deepening your feelings.

You can consult with a behavioral or vision therapy–oriented optometrist to prescribe weaker lenses for you. See the Web site referrals in the back section of the book for practitioners. Remember to explain to the doctor that you are using integrated vision therapy practices in addition to wearing the weaker-prescription lenses. Doctors may be reluctant to prescribe weaker lenses for fear of liability.

Natalie found that when she couldn't look at everything sharply she became more relaxed. This promoted her feeling more. Instead of being overly busy she would take time to sit and watch her flower garden, listen to the birds, and enjoy the colorful sky at sunset. Natalie imagined her retina and fovea both being stimulated by the incoming light. She also kept a daily vision diary and wrote all visually related discoveries in it. In this way she could begin remembering her life prior to getting glasses. Within those memories she recalled the times of her childhood when her eyesight was perfectly clear. Natalie could then consciously build on those memories for clearer seeing now.

## Patching with Reduced Lens Prescriptions

You remember that patching is typically done with your naked vision. In Natalie's case, her sight in her right eye was quite blurry. She could only see objects that were within about ten centimeters of her nose. This meant that in her naked vision she could "do" very little. She had to stop and feel. In this way, Natalie remembered how to be with herself. This was quite challenging for her, as it is for most people. In the beginning, the longest she could stay in her naked vision while patching her left eye was six minutes. She became irritable and restless, and she uncovered fear. Natalie wrote down her feelings. When she reread what she had written, she used her intellect to explain the reason underneath the feeling. As she did this practice over a period of a few weeks, her eyesight became more flexible. The letters on the eye chart became clearer to her.

Wearing a patch in her naked vision was more intense than looking through one eye while wearing her glasses. The reason is because being in one's total blur through one eye activates more emotion than looking through one eye with a compensating or therapeutic lens which produces more clarity. Natalie placed translucent sticky tape over the left lens of those glasses. The tape acted like a left eye patch, forcing her to look mostly through her right eye. She experienced less fear, and she could do more and still feel.

## Wearing Pinholes

In the comfort of your home, consider wearing pinhole glasses instead of your regular glasses. These special glasses hold lenses of plastic disks punctured by many little holes. (See "Products for Conscious Seeing" at the back of the book.) The pinholes produce about a 60 percent improvement in clarity over your naked eyesight. An additional advantage is that this sharpness is accomplished without the spatial distortions that occur with conventional lenses. Natalie found the pin-holes a relief after wearing glasses or patching. By remembering how she looked past the window in the exercise with the string, as described in chapter 7 under "The Practice of Seeing," she was able to look through the holes in the same way. She loved the feeling of expanding her focus beyond her normal comfort zone.

This outward, divergent stretching of her vision replicated a far-sighted way of being. When she removed the pinholes her visual world through both eyes was much clearer. While looking through the holes Natalie had to stay consciously present. If she became tense or overfocused, some of the little holes would merge and she would have double vision. In other cases, the holes would seem to get in her way of seeing. This feedback was excellent for her to fur-ther train her eyesight. Natalie could effectively monitor how the dif-ferent parts of her mind affected her seeing and looking.

> *A lens allows us to focus on that part of the mind*
> *that is waking us up to being or seeing consciously.*
> — THE AUTHOR

## Therapeutic Lens Prescription

In earlier chapters I mentioned how by further modifying the lens prescription the potency of the healing can be increased. In Natalie's case, it seemed prudent for her to spend time with both eyes open, training herself to look more through the right eye. This was accom-plished by weakening her left eye lens prescription with a new pair of glasses. Her eyesight through her left lens would be less clear than her eyesight through her right lens. This meant that when Natalie put on these glasses, her whole focus shifted from the normally clearer left eye to the more blurry right eye.

On the surface this may seem like a simple arrangement to get used to. On the contrary, this form of conscious seeing is deep ther-apy. This is why these lenses are called therapeutic. When you focus light more clearly through one eye, there is an activation of memory.

In Natalie's case, she accessed perceptions associated with her father and her own masculine side. Images and her past ways of looking and seeing emerged. Just as in patching, the wearing of glasses that simulate patching has to be done in twenty-minute increments. And, of course, it's necessary to develop a harmonious relationship with an optician or eye doctor who will support your use of such a training lens.

Another approach when there is more than 1.50 diopters of astigmatism is to increase the astigmatism by 0.75 in each eye. This has a very interesting effect. What is normally the least clear viewing orientation now becomes the clearest. This situation is analogous to the story of Sara and her father in the cave in chapter 1. Wherever the beam of the flashlight shines, that becomes the point of reference for looking. In the case of increasing the astigmatism, the light coming into the eyes has a particular focus, which lights up the normally darkened or shadow side of your perceptions. The impact of this will be further discussed in chapter 9.

## Seeing beyond Self

When Natalie wore the therapeutic lens prescription with the increased astigmatism, she started experiencing feelings she had been storing up about her brother and father. In her case, the lens design still allowed her to look more through her right eye than her left. She remembered how distant she felt from the male side of her family. As she started to allow herself to feel, her anger surfaced. As she increased the amount of time she wore these special glasses, she noticed a shift in her perceptions.

She began to value her outside world as much as her inner one. This meant that her attention and vision began to be split between seeing inwardly and seeing outwardly. At first this seemed very strange to her. Accompanying the feeling of awkwardness was a fear of stepping out of her normal inner comfort zone. Her secret, introverted nature shifted dramatically as she reached beyond the mountains of her own thoughts. For Natalie, climbing the orange mountain range was like the exultation of her first awakening in Tibet.

## Movement and Space Expansion

While standing with bare feet, look off into the distance. If you are outside, join nature through your eyes. If indoors, stand in front of a window where you can look out at the natural world. You may wish to make an eye chart on the window, constructed of stick-on letters, available in most hardware stores. In this way you can look through the chart into the distance.

Begin swinging your body from left to right. Close your eyes and imagine you are looking directly at your closed eyelids. Feel your body gently swaying back and forth. Use the in-breath, followed by the out-breath, and then pause. Take your time and deepen your sense of your feelings as you let go of your thoughts. As long as your eyes are closed, you are thinking less. Feel the pleasure of swinging. Imagine your body floating in space. Enjoy the motion. Become aware of how relaxing this is. Once again become aware of your breath and relax further. Imagine that the heavy weights of your thoughts are moving downward from your head toward your body. The heaviness is replaced with deep relaxation.

Continue the swinging for another thirty to fifty breaths. Then imagine you can look through your closed eyelids. You are remembering what nature looked like prior to closing your eyes. At first your vision reaches as far as the window. Slowly, with each breath, you stretch and expand your sense of looking further and further. You see the vivid colors and shapes in your mind's eye. You travel out into space, and your central view is perfectly clear. You also notice what is surrounding the central part of your looking.

Lastly, pay attention to the perceived motion of nature. Are you able to detect that the world appears to move in the opposite direction of your body motion? Verify this important visual distinction by opening your eyes and looking at your thumb placed before your eyes while you continue swinging. The world behind the thumb will appear to move very fast in the opposite direction that your body swings.

The goal of this practice is to use your eyes to occupy as much of your seeing space as possible. Looking includes seeing what is around the point you are focused on.

After a "swinging" session, look around the room or out in nature with your naked vision. Observe how you feel. Colors can seem brighter. Shapes may be more apparent. Then view an eye chart and notice if your eyesight has changed. Become aware of how your looking is different when you are in nature versus identifying letters. Re-create the feeling of expanding your focus and notice if the letters sharpen.

*My aim is not to be consistent with my previous statement on a given question, but to be consistent with the truth as it may present itself to me at any given moment.*

—MAHATMA GANDHI

## Farsighted Perceiving

While bringing the preceding practices into your daily life, consider how the consciousness of farsightedness works. Farsightedness means moving outside your head, seeing beyond where you stand. Think of your thoughts being inside your head. Spending time thinking crystallizes your thoughts. Now reach outside your thoughts by looking through your eyes at what lies beyond. In this way you expand your sense of self. You begin to realize that the world outside your eyes is part of you. Feel more than think about what you are looking at. Practice becoming part of what you are looking at. Imagine that there is no separation between you and the world you see, that the two are actually one.

## Expanding Vision Practice

Natalie used practices where each eye saw an image like in photographs 12 and 13 on pages 126–127. By crossing or uncrossing her eyes she was able to create a third image. This is similar to the computer-generated Magic Eye practices popular some time ago, where you first saw only an abstract pattern, say, of small, colored boxes or dots. But as you stared at the image, a photo of a famous person, or perhaps a word such as *love* or *see* emerged. You could never quite figure out why you could see it one moment but not the next, except that it had something to do with what you focused on within yourself.

The exercise I am about to explain works something like the Magic Eye images, except that the way you will be practicing will be more balancing and integrating, strengthening rather than puzzling you.

For nearsightedness, uncrossing will be the first step to master. Look past the two images in photograph 12. Identify a point in the far distance, say 100 yards or more away. Slowly move the photographs into your line of vision. Keep your full attention on the distant point. The two photographic images will appear to swim in your field of vision for a while. You may see four eye charts, with the middle two overlapping. Your goal is to see a third image directly in the center of the two photographs. This image may appear slightly larger and will have more depth. This will be particularly true in the appearance of the narrow street. Parts of the building and the fainter eye chart in the sky may be seen in different dimensions of depth. The alleyway will appear to be long and have depth. The eye chart will ideally have all the letters present. The buildings will appear closer than the sky. Let yourself relax and spend about three to five minutes staying with the final image, then palm your eyes and rest.

Write about your experiences. Share them with a friend. If you can, have a friend do these exercises and read this book with you. Observe how your eyesight seems different. What are you now able to consciously see—both outside yourself and inside? Over time, use the same practice but stand on both feet. What effect does standing have on your expanding your focus?

Natalie and her brother both became myopic living in their parents' environment. Perhaps the lack of feeling in the family contributed to their nearsightedness. Rolf was very happy wearing glasses. He did not have the same interest in conscious seeing as Natalie did. He stayed with his fully compensating lens prescription and enjoyed his profession and way of perceiving. Natalie, on the other hand, soon realized that her reduced and therapeutic lens prescriptions were a ticket to freedom from her thoughts. The more she entered into her feelings, the richer her life became. It was not always easy. However, conscious seeing brought her such a wealth of rich experience that she continues it even to this day.

## Children and Nearsightedness

Natalie had a daughter, Crystal. By age three, Crystal had been diagnosed as nearsighted. At first the diopters were not measurable in Crystal's eyes. This means that even in the presence of lowered eyesight, a reflection of her mind's eye, the camera eye had not recorded any dioptric changes that could be structurally measured. She had been sitting very close to the television, and she, like her mother, also loved books. Natalie noticed that her daughter was holding picture books very close to her eyes. So, with the help of a sympathetic doctor, she began to incorporate conscious seeing principles into Crystal's daily life.

Natalie remembers:

> The eye doctor was wonderful. He informed us that he would not prescribe glasses for Crystal since she was functionally projecting nearsightedness. He kindly explained that this meant that she was behaving like a nearsighted person and the structure of her eye was not affected. He said that the structural change in the eye comes later. The doctor encouraged me to work with Crystal at home. First we introduced visual hygiene practices. The concept is similar to dental hygiene, in that you take time each day to do something for your eyes. I designed a special reading area for Crystal on the couch, and provided lots of pillows to support her back. Crystal learned to sit up straight. I placed a bright 100-watt full-spectrum light behind the couch so that her book was lit up as

if the sun were shining. We put a digital watch with a timer next to the couch. Crystal is permitted to read in twenty-minute intervals. When twenty minutes have elapsed, the timer buzzes, and Crystal puts her book down and palms her eyes for twelve breaths. This takes about one minute. She repeats the same sequence when she plays her video games, watches movies, or plays with her plastic puzzles. Once a day she goes to an eye chart I designed, with animal pictures. I make sure that Crystal can see the smallest animals, and I change the animal pictures every few weeks by printing out new pictures from the computer.

Crystal is fortunate: Because her eyesight is close to 80 percent of normal, she does not need to wear glasses. Her visual demands for precise looking are minimal at her young age. Her supportive eye doctor and aware mother are both blessings in her life.

Like adults, children with nearsightedness can wear weaker lenses. At the same time, it is most important that they adjust their visual habits. They need frequent breaks. They need to rest their eyes by looking off into the distance, playing outside, and getting plenty of physical exercise. Sunshine and fresh air are most helpful.

Robert Kellum says, "The epidemic of myopia so prevalent at the completion of the twentieth century was associated with the consciousness of a nuclear family lifestyle. Each family was sovereign to itself. This was a foveal way of looking, not paying attention to the periphery." The solution might be to restructure our perceptions so that we "feel part of a larger community." For example, in the small community where I live, everyone shares garden implements and other tools. Rather than everybody on our street owning a separate lawn mower, we all share one.

Wouldn't it be wonderful if our educational system could be designed to encourage more farsighted behavior in children? Imagine nearsighted children being given their lessons outside in fresh air, where they are encouraged to look off into the distance. Would there be less nearsightedness if less demand were placed on activities that involved thinking and understanding? Could the incidence of nearsightedness be lessened by waiting longer until we teach children to read?

Most cases of nearsightedness in children require parents to get involved in their own conscious seeing. Our children amplify our own incompletions. We can choose to pay attention and consciously see or slip into the oblivion of the blur and see unconsciously. When I look at my children, I thank them for showing me the way to my conscious seeing, for it is their influence that has helped me to look beyond conventional practices.

# 9

## *Farsightedness: Centering and Clarity*

Most optometrists look upon the cause of farsightedness as an eye-ball that is too short. In such an eye, the rays of light focus at a point that would be behind the retina, causing a distortion in vision. While the farsighted person can see distant objects well, he cannot get close-up objects in focus. One variety of farsightedness can be considered a normal evolution in development. Skeffington, the grand-father of behavioral optometry, stated that a small amount of farsightedness is a good thing, since it serves as a "shock absorber" in times of distress. His point was that if we become overly focused on what's right in front of us, then a bit of farsightedness could protect us from moving into nearsightedness.

Think of farsightedness as a message guiding you to conscious seeing. The challenge is to shift your perception of farsightedness; think of it not as a problem but as a condition that can provide you with clues to see and heal incompletions in your past. With farsight-edness, you can peacefully reach into your future. If anger is an emotion that you need to work on, through your work with your farsightedness, anger can be transformed into a passion for life. Embrace your farsightedness as a way to expand and evolve your perceptions. Farsightedness is seeing life through eyes of brilliance, through a visionary perspective.

## Farsightedness in Children

Some children demonstrate transient farsightedness during their normal development. As the eye grows, the shape of the lens in relation to the length of the eye can produce farsightedness that is self-correcting as the child continues to grow and mature. This form of farsightedness is common enough to be considered part of a normal maturation process.

More acute farsightedness in young children may lead to crossed or lazy eyes. This form of farsightedness is also quite common. When the farsighted child has to focus on small details, he or she overfocuses the ciliary muscles. The action of the ciliary muscle, which is the heart of the focusing system, is known in visual science as "accommodation." It is controlled by a specific area in the brain, one that also centers the eyes so that they can work together rather than independently. When a farsighted child overfocuses in order to look clearly at close-up details, his or her natural centering ability can be disrupted, causing the eyes to cross. In most cases, one eye turns in more than the other.

At younger ages, children have ample reserves of focusing power and are able to focus and turn their eyes in a highly responsive way. Farsightedness in young children can therefore go undetected for years because they have ample capacity for compensating for it by overfocusing. Once a child is diagnosed as farsighted, the usual course of action is for optometrists to prescribe corrective glasses. The rationale is that when the child wears these glasses, the eyes cross less because they no longer have to overfocus. This makes perfect sense. If the child has to focus less, then the likelihood of the eye turning is reduced.

In severe cases of eye crossing, known as inward strabismus, physicians may pressure parents into a surgical procedure to correct the turning. There may be a valid reason for the surgery, such as a higher probability of better eye teaming; however, parents should be aware that the surgery may not result in binocular vision. Additional integrated vision therapy may be needed. Also, many surgeries are done for cosmetic reasons, when parents feel embarrassed about their child's vision problems.

When the farsighted person has very different focal lengths in each eye, the likelihood of a lazy eye, called amblyopia, increases. Focal length refers to the way light aims into the eye; a shorter focal length means that light rays don't focus as far behind the eyes as in a longer focal length. A child with this condition will probably suppress the vision in the more farsighted eye, and it may turn in as well. When this happens, doctors usually recommend patching the better eye in order for the more farsighted eye to gain experience with looking. Typically, this patching is encouraged at an early age, because physicians fear that brain cells associated with the suppressed eye may not receive the necessary light stimulation for ongoing cellular development. There is some validity to this concept. For the same reason many physicians persuade parents to have the surgery for their child to ensure the alignment of the eyes. It is hoped, then, the necessary brain development of vision will result. I have personally seen lazy eyes come alive even in adulthood, even in the absence of patching.

Farsightedness often is accompanied by astigmatism. The mechanism of astigmatism will be discussed in the next chapter.

In the following story, it is clear that a patient's farsightedness, as reflected in his camera eye, can be quite different from the symptoms projected from the mind's eye. Jeannie brought her two-year-old son Mathew to see me. Mathew's right eye turned in. He wasn't wearing eyeglasses or contacts. I asked Jeannie if Mathew was farsighted and she said he was, a little. His farsightedness was lower than would be expected for his degree of eye crossing. She showed me her son's prescription of +2.00 for each eye, which is not what I would consider to be a high degree of farsightedness — certainly not enough to explain the turning of the right eye for his age. Since it was Mathew's right eye that turned in, I asked Jeannie whether his father was present. She shook her head and said that the father had departed before Mathew's second birthday. Mathew's eye began to turn inward shortly thereafter. By patching the left eye, Mathew gained the experience of looking through the eye associated with his father—which I'll explain in greater detail in a moment. While he was undergoing this therapy, I coached Jeannie in dealing with her resentment over her husband's departure. She in turn brought this new awareness to her son, by speaking kindly to Matthew of his father and conveying a loving presence for the father in front of her son. Matthew's vision then improved.

Matthew's is not an isolated case. The real point of the story is that farsightedness and the resultant crossed eyes are not random events that occur independently of an individual's life experience. The human condition is intimately linked with the workings of the eyes. The physiology of vision holds a record of a person's life experiences, and each eye condition tells its story about how the person has adapted to the unique circumstances of his or her life. In the past, we needed to dig deeply and therapeutically to "fix" the original circumstance. This is no longer necessary. What is more useful is to change our perception. My real purpose in sharing these facts is to inspire you to begin taking steps to educate yourself and your eye doctor to look at what is happening behind your eyes.

Since you are exploring conscious seeing by reading this book, you are interested in something more than conventional vision correction. But bear in mind as you read that I am not proposing you abandon conventional eye care. The science of vision has contributed much to the development of complementary approaches to farsightedness as well as to other eye conditions. Conscious seeing makes use of therapeutic lenses, for example, to help correct the problem at its source. Farsighted lens prescriptions can be designed to awaken the deeper purposes of conscious seeing, that is as a path to larger truths in your life.

## To Be Farsightedness

Let's step beyond the physical condition of farsightedness. Following the concepts from earlier chapters, consider that farsightedness is a communication from the mind. Open yourself to the possibility that farsightedness is your brain and mind trying to get your attention.

Think of it as a state of reaction in the mind. If nearsightedness is an overreaction to thoughts and excessive thinking, then farsightedness is a reaction to emotions, usually anger. What I mean is that when we hold onto anger in our physical body, the energy builds up like a volcano and eventually tries to push outward. Looking at a certain content or seeing a past incident that provokes an angry feeling can fuel our vision to focus too far outward. This is a farsighted way of perceiving. One loses focus on the inward because it is too painful to stay in the clarity of the anger.

This does not mean that farsightedness is a bad thing. Nor does it mean that everyone who is farsighted is angry! On the contrary, the condition of farsightedness can be used to access the energy of emotion and transform it to a more useful form.

## Anger and Passion

Those who are farsighted often have a desire to push outward, an inner need to reach outside the self. They wish to be attentive to the forces of nature beyond self. Behind this soul-directed mission is a family history of high emotion. In most cases, the emotion sought by the farsighted individual as the source of why he or she pushes outward occurred during infancy. This raw, undeveloped state of emotion is reflexive and reactive. The farsighted person's challenge is to access the useful aspect of the emotion; this access is the doorway to the ground of centeredness and being. The farsighted person can then channel the energy of the feeling to enter their vivential state of being. If the emotion is anger, it can be transformed into passion. Each potentially negative emotion has its positive equivalent. For example, the opposite of resentment is love; the opposite of abandonment is nurturing; and of withdrawal, expression. Once the transition is made to the positive equivalent, the true nature of the person emerges and genius reveals itself.

As a clinician I have had the privilege of photographing many infants' irises a few months after birth. I repeated the process when these children reached two, three, and four years of age. From these photographs I was able to discern which markings on the iris are present at birth and which develop over time.

The evidence in these photographs suggests that each individual's pattern of emotion is present at or soon after birth. Flower-petal patterns or valleys are clearly visible in the iris within a few hours after birth. They form the first foundation layer that predicts the kind of vision the child will have, along with its concomitant emotions. The emotional pattern present in the petals on the iris seldom goes through any discernable physical change. On the other hand, the thinking markings of yellow, white, orange, or brown coloration on the iris are laid down like paintbrush strokes over time, occurring in conjunction with the child's development during the first seven years of life.

Because the iris reveals genetic influences, we can study the emotional markings in them and then correlate these markings to the refractive conditions of the eye. We also note that right and left eyes correlate with parental genders. The right eye iris patterns are linked to father; the left, to mother. And the iris holds even more information. Each eye has a particular region named the anger/passion position. For the right eye this is in the eight o'clock position. For the left eye, it is at four o'clock.

When I am with a farsighted person I like to observe their iris patterns for the presence of emotion. I am particularly interested in seeing the intricate formation of the iris structure. Looking from the pupil outward, I check to see whether the flower petal that forms there seems closed or open. Is it protected by steep borders? Is the valley at its center completely closed or open at one or two points? The more closed and isolated the valley, the more that anger will be protected and inwardly directed in the individual. Recall that while anger is the key emotion in farsighted individuals, there may be other, secondary emotions as well. These iris patterns help explain how a farsighted person will deal with anger. The more open the emotional pattern, the more accessible is the anger.

The shape of the pattern on the iris is genetically determined. I propose that when there is anger in the family tree, it is genetically passed down, like certain diseases. In earlier chapters I talked about how anger was present in my own family tree. It is also clear to me that each generation has the opportunity to deal with the emotion of anger. To the extent that each person accepts the challenge of preventing anger from controlling their life, the next generation can reap the benefits of this consciousness. I suggest that anger is an energy that, when used efficiently and consciously, can be useful in gaining consciousness, therefore guiding you to conscious seeing.

## The Wisdom of Anger

When you consciously see anger as having a potentially positive outcome, then you can see the wisdom of anger. For example, anger can help you cultivate an awareness of your passions. Michael's story, which follows, clearly demonstrates how conscious seeing can assist you in maneuvering toward taking responsibility for the way you see and behave.

As a farsighted person with good eyesight, Michael had known anger since he was a young child. His father would come home for dinner at night and scream at his mother and siblings. Michael's father always told his son that anger was part of their family heritage and he would just have to learn to live with it. Michael was a sensitive man who used his farsighted symptoms—in particular, eye crossing—to evolve past the genetic propensities he'd inherited from his father and his grandfather. He described his early years this way:

> I was always the pleaser of the family. I falsely perceived that my younger brother received more of my father's attention than I did. At an early age, I suppressed my resentment toward my father. I hated the way he doted on Solly, who was three years younger than I. Instead of acting my anger out, I stored it in my stomach and lungs. I became asthmatic and had terrible stomach cramps. I couldn't digest my life nor the food that I ate. The resentment inside me grew like a volcano waiting for the right moment to explode. Finally, there came a time when I could no longer suppress my emotions. Fortunately, my parents were wise enough

that, when I started acting out my resentment in angry screaming fits, they helped me redirect this energy in a positive way. I swam, and played tennis and hockey. In this way, some of the pain left my body. The part that didn't, left me helpless in reading. I saw double more than half the time I picked up a book. The words swam from a farsighted blur to a distorted astigmatic perception and then into double confusion. I was a nonreader who preferred to look far away out the window daydreaming of the perfect day in the future. Often my teachers called me back into the room, disturbing my far-off–looking, peaceful world.

I had trouble staying in the present. My resentment was strong. I was blessed to be appropriately directed by my teachers. I therefore never directed my anger in an antisocial way. I just sulked and burned inside from the ulcerous pain of resentment and anger.

The kind side of my father helped me to grow in creativity. He taught me how to paint. I felt so much love from this creative escape from the fire inside my belly. I became passionate about letting the paintbrush move effortlessly over the canvas. The strokes were the path for the anger to flow. I found the force of the inner volcano and it left me through my hands. I looked at the vibrant red and orange colors in front of me and felt relief. The energy of my anger was being converted to the passion of painting. This outlet was a big relief.

Then I began patching my eyes while I painted. First, the left eye. I directed my anger through the father right eye and let the canvas fill up with years of resentment. I repeated this process with many paintings. Each time I painted, I went deeper into my anger. I felt the hate and lifetime of pain and resentment toward my father and grandfather. After a few months, I could feel my resentment lifting. When I had emptied myself, I felt lighter and full of the.transformed energy.

I would then get on my bicycle and ride through nature, appreciating the summer flowers. I let this other form of emotion enter my being. I surrendered to a deep appreciation of my passionate nature. Life took on a new view. As I learned to integrate my two-eyed perceptions, I saw more deeply into myself through my eyes. I became aware of how I could direct consciousness from myself. By making space, that is, making myself feel large and significant rather than small and insignificant, and converting my resentment and anger into a useful passion, conscious seeing became available to me. Inside, I felt big, as though I occupied more of the true being of my self.

Michael speaks insightfully about the mechanism of anger. At first you feel resentment, he says. In the case of a deep valley structure in the anger/passion region of the iris, there is first a suppression of resentment. What is behind resentment is a fear of loss of love, abandonment, and fear of not being noticed. Just as eating too much sugar leads to discomfort, so resentment builds until the feeling is so uncomfortable that you explode in anger. For most of us, this anger is relatively harmless. Perhaps you shout at your children or partner. Maybe you use harsh words with a colleague at work, or perhaps a clerk in a store.

The danger with unskilled direction of anger is when the energy of the anger exceeds the person's ability to contain it. The energy eventually finds a place to emerge, sometimes not very pleasantly and safely. This happens more and more in our world, resulting in the growing problem of "road rage" on crowded freeways, for example, or when an angry person picks up a gun and shoots innocent people.

The way to heal resentment and anger is to seek a healthy and creative way to release them from the body. Like water flowing from a dam, anger may begin to flow from us with a single drip. Later, there might be a huge, rushing flow. Instead of destructive of life, the flow is now life-giving water.

For a farsighted person, the release of anger visually is to push looking outward, pushing vision out to look into the far-off space. This is partly to get away from the proximity of discomfort. The other process is to seek clarity of what is in the future. Another possibility is to find the answer in what the universal consciousness brings.

The farsighted individual looks ahead for answers. Part of the remedy for this farsighted looking is to refocus inwardly, into the present. This refocus can be helped by centering within, using eye-crossing principles. Crossing the eyes inward accentuates the focusing ciliary muscle action, producing more power and increasing one's capacity to be focused. This is particularly true if you are far-sighted in your late thirties, when you may begin to notice a decrease in your focusing ability. Also, if you are approaching your mid-forties and noticing small print becoming unclear, eye crossing is a perfect solution for focusing on self. As you cross your eyes, you can increase your focusing ability.

## To Be Centered

To diminish farsightedness, one must practice focusing deeply on self. This is what builds an energetically strong relationship with emotion. When the farsighted emotional person looks inward, he or she comes right up against unresolved emotion. Freeing the self from immature patterns of emotional resentment permits one to refocus inward and discover his or her true nature. The process of adjusting and balancing your perspective to the outside world is called "being centered." As a farsighted person you might find the centering or eye-crossing exercises to be demanding. You may resist the intense feelings they create in your eyes. The internal rectus muscles of your eyes may hurt at first, as they get used to the movement of focusing inward and remaining that way for five seconds at a time. And just for the record, your eyes cannot get stuck by crossing them inward! This is an old wives' tale.

To center yourself, cross your eyes. This requires you to access a place in your brain where messages are communicated to each eye muscle. The precision called for in eye crossing is exquisite. Each eye has to perfectly align itself so that each fovea receives the same image seen from a slightly different vantage point.

Centering prepares you for high-level, two-eyed viewing, where depth perception, seeing three-dimensionally, is developed. Conscious seeing involves being able to maintain this depth perception for longer periods each day. Within this depth you will find an ever-expanding repertoire of answers to life's challenges.

Michael learned that looking at his nose offered an excellent training practice for increasing his ability to focus more clearly on print and small objects. He started off by trying to see both sides of his nose. At first he could only see the left side. This meant that his left eye was dominating. He practiced covering his left eye to encourage the right eye to turn inward. After a few weeks, Michael noticed that for short moments he could see both sides of the nose simultaneously.

He shared his excitement:

At first my eye muscles hurt when I encouraged the right eye to turn inward. It was so difficult to see the right side of my nose. One day, while sitting on my patio watching the birds play in the trees, I managed to see a little of my nose through the right eye. It was such an exquisite feeling. It felt like parts of my brain were connecting. I felt so present. With practice, I saw more and more of both sides of my nose. The tree outside took on a multidimensionality I had never experienced before. What I saw wasn't that different. Instead, what I was looking at was in its right place relative to everything else. I could see at many distances at the same time. Objects that I normally see unclearly close to me now popped into focus. I felt so alive. I could see the pulsating consciousness of every leaf, and the movements of the birds.

As you practice crossing your eyes by looking at your nose, remember to practice integrated breathing. Breathe in when you look at your nose. When you breathe out, look off into the far distance. Then spend a moment in your distance view while you enjoy the pleasure of the pause before the next in-breath.

This near and far focus is very useful to improve farsightedness. One of my clients named this practice *zooming*. The brain organizes near and far movements by sending instructions to the eye muscles. In changing the way you focus, you are stimulating and relaxing the ciliary muscle. This change of focus is necessary to maintain accurate and flexible focus. With each shift of focus you are indirectly affecting a change in your eye's pupil size. In chapter 1 I mentioned that eye crossing has an effect upon the pupil size. When you look at your nose, you are stimulating focus and eye crossing at the same time. When convergence (eye crossing) is activated, the pupil becomes smaller, meaning the surface area of the iris increases.

Imagine an anger pattern stretching and being stimulated when the pupil gets smaller. This means that by engaging in vision practice, as in looking at your nose or other eye-crossing practices, you are activating emotion. If you need a break from the feelings that surface during these exercises, palm your eyes (place the palms of your hands over your eyes so that all light is blocked, allowing your eyes to rest for fifteen to ninety seconds) or look through a window into the distance.

At the level of the mind, crossing your eyes to look at your nose helps integrate thoughts with feelings. As you engage in this exercise, your attention is on the feeling and the imagery of the two sides of your nose. What happens when you enhance your focusing skills is that you think less and enter into the experience of using your eyes in a conscious way.

## Farsightedness after Forty: My Arms Are Getting Too Short!

I remember when I approached the age of forty, I faced fears of becoming old. As the humorous birthday cards point out, I felt like I was "over the hill." When I was sixteen years old, my parents took me to our family optometrist. He examined my eyes and stated that my vision was good. But, as I was leaving, he casually proclaimed: "Your eyes are good now, but when you turn forty, you'll need reading glasses."

As forty loomed, I could hear this doctor's comments ringing in my head. I felt so much anger. How dare he brainwash me in such a demeaning way! I wondered why I felt so much resentment, and then I remembered the relationship between farsightedness and anger.

I laughed. I was feeling my anger and I suddenly noticed that my arms were indeed shorter!

I recalled my first experience of unclear vision, difficulty reading small print outside a cinema. I cursed the optometrist for his self-fulfilling prophecy. Once I realized the joke was on me, I turned the anger into passion. I vowed that I would develop a series of exercises to train my focusing. I was not going to let presbyopia, as age-related farsightedness is called, get the better of me.

For the next ten years I practiced eye crossing in its myriad forms. I could do marvelous things with my eyes. I used photographs 13 and 14 on pages 127–128 to reach the point where I could stand to move the book and still hold the third image. Perhaps you can devote time to practice eye crossing with this photograph until you can do the same. My normal double vision disappeared and I never needed to wear reading glasses. And, yes, my arms did seem to be getting longer!

I teach others that how we use our eyes is a choice, yet I must confess that I am presently not following my own best advice. For now, at fifty-two, I do need those reading glasses. My lifestyle has become complex. Traveling every four weeks, dealing with jet lag, working frantically on a laptop computer, writing books, and spending hours composing digital photo collages have all taken their toll. The demand on my eyes in near-centered tasks far exceeds my level of vision fitness. But I have made plans to modify my lifestyle.

I can choose to continue undertaking projects that place a high demand upon my using my eyes for reading and computer tasks as long as, at the same time, I practice conscious seeing. My approach is to use the weakest possible lenses for the computer. These are usually 0.25 or 0.50 weaker than my reading lens prescription. During my workday, I take frequent visual breaks. I practice one or more eye-crossing techniques, close and rest my eyes, look out the window, palm my eyes, and stand up and do the body swing meditation described in chapter 7. On my last vision examination, my optometrist estimated my near vision was equivalent to that of a forty-four year old.

One of the easiest and most conscious practices is to notice when your eyes are becoming tired. Observe when the print begins to swim or blur or if your attention wanders. Are you able to maintain a picture of where you are not looking? Remember to keep your seeing space wide open.

If you are farsighted and under the age of forty, you might want to consider reducing your plus lens prescription by as much as will permit you to see small details at a close distance without straining. For this kind of farsightedness, you can usually reduce the lens prescription by more than one diopter.

When I am working on a more relaxed schedule I spend twenty-minute periods reading using pinhole glasses. Unlike reading glasses that can make my naked reading performance seem less clear, after looking through the pinholes, my naked eyesight is clearer. This practice gives me much satisfaction. My eyes and the way I see no longer are a source of anger. I thank my family optometrist for saying what he did. His statement was the exact homeopathic medicine I needed. I love the way I see. My future is clearer than it has ever been. I am close to my self.

## Farsightedness and Light

The key to clear eyesight and conscious seeing is light. All light has the effect of reducing the pupil size, which in turn leads to greater depth of focus. Consider that the ability of light to constrict the pupil is a useful practice.

In farsightedness after forty this is particularly true. On a bright, sunny day, most presbyopes can adequately read outside without glasses. Spend time early in the day and later in the afternoon taking advantage of the beneficial effect of sunlight on vision. Close your eyes and face the sun. Feel its warmth and light on your face. Breathe and feel a wave of relaxation moving the energy from your head toward your feet. Invite the light into your eyes. As long as you are relaxed and consciously remembering the benefit of the light on your well-being, the sun's rays can't damage the eyes, or the skin, for that matter. When you are unconscious about your well-being, harmful effects from the sun are more likely to be experienced. On the other hand, when you are present to your self, you are more cognizant of when it's time to take a break and perhaps cover your eyes with sunglasses.

Feel the light traveling through your closed eyelids bring a wave of deep loosening to the many fine muscles in your eyes. Imagine the seven colors of the rainbow being present in the white light inside your eyes. Visualize your pupils being able to efficiently change from large to small and large again. Recall that crossing your eyes helps reduce the pupil size.

In the winter months, you can make use of a sixty-watt light bulb in front of your closed eyes to simulate the sunlight. Use a brighter light source for reading. No matter what the season, try to read during the hours when natural sunlight is present. Using your eyes at the computer is much better with natural daylight. Reduce the time you read or work at a computer at night. My favorite advice to my clients is that the night hours are for slowing down and resting.

## Intimacy and Seeing Close

One day while working with one of my clients, Joseph, he shared an experience that prompted me to look more deeply into farsightedness after forty. Joseph was forty-two, a professional in the healing arts, and he was practicing looking at a letter chart. He was dating Penelope, a nearsighted, astigmatic woman in her middle thirties.

He shared his experience:

My girlfriend tends to get very close to my face when she talks to me. Usually, she takes off her glasses and looks me in the eye. The last time this happened, I noticed I couldn't clearly focus on her eyes. She was about fifteen centimeters from my face and everything was a blur. This practice of looking at small letters reminds me of that. The first feeling that went through my body was that I needed to move away.

I said to her, "Penelope, you're too close. Please move away." At that precise moment I felt resentment. She was invading my space. As I have learned from conscious seeing, I stayed with my feelings. The next feeling was a tightness in my chest. I recalled this feeling from the earliest days of being a young boy shutting down my heart around my mother. I even remember doing the same thing with girlfriends. And now my eyes were revealing this mechanism to me. When I close off my heart, how I see close is blurry.

I explained to Penelope what had happened. As I talked, I began to cry. Penelope held me in her arms. I felt so heard, under-stood, and loved. As I raised my head to the same twenty-centimeter distance, I had a very surprising discovery. I could see Penelope's eyes perfectly in focus.

Joseph's experience is not an isolated incident. I have for years been evaluating the relationship between intimacy and the ability to stay clearly focused. It appears that when the fear of closeness is fully experienced, the heart opens. Looking from the heart provides a way to be closer to and clearer with yourself. Is it possible that presbyopia is a time of looking closely at self? At forty, you have completed a twenty-year cycle for the second time. Forty is a time of rebirth. During this period, you are moving further away from the way you grew up under your parent's direction. Is it a time for gain-ing more independent focus? Conscious seeing at this age is having the flexibility to see the future and being close to yourself at the same time. This may further necessitate you examining your fears of being intimate with yourself and with others. Joseph took on this chal-lenge with wonderful results. You can do the same.

## Independence

It appears that age-related farsightedness has a specific message. This idea fascinates me because I am at precisely that age where I can con-duct my own experiment. And you can as well. If you are near-sighted, the task is relatively easy. If you have a small or moderate amount of nearsightedness, you can take off your glasses and see very clearly the close distance. This is not the case for people who are clear sighted at far distances. When they attempt to read the label on the toothpaste container, it is not clear. The older we become, the further away we need to push the label in order to see it.

We who are experiencing this change in our vision should ask ourselves, What else are we metaphorically pushing away? A colleague of mine made me think more deeply about this relationship between presbyopia and independence. One day Phillip said to me, "Look at the physical to explain what is happening inside the eyes." I listened. "People after age forty move reading material away from themselves. What does that tell you?" asked Phillip. I considered his point for a moment and asked for an explanation.

Phillip offered this concept:

Up to age forty we need to focus closely on nearby objects. Our parents and teachers are close to us. They and others influence how we construct the content of our lives. In our first forty years we build a strong sense of what gives us physical security. Our careers are foremost in our minds, as is gaining the necessary knowledge to succeed in becoming independent and earning money. The next step is creating a home, family, and security for the future. These activities require the clear focus and dedicated precision of looking at the near-centered details.

Usually after forty, the construction of the material life is cemented into a concrete form. A steady income is flowing and a pension assures future security. Now a certain amount of relaxing can occur. It is time to enjoy the fruits of one's labors. The evolution now is in the direction of not necessarily learning so much about life. There is a move toward a spiritual questioning of the meaning of life. This requires a certain amount of independent search. In most cases this happens through experience rather than through the acquisition of more knowledge and understanding. This is also the time of the so-called midlife crisis. Perhaps the changes that occur during this time are part of the reclaiming of the authentic self?

What Phillip said makes sense. At first we cultivate thoughts and mental understanding as a way to explain life. Then we enter into feeling what we think. Lastly, we discover the exquisite pleasure from experiencing just being in the excitement of our vivential nature of life. Perhaps, from age forty onward, we are further entering this vivential phase of spiritual and material evolution. Is it possible that presbyopia is a reminder that what we read is not as important as what there is to see in life? I think so.

## Reading: What Else?

My clients are usually horrified when I suggest they consider reading less. My most conservative approach is to ask how many hours they read for pleasure. The range is from one to four hours per day. Retired people routinely have more time for reading. I have fun by asking them if they would be willing to reduce their reading time by half. Quite often this provokes a strange and sometimes an angry reaction. "What will I do with myself all those hours?"

I delve a little deeper. What kind of reading are you pursuing? Is it reading for escape? Does the reading promote a deeper appreciation of spiritual evolution? Do you choose books to gain more knowledge? From their answers, I gauge how much less reading should be considered. My clients again complain: "What am I to do when I'm not reading? I'll be bored." First, I encourage them to engage in their vision practices and give their eyes a break from reading, and to remember that the eyes were never designed for extended periods of close focusing. Eye physiology suggests we need to balance between near and far viewing, like that provided for with the zooming vision practice.

I suggest you spend more time moving your body to increase muscle movement and blood flow. Go into nature. Spend time looking at forests, lakes, oceans, and flowers. The most conscious way to use your eyes is in nature—that is the world they were designed to see. Your eyes are part of your inner nature. Let them join with outer nature. While looking and seeing into outer nature, and from the present moment, contemplate your future. Your farsighted way of going to the future is present here, now. See what is right in front of your eyes, just like my friend Jerry did in chapter 1. Remember, he was the man who finally *saw* the photograph of his friend and his friend's baby after the hundredth time of *looking* at it.

Don't delay your conscious seeing one day longer.

# 10

## *Astigmatism: From Distortion to Integrated Wholeness*

Of all the conditions of the eye, astigmatism most clearly illustrates manifestation of the survival personality I discussed in chapter 3. First, let's address astigmatism as it relates to the camera eye, that is, the attributes of the physical eye itself. The shape of the cornea with the nonastigmatic eye is a perfect sphere; on the astigmatic eye, the surface of the eyeball is less than perfect, resulting in what amounts to a slight warping of the cornea. There can also be variations of shape in the lens of the eye that can contribute to or lessen the effects of the corneal astigmatism. Ninety percent of the time, astigmatism accompanies nearsightedness or farsightedness.

Imagine the cornea as a dome covering the outer structures of the eye. Its curved surface will be equally shaped in all directions, perfectly symmetrical. Astigmatism exists when the shape in one direction differs from its counterpart ninety degrees away. The following demonstration I do with my clients gives a direct experience of this very interesting refractive condition.

### Experiencing Your Astigmatism

Take a piece of stiff cardboard about the size of a business card. Using a sharp knife, slice out a narrow slit about one millimeter in width (just under 1/16 inch) and three or four centimeters (5/8 inch) in length. Round the edges of the cardboard so it won't accidentally poke you in the eye. Cover one eye, and without your glasses or contact lenses, place the slit in the vertical position before your open eye. (See Figure 10.1.)

**Figure 10.1**

Peer through the slit in the card at either a calendar or a book at a distance where you can just make out the details. Do the letters appear clearer through the slit than they do with your naked eye? Begin rotating the card so that the slit is eventually in a horizontal position. (See Figure 10.2.) Do you see more or less clearly when the slit is in the horizontal position? Experiment with positions other than vertical and horizontal. You may find a clearer position in one of the diagonal directions.

If you observe no difference between any of the positions that you turn the slit, then you have no astigmatism. A difference in clarity between any two meridians indicates that you have an astigmatism.

Note where your greatest clarity is located. Is it when the card is in the vertical position or when it is in the horizontal position? This position—vertical or horizontal—has significant implications in terms of your journey toward conscious seeing. We will come back to this point in a moment.

Figure 10.2

## Where Do You See Clearest?

For the following exercise, think of a clock face superimposed over a person's eyes. (See Figure 10.3.) If you are doing this exercise alone, you'll have to imagine these instructions from the vantage point of a person facing you.

For the right eye, a perfect horizontal line would run between nine o'clock and three o'clock. That's where you start your evaluation. Slowly rotate the card slit so that you are moving toward ten o'clock, then eleven o'clock, then twelve o'clock, and so on. If you

Figure 10.3

find that your vision is clearer in one position as you rotate the card slit in a clockwise direction, write down the point at which that clarity occurs. Is it at two o'clock, three o'clock? Write down your findings in your journal. If no place is clearer than another, write down notes to that effect as well.

Evaluate both eyes in this way.

## Compensation with the Help of Corrective Lenses

Optometrists and ophthalmologists measure astigmatism in more sophisticated ways than with the slit card you just experimented with. A *computerized auto refractor* scans the optical elements of the eye and prints out a report for the overall astigmatism exam. Also, a special instrument called a *keratometer* measures the corneal curvature in the two primary meridians, providing an extremely accurate measurement of the astigmatism of the cornea.

It's important to remind ourselves that all these measurements with the keratometer and the refractor work assume that the astigmatism is in the eye itself, in the camera eye. But is this really the case? Is the eye itself the origin of the astigmatism, or might we find the origin elsewhere? By exploring the origins of your astigmatic perceptions, as we'll be doing in this chapter, you will gain insights into how you might better generate flexible perceptions that are more aligned with your conscious seeing.

Taking the measurements found by the keratometer and refraction, a prescription lens can be made to compensate for the asymmetric shape of the cornea and lens of the eye. But the lens very rarely corrects, or cures, the condition of the camera eye. If the lens actually corrected the astigmatism at its source, there would come a time when the astigmatism would no longer be measurable in the eye. Doctors rarely see that occur. In most cases involving a compensating lens, the astigmatic measurement either stays the same or worsens with time.

What exactly does the lens accomplish? Let's say that when you look with one eye at two black lines, a straight vertical line and straight horizontal line, the astigmatic eye sees the vertical line as blacker and clearer than the horizontal one. This is one variety of astigmatism. In a second variety, the horizontal line would be blacker and clearer. Obviously, then, if one eye sees one line clearer and blacker than the other, it can mean that you end up with two images in your brain that are not quite consistent.

Let's say that through one eye you see a perfectly vertical line while the horizontal line is unclear and gray. Your brain will decide to stay present with the blacker and clearer image. The compensating lens can make the two lines appear equally black and clear, which results in a single point of focus on the fovea. Presumably, this would make the image that you perceive clearer so that your brain ends up easily accepting both lines.

If you have an astigmatism, the experiment you did with the cardboard slit revealed that, as you rotated the slit, you saw more clearly at certain positions than at others. Let's say that you had the clearest vision in your right eye when you held the slit at an angle corresponding to the ten o'clock position of the little hand on a clock. In other words, your astigmatism ends up showing you that in one meridian or view of life you have greater clarity than you do ninety degrees further away, or at four o'clock. Here's the tricky part: Wherever you experience lack of clarity, you will find that the blurring in this area translates into greater near- or farsightedness. For example, Joe has perfect clarity in one eye at ten o'clock, but is nearsighted at two o'clock. In terms of the inner influences we've been discussing, this means that in one specific view of Joe's life, the two o'clock position, he is more contracted or restricted than in another. Why would this be?

## Astigmatism and Survival Perceptions

The most common variety of astigmatism is where there is the most unclearness in the twelve o'clock meridian. This kind of astigmatism has been called "with the rule," since most people have this variety. This means that the greatest restriction is associated with perceptions of a particular part of your survival mind.

At the level of the camera eye, you will usually observe one level of unclearness that can be traced to an astigmatism. From a conscious seeing perspective, you will notice that because of the interaction between the mind's eye and the camera eye, variations in clarity may also occur depending on how you are breathing and whether you are straining to see.

Your astigmatic view of life need not be a permanent situation, however. As I've explained throughout the book, the state of your mind's eye will affect you at the level of your camera eye. Thoughts, fears, perceptual distortions, feelings, beliefs, and emotional variations are integrally woven into the way you come to life through your eyes. Also, you can construct nonastigmatic perceptions that will alter your life view moment by moment when you observe life through your eyes of vivencia. This chapter will guide you to this way of seeing.

The more the astigmatism is structurally embedded in the camera eye—that is, it has actually caused physical changes in the shape of the eye—the more you might be using the astigmatic blur to suppress part of your mind reality. In your naked vision, the slit experiment reveals the likely location in your mind where this is occurring. By exploring how you see through the slit, you can find clues about the causes of your astigmatism. When the astigmatism is built into the camera eye, it means that the struggle with a particular part of your reality has been present for a long time in your life, long enough to cause a more or less permanent distortion of your eye's cornea and/or lens.

Wearing a lens to correct structural astigmatism provides you with a clear focus for the view of the outer, projected world. This sharp camera eye focus directs your attention outside yourself for the answers to the astigmatic enigma. This artificially focused light does not illuminate the inner mind where the more complex source of vision is housed. Even in the presence of sharp eyesight, the inner "slit" of vision can remain unclear. This is called a "suppression," and in this case a part of the retinal field of vision can be blocked. Depending on the needs of the survival personality this visual field suppression can be partial or complete.

When your mind's eye is projecting more astigmatism than the camera eye, as witnessed in the retinoscopic finding described in chapter 1, it indicates that you are under duress. The consciousness of your perceptions are being distorted in order for you to cope with a particular situation in your life.

The following chart will help you more deeply examine the results of your perceptions through the slit. The axis and degree number, as noted in the chart, can be found in your eyeglass prescription from your eye doctor. By addressing the words in the third column, you can consider which survival perceptions apply to you. While undertaking the practices for astigmatism mentioned later in this chapter, begin using the descriptive words in this chart as a way to create healing sentences and thus more flexible perceptions. I'll explore this in depth later in the chapter.

| Astigmatism axis | Clock dial | Survival perception | Flexible perception |
|---|---|---|---|
| 180 | 12 o'clock less clear | Stubbornness, inflexibility, impatience | Yielding, flexible, patient |
| 90 | 3 and 9 o'clock | Lack of commitment, voicing truth, love | Being committed Fully expressive, nurtured, and loved |
| 045 | 2 o'clock *Right eye* 10 o'clock *Left eye* | Unresolved anger Resentment | Passion for life Humility |
| 045 | 2 o'clock *Left eye* 10 o'clock *Right eye* | Strong or weak willed Sexual issues | Integrated will with power Spiritual perspective to sexuality |

For example, in the chart the axis 180 corresponds to the 12 o'clock position for the most unclearness. The survival perceptions might relate to the words *stubbornness*, *inflexibility*, and *impatience*. If this is where your astigmatism is, first examine how these words are related to your survival personality. Discover how and why you possibly developed astigmatic projections for seeing this survivor part of your life in this way—be it near- or farsighted. Then, use the words *yielding*, *flexible*, and *patient* from the next column to create a new way of seeing the same content of that part of your life in a fresh way. The experience can be deepened by using the sentence sequence mentioned in more detail below.

Another practice I suggest for astigmatism is a *patching paradigm*. This consists of completely covering the spectacle lens of one eye with translucent tape. Cover the dominant perceiving eye or the eye that has the greatest clarity, as you determined with the slit exercise. For the other eye, cover your spectacle lens with the same tape, but create a slit to look through at an angle that matches the angle where you found the least clarity in your slit exercise. Your conscious seeing is to practice looking through the eye that now has the adhesive slit before it. Actively spend time looking through the slit. Imagine focusing this light as healing energy that is able to awaken your perceptions of your astigmatic unclearness. Consider the survival words from the preceding table and become aware of the survival aspects of your own past. Once you have recorded your notes in your journal, use the words under the flexible perceptions to create new perceptions of your former survival experience.

An example in this practice might be that as you are looking through the slit you realize that you are not really committed to your job. Notice that commitment is when the slit for one eye is along the nine and three o'clock position. This is when the astigmatism is axis 090. You would make a slit with adhesive tape to look through this eye along the nine and three o'clock position. Through your exercise looking through this slit, you can uncover your inner reasons for the lack of commitment, like not being challenged enough. This can explain the blur and the distortions you experience. Use this patching in the comfort of your own home and be careful on stairs and in the kitchen, where you might encounter hazards. Be warned that your depth perception is affected in this practice. You can safely patch in this way for twenty-minute periods and extend one minute per day up to a total maximum wearing time of three to four hours.

## Constructing Flexible Perceptions

You can look at the iris patterns that correspond to the area of astigmatism in your eye. Ask questions associated with that particular area of the iris. Using the descriptive words in the preceding table, create phrases and sentences for yourself to use while doing the practices described later in more detail. For example, *nurturing* is a descriptive word. The corresponding slit for this is the horizontal, nine and three o'clock position. For the following incomplete sentence, "The way I prevent myself from being nurtured is ...," you would complete the sentence in your own words. So you might say, "The way I prevent myself from being nurtured is by not eating properly!" Once you have mastered this process, repeat the sentence while doing one of the practices I'll describe, each time adding a new ending. It is important that you not repeat the same ending twice. When you cannot come up with any new completions, you will have either completed this phase or you are resisting going deeper into your feelings and emotions. To determine whether you're resisting, look deeply to see if you have any uncomfortable feelings. If so, resistance of feeling and emotion is manifesting itself. Continue with the practice.

If you feel complete, then you are ready to undertake the flexible perception part of the practice, where you might say, "The conscious way for me to be nurtured is ..." Your completion might be, "The conscious way for me to be nurtured is to take time each morning and evening to fix good food for myself and take the time to fully enjoy it." You then repeat the sentence and keep finding a fresh completion. This is a very effective training practice for developing conscious seeing. First the survival astigmatic perceptions that prevent you from feeling nurtured are dealt with. You then generate clear-sighted perceptions by finding a conscious way of being nurtured that is congruent with seeing your life in a clear-sighted way.

## Therapeutic Astigmatic Lenses

Assuming your journey toward conscious seeing progresses well, you can go even deeper into the process. You will need to find a supportive eye doctor or optician, or perhaps a behavioral optometrist. You can find referrals in the Web site links at the back of the book to practitioners who can design lenses that focus the light into your eyes in a similar manner as looking through a slit. The difference is that there will be no slit present, just the lens effect of looking through the slit.

Interview the practitioner on the phone or in person to determine how open he or she is to helping you in a way that is compatible with the tenets in this book. Explain that you are undertaking an integrative vision therapy process called "conscious seeing." Let the professional know that your intention is to use therapeutic glasses in a conscious way during your practices and that you will be happy to sign a disclaimer type of agreement to wear your regular clear-sighted glasses for activities such as driving or operating any kind of machine. This disclaimer should alleviate any fears the practitioner might have of being liable if you were to have an accident or otherwise hurt yourself while wearing the therapeutic lenses.

If you are nearsighted, mention to your eye doctor or optician that you wish to slightly increase the *astigmatic cylindrical compensating lens* prescription while reducing the *spherical component*. You may not fully understand what this means but he or she will know what to do from an optical point of view to help you reach your goal. What therapeutic lenses will do is provide you with the clearest image focused where the slit used to be; that is, along the meridian of least clear vision. This is exactly the therapeutic advantage you are seeking. With this correction, your survival perceptions will be activated.

If you are farsighted, the same effect of focusing the light rays on the most blurry meridian is accomplished by reducing the astigmatic component of the lens prescription. In either case, get a separate therapeutic lens prescription and still keep your regular corrective eyeglasses for night activities, driving, and the movies. In this way, you can consciously choose which lens prescription you wear, depending on the activity you are involved with at the moment. Begin wearing your therapeutic lenses at home, where you can more adequately process the feelings that surface. Keep a journal of your experiences and each week reread what you have written, to help you link the old and new perceptions.

You might be wondering about the cost to change your lenses more often than before. Certainly you will need to budget for new lenses. Find a willing optician who has discount frames and good prices. Also search on the Internet for discount facilities where you can order inexpensive frames and lenses online. Most online providers will accept a faxed copy of your doctor's lens prescription. This approach will help keep the overall cost of your therapeutic lenses to a minimum.

## Following Your Thumb

If, from your experiment using the slit, you discover that one of your eyes has more unclearness in a particular meridian, then this is the eye you want to practice looking through as you patch the opposite eye. Wear a black patch over the clearer, dominant eye. For the other eye, wear no lens or patch but instead look with naked vision; thus, you will be wearing a patch over the clearer eye with nothing at all over the astigmatic eye.

Position one of your thumbs at a distance of twelve centimeters before your open eye. Recall the orientation of the slit for the meridian of the most unclear vision for that eye. Let's say it is the vertical twelve o'clock position. Now, holding your thumb as if pointing it toward the sky, move it vertically (up to the sky and back down toward the ground) up and down in front of your open eye, while maintaining the distance of twelve centimeters. Move the thumb only as far as you can see it. (See Figure 10.4.)

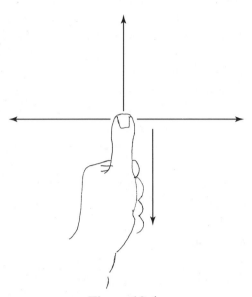

**Figure 10.4**

The movement can be in three forms. First, move your eye to follow the moving thumb. Let this movement be flowing and effortless. As you do this, breathe in the integrated way, with the in-breath followed by the out-breath, and then a pause. Follow your moving thumb with your open eye, being careful not to move your head in the process. As you do so, notice the movement of space beyond your thumb. In which direction does the distant space appear to move while you are looking at your thumb? Do you have any feelings of dizziness? How does it feel to keep up with the moving thumb and not lose focus and attention?

Now continue to move your thumb in this way, except this time let your head follow it while your uncovered eye obviously joins the head movement. This may seem awkward in the beginning but with time it will be easier to do. Remember to breathe at the same time.

Thirdly, choose a point beyond the thumb to look at. Keep your focus directed at this point. Begin moving your thumb, but this time don't actually look at it; remain focused on the point beyond the thumb. Just notice and see the patterns of movement.

Experiment with movements in other directions and note the differences you experience. Write down these experiences. Recall that you are activating memories in this practice and you may need some quiet time in between the different levels to process these feelings. You may also use the sentence-completion process to deal with content around your survival perceptions that might surface.

Palm your eyes if you become tired. While palming, use the flexible perception words to create sentences to complete. Upon completion of each session, recheck your eyesight through the slit along the direction of unclear perception you have been training. You might be surprised to find your perceptions changing. Note how this increased clarity makes you feel, and record any changes in your journal.

## Fusion Photographs

I have designed a series of photographs for reintegrating the left and right eye images for astigmatism. (See photographs 15, 16, and 17 on pages 129–131.) Notice that each photograph has a particular part that is out of focus; there are vertical, horizontal, and diagonal places of blurring. These unclear positions of the photographs correspond to the different clock positions that you have already determined for yourself using the slit.

The goal with each photograph is to successfully cross your eyes and create a middle, third picture, as you have practiced in earlier chapters. (See photographs 13 and 14 on pages 127–128 if you need a reminder.) In order to see the third picture, look at your finger held thirty centimeters in front of your open eyes. While keeping your focus on your thumb, notice and see the two pictures behind your thumb as it sits directly in line with the pictures. At first you may see four pictures; the middle two may even be moving. By varying the distance of your thumb toward and away from your eyes, you will notice a point where the four pictures will become three. When this happens, practice removing your thumb and holding the three pictures in your mind's eye for as long as you can.

The next step is to relax and let yourself move into seeing the third picture more deeply. When you are able to stay present looking through the fovea of each eye, and maintain a presence of peripheral space with your retinas, all the parts of the middle image will appear undistorted and clear.

Start the preceding exercise with the photograph that is the easiest for you to work with. Then move to the more difficult ones, that is, the photographs in which you have the greatest trouble seeing clearly. (You may see your task as making the blurry and distorted parts of the picture disappear.)

The longer you are able to look at the third image while remaining relaxed and breathing, the more you see from your eye of vivencia. You may notice many variations of depth in the pictures, and observe elements of the picture that you had not noticed or paid attention to before. In addition, you may access a deeper perspective about yourself via new realizations and expanded inner awareness.

## Orientation and Consciousness

Justine was eleven years old when she first visited me. Her mother, Laura, who was a therapist herself, was concerned about the recent eyeglasses that had been prescribed for her daughter. Justine had astigmatism and her most unclear perceptions occurred while she held the slit along the horizontal nine and three o'clock position for both her eyes. She had been given farsighted eyeglasses that compensated for the 3.25 diopters of astigmatism.

Justine demonstrated a pushing-away farsighted behavior along the horizontal meridian of her vision. This kind of farsighted astigmatism is called *against the rule*; it is the least common type of astigmatism. I looked at her iris patterns and noticed emotional valleys along this horizontal meridian. The structure of the pattern revealed to me that an emotion was deep and protected in Justine's mind's eye.

With the information about Justine's farsighted astigmatism and the deep emotion associated with joy, nurturing, and commitment that was present on the horizontal meridian, I had a starting place to explore the reasons for her astigmatic eye condition. What was Justine's survival personality about? Which parent was the likely influence? What kind of survival vision was Justine projecting through her eyes to produce this kind of distortion? The information in her iris and lens prescription prompted me to ask deeper questions. You can do the same by using the preceding table.

Justine was unable to cross her eyes. Each time I brought an object toward her, the left eye closed and wandered off to the right. What I saw was that Justine favored her father eye and literally shut off the left, mother eye. The next step was to learn about her father. Because she favored the right eye, I suspected that she was closer to her father than her mother and was angry toward her mother. Since our first visit only lasted an hour, I chose to stay with the physical approach and suggested that Justine learn the integration practice of crossing her eyes, through looking at her nose and focusing on seeing both sides. I assumed that if this practice were successful, Laura and Justine would return for additional visits.

Eighteen months later, Justine and her mother were back in my office. Justine had attempted and mastered looking at her nose with 60 percent proficiency. She now noticed she felt more comfort and maintained better concentration with her schoolwork. Justine was still having difficulty keeping her attention focused on reading assignments. There were other issues at hand. She had entered puberty and was fighting a lot with her mother. I worked with Justine for half the session and then spoke with her mother alone.

I was correct in assuming that Justine's angry, farsighted pattern was at first directed toward her mother. The other factor I felt was having a negative effect on Justine's vision was the busy life of her father and the absence of nurturing from the man she had dearly loved when she was younger. In addition, Justine had earlier in her life sensed the unhappiness of her mother's and father's love life, a common theme when the two eyes do not fully work together in binocular, or *two-eyed*, vision.

Justine's father had had a lover for a few years at about the time Justine's astigmatism first projected itself, when she was eight and nine years old. He had died suddenly between Justine's visits to me when she was twelve. Now, at twelve and a half years of age, Justine's lowered school performance, I concluded, was another symptom of her inner unhappiness and reflected by the inability to stay centered and focused in a conscious way.

When the mind's eye has to make survival choices, as in Justine's case, the camera eye prints out a specific astigmatic prescription. My clinical experience strongly suggests that by dealing with the camera eye astigmatism in the manner I have suggested, we can determine and remedy the survival perceptions of the mind's eye. When this is accomplished, the eye of vivencia opens and conscious seeing is available. This kind of vision is clear and real.

## Self-Esteem

Building self-esteem is one of the greatest challenges many of us face in youth. One region of the iris is called self-esteem and is located away from the vertical meridian at eleven o'clock for the right eye and one o'clock for the left eye. By referring back to the chart on page 213, notice that the vertical positions of unclearness are associated with the axis 180 (with-the-rule) form of astigmatism. My findings reveal a very strong relationship between with-the-rule astigmatism, self-esteem, and its next-door neighbors, sensuality and sexuality.

Healthy self-esteem comes primarily from having plenty of positive reinforcement and being exposed to positive models from our parents when we are young. Positive self-esteem, in turn, promotes self-determination, allowing us to take on challenging projects and develop good decision-making capacities.

Any form of negative criticism in childhood literally erodes self-esteem. My clinical evidence suggests that a person develops a with-the-rule orientation of astigmatism as a way of defending his or her low self-esteem. In this way, the person avoids facing the reality of emotional hurt and pain. Twisting reality in an astigmatic way is a perfect adaptation to avoid feeling.

Jonathan had such an experience growing up. His father, Maurice, was a critical man. Maurice loved Jonathan, but from a point of view that was quite immature, projected from a place of his own low self-esteem. One of the ways Maurice transferred his own weakness to Jonathan was telling Jonathan from an early age that he was not smart.

Jonathan shares his story:

To be with my father was a nightmare. He was so critical of everything I did. How I dressed, cut wood with a saw, did my homework, rode my bicycle. He picked on me like a sergeant in the army. I learned at a very early age that nothing I did was right. Soon, I felt stupid and lost all confidence in myself. I developed astigmatism that gave me headaches when I tried to read. I also had difficulty integrating my two eyes together. When I was a boy I loved my father but couldn't understand why he was so cruel. I filled myself with terror, waiting for the next attack. Later, during conscious seeing experience, I realized that I even attracted teachers who treated me as my father did. It wasn't that my father disliked me. He only wanted the best for me because of his own inadequacies. The problem was that he projected his own warped way of coping onto me. I took on his visual and survival characteristics. I had a difficult time making decisions. I didn't trust my instincts or my intellectual abilities. Life was miserable.

I had to learn to trust the instincts of my emotions. I undertook many processes to face the deep fears that had led to distortions in my vision and body. One of my favorite processes was using my body to learn about fears and perceptions, which I began doing at age thirteen. In our town that year a new swimming pool had been built. It had three diving boards: one, three, and six meters. I learned to overcome my fear of hurting myself by facing heights and diving off the one-meter board. I discovered that by positioning my body in exactly the correct posture, I could gracefully enter into the water. If any part of my body was not in its exact, correct position, I would feel a sting on that part when I hit the water.

I mastered feeling my body position. When I forgot, the stinging sensation reminded me of my lack of presence. I then ventured to the three-meter board. Now I had to readjust my looking to see the distance between myself and the water. Entering the water was another visual discernment. I had to see when to angle my body to gracefully enter in the exact vertical position. The rushing by of the water on my body provided me with a wonderful kinesthetic experience. I felt the space of my body in the vertical orientation. I later found out that this was like the vertical alignment of my astigmatism in my right eye.

Next was the six-meter board. Here I more deeply entered the water's depths and at much greater speed. The massage effect of the water brushing against my body awakened a particular feeling much deeper inside. In addition, I faced my fear of diving from such a height. I decided for myself when to dive. I trained myself to access my inner resources to direct myself through space. This prepared me in many ways for later life.

It was during a conscious-seeing training session that Jonathan made the connection between his body awareness and the vertical space of his vision. When he dove, he experienced the same feelings in his eyes and body as when he followed his thumb moving up and down in front of his open eye. As he did the exercise, Jonathan felt as if there were an energy moving up and down his body, from his head to his feet.

One might wonder if Jonathan's early diving experiences kept him from developing greater degrees of astigmatism. Jonathan remembered that as a teenager, growing up in Perth, Western Australia, he also loved to bodysurf. He described how, by positioning his body, he would get on top of incoming waves and spend hours riding them to shore. Jonathan realized that this was his way of mastering the inner, stored feelings and emotions armored into his musculature.

He explains:

> When I am centered in myself and use my visual awareness, I can gauge the strength of the wave, when to shift my body weight, and stay moving forward. This process integrates my senses with my body musculature. When successful, I can calmly glide on top of the wave, experiencing bliss and elation. If I become disintegrated between my feelings and thoughts, the force of the wave takes over and throws my body around like a tree branch in a raging river. I realized that being out of control in the fury of the wave was like being with my father when I was a youngster. I was at the mercy of an influence outside myself. Now I have mastered myself in order to effectively deal with an external force. When I am integrated and being conscious I feel and see consciously. Bodysurfing showed me how to access the horizontal space of my body. I learned how to integrate the left and right sides of my body and brain hemispheres. I re-experienced this feeling while watching my thumb going from left to right.

## Oblique Astigmatism and Sexuality

In this variety of astigmatism the unclear vision occurs along the ten o'clock (right eye) and two o'clock (left eye) meridians. This form of astigmatism can be considered an advanced adaptation compared to the "normal" nine, three, and twelve o'clock varieties because, in addition to the unclearness along the vertical or horizontal positions, a person with this type of astigmatism further distorts the unclearness through the survival possibilities of the mind's eye. This is manifested in the camera eye with the most unclear view away from the horizontal and vertical positions.

For many years I asked the question, Why would a person go to so much trouble not to see? I didn't pay much attention to the origins of oblique astigmatism until I began looking at iris patterns in the right-eye ten o'clock and left-eye two o'clock positions.

These locations in the iris suggest potential restrictions that are buried deep in the unconscious parts of the mind's eye, where memories are more difficult to access. These survival perceptions originate from the genetic factors that are mapped on the iris and correspond with sensuality and sexuality. As a clinician interested in vision, it was awkward to begin approaching my patients with questions about sexuality. So, while I was a clinical professor of optometry at Pacific University in Portland, Oregon, I collaborated with a social worker to investigate the matter of sexuality and astigmatism. The social work professional began conducting in-depth case histories of individuals who measured astigmatism and other refractive conditions.

In our studies, we found that 75 percent of the total population of the United States has early "dysfunctional" experiences that create confusion about sexuality. These experiences range from physical or emotional abuse to avoidance, confusion, trauma, and a distaste for sexuality. This figure correlated with my findings: 75 percent of the patients who were nearsighted and demonstrated astigmatism had experienced a form of sexual dysfunction.

In the ensuing years, in my consulting practice and workshops I developed an ease in being able to discuss with patients the links between astigmatism and sexuality. I observed that when people do the exercises described in this chapter, face their survival perceptions, and create flexible ways of perceiving, their camera eye astigmatic distortions diminish. In some cases, deeper counseling work with a therapist is necessary. When the person is free of the controlling influences of the mind's eye, he or she is more able to see from the eye of vivencia. Conscious seeing reinforces a healthy way of using the camera eye that in many cases can lead to a freedom of the addictive power of compensating lens prescriptions.

Sex can be used in an addictive way, to help the individual feel better when he or she is depressed or suffering from low self-esteem, or to protect him or her from feeling anger. As long as sex is used in these ways, the person doesn't have to look closely at the source of the uncomfortable feelings. I speculate that astigmatism, coupled with difficulties integrating the perceptions of both eyes into binocular vision, offers a survival mechanism that can keep uncomfortable perceptions toward sexuality locked away in the mind's eye.

A significant number of women in their late forties to mid-sixties who are committed to conscious seeing have stated that they find it quite easy to suppress their sexual needs. They live partially in denial of their eroticism. Does an avoidance of a part of our reality lead to that part speaking louder in order to get our attention? It appears that this is so, that when we suppress the emotionality of sexuality, astigmatism reveals the part of our life view that is unclear. Conscious seeing is taking the steps to uncover how astigmatism can lead us to the places of our visual denials. In that way we can face our lives with renewed clarity of eyesight and find fulfillment and the bliss we all so richly deserve.

## Posture and Astigmatism

The evolution of astigmatism has so far been linked to suppression or blockage of a part of the mind's eye space. The inner distortion successfully creates a visual distortion of our outer visual reality, projecting a change in the structure of the camera eye. As a result, our perception of reality is falsely warped to match an inner inability to cope with what is impinging on our consciousness through our eyes.

Behavioral optometrist Paul Harris's clinical findings suggest that the same process of distortion can occur when the body is not aligned in a vertical orientation. Dr. Harris found astigmatism in concert musicians whose posture while playing is contorted; for example, as in the case of violin players who typically twist their heads in the direction of the violin.

Other reports indicate that when people are in occupations where they move their eyes in one direction more than another, they develop astigmatism. For example, consider the differences between a postal worker and an assembly line worker. The postal worker sorting mail moves his eyes in the vertical direction more than the horizontal as he sorts mail in an up-and-down fashion into different slots; an assembly line worker moves his eyes in primarily a horizontal plane. Interestingly, the postal worker shows less clearness in the horizontal; that is, he tends to have against-the-rule astigmatism. The assembly line worker develops with-the-rule astigmatism, with less clarity in the chronically unpracticed direction of movement, namely the vertical.

The point is to be conscious of maintaining a good vertical alignment of your head, spine, and eyes when reading, working at a computer, or doing desk-oriented activities. It is unwise to lie in bed and read with the book to one side. While at a computer, use a chair with pillows if necessary to support your back. Keep checking that your spine is comfortably erect and not distorted in any manner. Take frequent breaks by stretching your arms above your head and straightening your head and spine.

I have presented astigmatism from my personal experience with many clients. This approach has been useful for them. But as you've begun to see, the topic of astigmatism is complex. Astigmatism is fertile ground for self-exploration. Take the challenge to consciously see all your obscurations and distortions from the past so that you can enjoy clear, conscious seeing in both your present and your future.

# 11

## Eye Diseases: Wake Up and See!

### From Blindness to the Light

The painful words, "You are going to be blind in your right eye within three years, so just learn to live with this," sounded to Françoise like a life sentence. The ophthalmologist who uttered these words offered no treatment other than control checks to monitor her visual deterioration. At age nine she had been diagnosed with astigmatism, but she didn't need glasses all the time, just for reading and homework. The prescription for the right eye was +1.00 −1.00 axis 030 and the left +1.00 −1.00 axis 150. Relative to the axis of the astigmatism, the axis is aligned with the regions of the iris associated with sensuality and sexuality that I discussed in chapter 9.

Françoise, at thirty, didn't let this harsh diagnosis prevent her from appealing her case. She researched alternatives and found her way to conscious seeing. She remembers:

My eyes were never a problem, but at age twenty-three I began to have problems looking for an object in my field of vision. I was busy, so I didn't take action. When I was twenty-five, the symptoms were bad enough that I went to an eye doctor. I couldn't see 100 percent in my right eye. The ophthalmologist thought it was a color deficiency, but I had never had that problem before. She said

I had an eye disease, maybe a *seizure* in the eye. Although she couldn't help me, no referral was made. I followed up on my own, visiting a neurologist and having brain scans to rule out the possibility of a brain tumor. The doctor said my optic nerve was healthy and there were no tumors.

A second consultation with another ophthalmologist led to the diagnosis that I would be blind in three years. I was told to be strong. I told my parents, even though I couldn't get specific information about the condition of my eye. In the summer of 1996 my father took my medical records to a well-known medical school. Three doctors became involved in my case. Finally, a diagnosis of rod cone dystrophy was made. The rods for night vision were more affected. I was referred to a retinal specialist where I had to wait six months for an appointment. I felt relieved because finally I met a doctor who was aware of the condition of my eye.

He said that the rod cone dystrophy was evolving slowly. He couldn't explain why I had this disease. He called it genetic but no one in my family had this condition. He advised me to be very careful of sunlight because the ultraviolet light could further damage the retina, and to wear sunglasses in sunlight. I did this.

After the consultation with this specialist I sold my car and stopped driving. I could still read and function pretty normally. I was to see him in two years. I tried to be strong about my disease. Everybody kept telling me to find a job that would be more secure, like in administration. This was not the life I wanted. For these two years my state of mind and morale seesawed. Two years later, the doctor said the condition had not deteriorated.

I began realizing that I needed to find a solution myself. I met a man who helped me work on my self-development. My mind opened to ways I could improve myself. I read helpful books about conditions of the body and how they are metaphorically linked to the mind. I had begun working on other physical problems. I asked myself, if I could get good results with other parts of my body, why not my eyes? This idea was a breakthrough for me.

I researched books on eye diseases. I found out about Dr. Roberto Kaplan. I visited him, and during two hour-long consultations, much happened. I started to cry tears of happiness. I began to release things from my past. I followed his suggestion of wearing a patch over my dominant, clear left eye. I listened to self-healing audiotapes that he designed about letting go.

I found that the right eye was connected to the father, or male, side of the family. I realized that my right eye condition reflected the confusion I had with men in my life. In my dreams I wanted to be in a profession that was more creative, like dancing, singing, and making movies. I wanted to work with people. I could help them. My disease was telling me about something I hadn't fulfilled in my life.

My diet was good. I didn't eat much dairy and meat. I began to use a stimulating color before my right eye to increase the self-healing potential of my body and mind. In addition, I supplemented with antioxidants in the form of sublingual spray. Contrary to my earlier physician's warning about the harmful effects of sunlight, I began a practice of lovingly inviting the sun into my eyes. I sat with my face toward the sun and with my eyes closed, in the early mornings while I waited for the train. I loved the warm feeling of the sun.

After a while, the sun felt so good for my eyes I began to stop wearing my sunglasses. Of course while skiing I used them. The sun became my friend. It was no longer the enemy. I realized that the more conscious I am, the less the sun can burn me. I continued listening to the self-healing audiotapes for nearly two months. The content and information shook up my mind. I began to stand up for myself. I no longer was willing to feel abused by people.

The combination of the audiotapes and wearing the patch helped me have flashbacks to memories of my childhood I had forgotten—memories that I did not remember and see. For two weeks I felt very vulnerable. My crying allowed me to further let go.

My goal was not to hurry my life anymore and try to find a job. I would take care of myself first. I would only take jobs that interested me. I worked in film and my eye improvement continued.

I wanted to know what the emotional blockages were that may have led to my eye disease. Roberto Kaplan invited me to a three-week self-healing retreat he and his partner were leading. In the retreat, deeper changes happened. I began to patch again. I found it really difficult at first. I felt emotions connected to my father and this affected my breathing. As I more consistently wore the patch, another emotional world emerged. Every day a different emotion surfaced. In one moment my heart was pounding like I had run a marathon. Next moment, my chest was on fire. Then I would calm down. Day after day I went through a purging of emotions. I had firmly locked up deep childhood feelings toward my father in a box.

At first wearing the patch on my left eye led to my world through my right eye—it seemed dark and gloomy. There was a dark compact area in the middle of my vision. It looked like an impression of an eye. In the retreat Roberto led us through a healing ritual of examining our restrictions. I placed myself between the ages of six and eight. Lots of memories returned. One evening I was encouraged to act out my restrictions. I could feel when I was six years old. I hated when my father hugged me or touched me. My sister had been abused. I had to lock what I sensed back then into a box so that I wouldn't get hurt. I stayed with the feelings even though it was very frightening. I lay on the floor and moved, made sounds, and then danced. I acted it out. In a matter of seconds I lived again being six. Then everything came out.

At that moment, I burned the restrictions in me. I realized that I had been abused. I had recreated this pattern of being a victim with my boss. Now, all the related feelings and emotions do not bother me. I am able to feel them and let go. My past doesn't hurt anymore. I feel good about my father. There is no blame. Now this is all behind me.

The day after, I was so relieved, so happy. I was a new person. I noticed my right eye became filled with light. The compact dark area was dissolving. Now it was a nice blurry veil, and was getting lighter and lighter. I could feel the light coming into my right eye.

Every day it gets better and better. When there is lots of light, I am really happy as I can now read with my right eye. While patching I can see people's faces and their eyes. I am healing my eye condition and am free to pursue living in a conscious way.

## A New Beginning

Françoise's story poignantly shows how, in the presence of adversity, when you allow your deepest light to direct your seeing, the eyes regain useful function. While this concept is relatively foreign in conventional medical practice today, people like Françoise are lighting the path for future vision care. Invasive surgical or medicamental approaches certainly have their place, in cases of trauma or when improvements in eyesight do not result from the methods described in conscious seeing. However, it is time to reinvolve patients in their own self-healing.

I tell my clients that the body is a perfect, finely tuned, self-healing instrument. Due to the intensity of living in our fast-paced world, every now and again we might be reminded through our aches, pains, and symptoms to recalibrate this instrument. This body of ours is in the process of regenerating every minute of every day, nonstop. To consciously see is to become observant when our eye symptoms reveal a state of imbalance.

In most cases of eye disease, there is a new beginning lurking in the dark shadows of the blinding condition. Cataracts; glaucoma;, macular degeneration; and optic nerve, retinal, and corneal conditions often present themselves to alert us to pending physical blindness unless we alter an aspect of our out-of-balance life. This physical symptom of nonseeing often invites us to examine what we are blind to in life. If we deny our symptoms, the eye condition will stop us in our tracks to get our attention. This blindness has been likened to a "mini-death." A part of our lifestyle needs to go through a death process in order to birth a new vision of living.

This death usually involves entering into feeling more deeply. Invariably this means facing the emotional side of our personality. To be conscious, to see consciously, demands that we leave no stones unturned if we are to free ourselves from the incompletions of the past.

## Body and Mind Out of Balance

As a doctor trained in optometric visual science, I would never have guessed my practice would one day be devoted to educating people with eye diseases. My specialty was to refractively measure the visual system and provide vision therapies for two-eyed and learning-related problems.

In the late 1970s, my own desire for conscious seeing led me to Seattle to find a solution. I was frustrated. Patients at the clinic where I was supervising vision therapy repeatedly asked me if there were specific therapies they could use to improve their nearsightedness. Occasionally, someone with an eye disease prompted me with the same question: "Is there something natural I can do for my glaucoma or cataracts?" I would reluctantly shake my head in ignorance.

A colleague and mentor, Raymond Gottlieb, was visiting Seattle to talk about an unknown branch of optometry known as syntonics. He and other doctors had used colored lights shone in the eye to treat refractive and two-eyed conditions. He believed that color could be used to manage certain eye diseases and conditions.

As a clinical professor, my skeptical buttons were pushed by these comments. There was no way that colored light could influence biological tissue. "Show me the research," I demanded. If his claims were valid, I and thousands of other doctors would have to admit that we were not telling our patients the complete truth. We would have to face the lie that medication and surgery were the only solutions available for eye diseases.

Dr. Gottlieb looked me in the eye and said, "You want research, why don't you do it?" I was stunned by his boldness. But I was in the perfect situation, in my optometric clinic, to conduct an investigation. The next day I was browsing in an alternative bookshop and came across a book by the German physician William Luftig, *The Natural Treatment of Eye Diseases*. I could hardly believe my eyes.

I walked out of the shop protectively holding this treasure as if it were gold. I intuitively knew that this man's writings were to open my eyes to a whole new world of possibilities.

The next morning at the clinic I was approached by Sharon, a nearsighted woman in her late thirties. She had been diagnosed with a retinal detachment. In an attempt to have the retina reattach itself, a scleral buckle had been surgically placed in her right eye. Sharon pleaded with me to take her case on. She desperately wanted to learn self-healing practices to heal this detachment and prevent the same thing happening to the other eye.

I felt uncomfortable because Sharon was asking me to go beyond my usual way of practicing. I resisted. What would my colleagues say? What would happen if it didn't work? If Sharon's eye condition improved, what then? I would have to revise my entire way of thinking about eye treatment. My mind galloped with these questions. That evening I began reading Luftig's accounts of how he worked with his patients. I stayed up into the early hours of the morning, totally fascinated by his approaches of using light, homeopathic remedies, and modified eating practices to awaken diseased tissue of the eyes of his patients.

The conventional Western form of medicine promotes the idea of age and illness being a natural consequence of living. Yet, there are many people in our world who happily live past 100 years without major disease, maintaining good health to the very end. Certain cultures eat very simple diets comprised of fruits, vegetables, nuts, and seeds with little meat or dairy products. These people are vital and free of illness well into their eighties and nineties.

Luftig considered that the body needs to be in balance. If its delicate constitutional balance was upset by an unhealthy lifestyle, poor eating, overworking, unhappiness, abuse, and lack of natural light, then this could be seen in the eyes. This way of thinking made so much sense to me! In the deepest part of my being the words of Luftig struck a very deep resonance. I knew then that this was my path.

The next morning, I phoned Sharon and told her that I would take her on as a single case experiment. I read about the medical use of visualization. A number of doctors were using pictorial stories for their patients to heal conditions ranging from raised blood pressure to cancer. Why couldn't the same approach be used for the eyes?

I designed a self-healing script that awakened the healing potential of the retina. I read the script to Sharon while she palmed her eyes. In a vivid journey, she traveled through her eyes, gently talking to each of the structures until she arrived at the retina. Here Sharon was instructed to visualize healthy blood being pumped from her heart to her eyes. She imagined eating healthy food, with her clean blood carrying the vital healing nutrients to her retina. In this way the reattachment of her right eye would be engaged by her active participation.

I discovered that this approach provided another important benefit. When Sharon started the project, she presented a fearful behavior. The integrated approach I used with her helped neutralize this fear and created a very important change in Sharon's mind. Her fear was replaced by what some would call hope or faith. I call it the *excitement for what is possible*. Sharon intended and expected that her work with me would be helpful. This "mind" shift of claiming intention and self-responsibility is potent medicine. It sets the inner stage for natural healing to take place.

In conventional medical practice, this aspect of self-regulated healing is shrugged off as unscientific. Research purists seek a direct cause and effect for measurable changes in function or behavior. I find that each individual needs his or her one particular remedy to have the mind make the shift in consciousness. Also, by each person taking responsibility for their own well-being, they begin to live a life congruent with their own rhythm and personal needs.

## Slowing Down

Eye disease conditions like Sharon's literally stop us in our tracks. If you have an eye disease, you know how your life suddenly stops as you face the seriousness of your condition. Sharon had a career, was a mother and wife, and had a busy life. She had to stop and take time to have eye surgery and reevaluate her life. She could no longer drive, and her cooking and reading slowed to a snail's pace. From a "normal" life in the fast lane, her eye condition forced her into the slow lane. Part of her visual healing compelled her to ask questions about the various parts of herself.

I had her examine her perceived degree of happiness in her marriage, in her career, in her overall health, in her creative endeavors, and in her home life. The reason for engaging Sharon in this process was to have her find a way in her personal life to apply her conscious seeing. The idea is that, when you begin seeing consciously how you have constructed your past, life may not look the same.

Conscious seeing reveals the faulty perceptions of the past. You are forced to examine the illusions of your former vision. Part of the visual healing of eye diseases is to reconstruct the above aspects of your life aligned with your true viviential nature. There are two processes working in parallel. On the one hand you are making use of practices like Françoise and Sharon did, listening to self-healing audiotapes. Simultaneously you are examining your outer life process. In this way the inner healing is setting the stage for the creation of new perceptions that are in reality part of your real inner nature. Your soul speaks through your eyes and you literally see your life more clearly.

As it turned out, Sharon was not fulfilled in her marriage. In fact, she was able to face the fact that her eyes had already begun wandering to other men. Sharon blamed the lack of connection about sexuality as her husband's fault, noting, "Jim is a good man and father, but he comes home at night and just wants to smoke marijuana. My interest is a healthy lifestyle. I feel we are separating in some way that I cannot explain."

I had Sharon examine her statements. I pointed out that an inner belief of separation is a form of perceptual consciousness. By asking her a series of questions and guiding her to examine exactly how she had expressed herself, Sharon explored the feelings of separation from her husband with her retinal separation, which had led to her retina's detachment from the layers at the back of the eye. Is it possible that feelings of separateness from our loved ones represent mental detachment, too? As in the case of astigmatism and near-/far-sightedness, the retinal reflex prints out the mind message. In this case the structural detachment of the retina does the same thing.

Sharon began directing colored light into her right eye to deepen the self-healing process.

I obtained a lamp used in theaters, the kind where you can place colored filters in the front end. I mounted it above my bed. After combining a blue and violet filter I would lie on my bed and look at the light from a distance of fifty centimeters. At the same time, I listened to the deep self-healing audiotape for the retina. The combination of the light, healing food, and the taped messages opened up in me a sense that I was participating in my own healing. I wasn't only dependent on my eye doctors.

In this way I examined my dependence on my husband for my own satisfaction. During the ensuing months of intense inner searching, I reached an awareness of how I had been neglecting my painting and art work.

At my three-month checkup, my doctors were surprised at how well the retina had reattached and that my visual field was much broader with fewer blind spots. The eyesight and nearsightedness in my left eye were stable. There were no symptoms such as flashes of light. The likelihood of retinal detachment was deemed to be low.

Jim and I went on holiday and once again found the connection that brought us together in the first place. My physical eyesight was improving. I reduced the nearsighted diopters by 1.50 and my inner vision, that is my feelings toward my husband, were much clearer. My eye condition had revealed a state of mind that I had been blind to. Jim also became more conscious.

## A Shift in Perception

With his patients, Luftig used healing food, homeopathic remedies, colored light, and physical body practices. Perhaps this combination produced a certain awareness in patients. I began experimenting with the effect upon consciousness of eating differently and using self-healing color and audio suggestions. With Sharon and other clinical patients, I slowly introduced these healing principles into their lives. I had them keep diaries, and the social worker and I conducted interviews with them.

At first, the patients believed that the purpose of the preceding healing modalities was to fix their eye problems. They therefore did what I, the doctor, told them. Typically patients believe what their doctors tell them. A doctor's recommendation has power, like the medicine that is prescribed. I speculated that there is also powerful medicine in the patient's intention to be well and live and see in a conscious way.

In my treatment of my clinical patients, I integrated both African rituals from my own background and my training in Tibetan philosophical practices. These practices centered on offering gratitude for whatever reveals itself in your life, and spending moments each day seeing what is present in your life and acknowledging it through eyes of love. The goal is to let your heart guide your seeing the consciousness of all before you.

I guided my patients to see eating as a sacred rite of passage to wellness—a time to bring healing food and energy into the body. Some patients needed to be made aware of how to prepare one healthy meal a day for themselves. Some needed to learn to honor the act of eating as an important daily ceremony: sitting down for meals, making use of linen napkins and placemats, bringing out the best crockery and cutlery. They even learned how to chew differently, chewing their food with presence, as in the viewing of the candle or the fusion pictures. They practiced breathing and consciously letting their organs digest the food with love.

This process resulted in profound changes for the patients. Consciousness emerged in their seeing; they were no longer concerned only with fixing their eye problems. Their eye condition became the catalyst that helped them discover how they wished to see their new life. They became aware of their former unconscious, robotic way of perceiving. Because the parts of their lives took on a richness, they developed an intention to live in a full and passionate way.

My experiences with these clinical patients dramatically affected my approach to eye problems. I learned that eye diseases or unhealthy conditions were no longer a problem. Instead, they were an opportunity to be conscious and to see from the deepest self.

## Self-Healing

One client, Heather, was a delightful person who had just celebrated her seventieth birthday. She had cataracts in her eyes. Although her doctor assured her that a simple lens implant would correct her vision, Heather was reluctant to undergo the surgical procedure. She consulted with me to find ways to improve her eyesight.

In such cases, I first present the patient with her options. I assured Heather that the lens implant was a relatively safe and well-tested procedure. I recommended she verify with her consulting doctor the health of the macular fovea region of the retina. She replied that, at her last doctor visit, there were some minor alterations in the macular area, and the physician was not overly concerned.

Here are Heather's comments on our one-hour session:

> Dr. Kaplan guided me into my life. I examined the areas where I felt loss and unhappiness. I missed my family so much. I live alone in the big city of Frankfurt. My children and grandchildren all live in Australia. I feel so much love from them and they are so far away.
>
> Roberto took my hands and turned my palms face up. He placed his palms on my hands and asked me to feel the warmth. He closed his eyes and began breathing. Within seconds I felt warmth entering my palms from his. It felt like I had my hands near a warm stove. Roberto encouraged me to breathe in unison with him. First, a full in-breath, followed by a longer out-breath. Once I could join him in this way, we introduced a pause between the out- and in-breaths.

I continued to feel the warmth through the hands. After a few minutes, Roberto asked me to feel my family's love. I cried tears of joy at this suggestion. I poured this feeling of love into my palms, like a healing nectar. Roberto then directed me to place my warm palms over my closed eyes. I rested my elbows on my knees.

The sensations in my eyes were amazing. I could feel warmth entering my eyes. It appeared to change from bright yellow to orange. Roberto spoke in a gentle, healing voice. I took the colored light and passed it through the lenses of my eyes. Like a laser beam, the colors and warmth began to dissolve the cataract material. Then I sent the light further back into the retina. I imagined the rays activating healing and blood flow to what Roberto had called the macular area.

After removing my palms, everything seemed so wonderfully bright. I looked at Roberto and hugged him—something I have never done to a doctor before. The gesture felt so spontaneous and right. I left with healing tears of joy in my eyes. I knew in my heart that this was the exact medicine I needed.

## Eyesight Can Improve!

Sandra Merideth is a vision mentor. She provides counseling and education for individuals who have vision problems. She herself had an eye condition called keratoconus, in which the cornea can develop a cone protrusion. The resultant corneal deformation produces extraordinary astigmatism. Sandra described her vision with this condition:

There is a fracturing of the visual field in which points of views proliferate. A person approaching a keratoconic may appear to be coming forward, then retreating. He may have two noses and three or four arms. If something like buttons on his shirt catch the light, the light will be splintered in many directions—each button will appear as several buttons, each of them in turn sending out spidery rays of strange luminescence.

Sandra's lens prescription for her right eye was –17.00 diopters. With this lens prescription, she could make out the big E on the eye chart. This is equivalent to approximately 10 to 20 percent of useful eyesight. With her left-eye correction at –9.00 diopters, she could see at about 20/40, giving her about 50 percent useful eyesight in that eye. It is not uncommon in cases of eye diseases, by the way, that vision cannot be corrected to 100 percent.

Sandra reported to me that she visited her ophthalmologist, who prescribed glasses that she could wear after removing her contact lenses. Instead of wearing the fully compensating prescription, Sandra had a –5.75 diopters correction put into her old frames, as she was committed to reducing the amount of diopters before her eyes and increasing her eyesight potential. She entered her world of blur.

She remembers: "I began taking long walks without the –5.75 lenses. At first the world was quite surreal. I remember meeting what appeared to be the Elephant Man pushing—or was it pulling?—some kind of three-wheeled brown wagon. I was stumped as to what it was, until one of the wheels barked...just a man walking three dogs!"

At first Sandra noticed that her naked vision eyesight was quite unclear. This is quite common. Over time, especially if the earlier practices and use of the photographs mentioned in earlier chapters are used, this unclearness begins to lessen.

"And just a few weeks after that, a backyard that had always looked like an abstract jumble of color suddenly organized itself into recognizable objects. I recognized a toddler's bright orange Big Wheel trike; a lawn chair, turned upside down; a garden hose; and a rusty barbecue grill."

Sandra's eyesight improved to such a degree that she decided to see if her eyesight was significantly good enough to drive looking through the –5.75 glasses.

I took my distant vision test to have my driver's license renewed, wearing my prescription –5.75 diopters for each eye—and passed! For a moment, the letters were a bit blurry, and then I heard the voice of the ophthalmologist who had originally diagnosed my keratoconus. "You'll be in hard contacts the rest of your life," he had said. When I re-heard these words, every line on the chart came into crisp focus. Since then, my prescription has been reduced to –4.25 diopters. With these glasses I consistently see at least 20/32 two-eyed vision [about 64 percent]. With my right eye, the one with the larger cone, I can usually see 20/70 to 20/100 [about 20 to 28 percent]. I find it remarkable that at one time, with –17 diopters of lens prescription in front of this eye, I could hardly tell there was an eye chart at all! And with my left eye, even though it also has a cone, I can see 20/40 [50 percent].

Sandra gives credit to the integration practices (like you have been introduced to in photographs 9, 10, 12, 13, 14, 15, 16, and 17) she used to encourage her two-eyed vision: "This fusion of both eyes, integration of both sides of the brain, and in fact, bringing into harmony the many aspects of one's life, is the single most helpful theme for the reduction of keratoconus."

## Color and Healing

The results of these individual case experiments convinced me to accept Dr. Gottlieb's challenge and conduct clinical research on the healing benefits of color. I received a grant to investigate the use of color to expand the visual fields of children who had reading difficulties. (These findings were discussed in chapter 3.) The results of this study convinced me to include color balancing into my healing repertoire of activities to increase functional vision for patients with eye diseases.

We know that the body functions best when its acid and alkali levels are balanced. A balance between the fire, water, air, and earth elements is also needed. The autonomic and central nervous systems of the brain help regulate these balances. When we are out of alignment with our true nature, the body, in turn, can quite quickly swing out of balance.

In the same way, wounded states and distorted fear/anger emotional imbalances can result in organs of the body losing some or all of their functionality. I see eye disease as an indication of either over- or underuse of certain tissue. For example, in the case of astigmatism there appears to be a loss of energy flow in the eye structures.

Introducing colored light into the eye increases the flow of energy in the eye tissue. Certain colors increase the vibrational quality of blood flow and the delicate cells. The cooler colors slow down the vibrational energy.

For example, eyes suffering from conjunctivitis have a highly inflamed pink or red color. A cool color like indigo, a mixture of blue and violet, has a slowing-down effect upon the conjunctival structure. The cool color takes away some of the heat of the eye condition. The patient reports that his or her eyes feel more comfortable.

The opposite is true in the case of a macular degeneration. As the name implies, the macula is in a destructive, degenerative process. It needs stimulation by a warm color such as yellow or orange.

In my other books, *Seeing Without Glasses* and *The Power Behind Your Eyes*, I provide more detail about color balancing, and which colors and food are linked to specific eye conditions.

Consider color as a way to create the ideal balanced condition for your body, a condition that creates the perfect environment for the evolution of your conscious seeing.

Food also contains vibrant healing colors that impact your wellness. Spend a few moments while eating to acknowledge the presence of the color. Invite the energy of the food to nurture and heal your eye disease.

The balancing of the nervous systems helps individuals to reach the deeper parts of the mind. Hanna, at age seventy-seven, led a very active life. She and her husband, Klaus, were both medical doctors. They had shared a busy medical practice. Over the years they had drifted apart. Klaus became more distant and even spent time away from Hanna. Her children were nearby but they had busy lives.

When I first met Hanna she looked depressed. "I got my first glasses at age seventy-two," she reported.

But my eyesight became so bad I went back to the eye doctor. He diagnosed a cataract. I waited six weeks for the surgery on my left eye. But after surgery, my vision was worse. I could no longer see the shapes of what I was painting. The doctor then said that the right eye needed an operation. There was also a cataract in it, which he said had been induced by medication I had been taking. He operated on it, and I saw very well afterward. I went on holiday, skiing. On the last day I fell on my head. I was unconscious for some seconds. After one week, my sight still hadn't returned to normal. I couldn't see well again. I went back to the surgeon. He told me I needed laser surgery. He took a photograph of the eye and a diagnosis of macular degeneration was made. He could do nothing further for me. At that point, I realized that I had to do it for myself.

When Hanna didn't pay enough attention to the message behind the first eye condition, a second one appeared, macular degeneration, to let her hear the knocking more loudly. Sometimes we all need second and even third reminders before we pay attention to our inner life and examine where we are out of balance or are denying our deeper feelings and emotions. This is quite common. But we must remember that the sensitive structures of the eyes are linked to the wisdom of the soul. Each time our eyes communicate a symptom, it is imperative that we stop and pay attention to the message. Imagine someone knocking on your front door. If there is no response, they will knock more loudly. In the same way, our eyes persist, with louder and louder symptoms, in drawing our attention to what lies behind them.

At first, Hanna simply let the doctor do the surgery for the cataract. Despite her surgically addressing her cataract issue, the macula was already preparing itself to increase the loudness of the knock in order for Hanna to look more deeply into her life. When Hanna had to stop her painting and felt restricted in her mobility, she finally took on the responsibility of taking care of herself. She finally decided to really look at her life.

This is when I met Hanna. I coached her in the principles of self-healing. After a three-week intensive healing, Hanna was able to let go of the death of her former life and blindness to her needs. She needed to reintroduce daily painting into her life, and acknowledge that her husband was no longer able to provide for her nurturing needs. I wrote about Hanna in my notes: "She purged the dark energy of pending blindness and death in her appearance. She invited in light and spirit."

After our sessions, Hanna felt newly born in perceptions of her independence. She faced her future by asking Klaus for what she wanted from him, which was to have daily time to paint and not be his personal nursemaid and cook. After she had addressed the underlying reasons for her loss of seeing, her vision improved sufficiently for her to travel on a plane or train on her own. Her paintings carried the message of her dark, restricted past, but peeping through them was the colorful future. When I waved goodbye to Hanna for the last time, I gave her this poem.

*Opening my eyes*
*invited by the spirit*
*Being in light — love*
*and sharing together*
*I begin to know*
*who I am*
*I begin to feel why I am*
*I begin grow into light —*
*into love — into joy —*
*into color*
*I grow every day fast*
*into myself*
*I am happy and thankful*

The photographic collage number 18 on page 132 is a visual representation for you to access your deeper feelings and emotions. As you get into your feelings, the images will guide you to discover the issues behind your eye disease or condition. Spend five minutes a day for twenty-one days letting the individual images and collective collage touch you. This is healing.

Begin with the three irises. The pupil of each iris has been replaced with an image. Observe the iris image on the right. There is an image of an old church window superimposed over the iris. This represents the sacred geometric form of the eye structure. See the blue bubble as the dome window entrance to your eye known as the cornea. The curved bubble is the power constantly available for you to discover.

Then focus on the brown iris in the bottom left. Notice the markings of the iris representing your family tree. The image in the pupil is of the retina as if you can look right to the back of the eye. This is how it actually looks when you enter the pupil using the doctor's ophthalmoscope. Realize you are looking at pumping blood vessels, those veins and arteries carrying the healthy blood. Let this be your own eye.

Notice the triangular sunlight linking the three iris structures. You and your family are forever connected, crossing all time and space barriers. See the unborn baby inside the triangular light as your pre-birth experience. See if you can find the two images that speak to death. The cross against the sky in the lower right corner and the skull in the pupil òf the top left iris allow you to focus on death of the old pain and suffering. See the black-and-white image in the top left corner. A little boy has anguish on his face. The blindness (two persons with patches on, below the black and white image) reminds us that what we don't see on the inside reveals itself as disease in the eye. Deep emotion that is not felt one day explodes like a volcano. (See the image of Earth's volcanoes taken from outer space—lower left corner.) Once we are born from the former death, we see love (a boy being kissed, top right corner).

The naked body is our vivencial nature fully exposed.

# 12

## *The Future and Conscious Seeing*

*You never change anything by fighting the existing. To change
something, build a new model and make the existing obsolete.*

—BUCKMINSTER FULLER

Buckminster Fuller was literally and figuratively a farsighted visionary. He had an eye condition called strabismus, which, if you recall,
means that his eyes turned inward. It would seem plausible that Mr.
Fuller accessed his conscious seeing because he was able to transcend
the physical limitation of his camera eye and bring forth amazing
insight and vision. Similarly, Mohandas K. Gandhi was farsighted.
His vision was one of truth and peace. Both of these exceptional men
probably accomplished conscious seeing by not altering their camera
eye but by seeing through their eye of vivencia. It was through their
being human that they made their most impressive contributions.

I believe that conscious seeing is the new model of vision care,
and that it will eventually be adopted by optometrists and ophthalmologists everywhere. Others before me, like ophthalmologist
William Bates, proponent of better eyesight without glasses, and
Skeffington, the grandfather of behavioral optometry, introduced a
new way of looking at vision. Even though their ideas were not fully
embraced by all eye doctors, they left an indelible impression on
human consciousness. Conscious seeing is the new paradigm of
vision for the twenty-first century. It is not designed to make the
"existing obsolete," as Fuller suggests. Rather, as Gandhi said, "Truth
is like a vast tree, which yields more and more fruit, the more you

nurture it." The truth of conscious seeing will speak loudly because it is aligned with universal truth.

I sense that if we each are aware of seeing consciously, then a critical point in time will come soon when it will be considered normal to practice conscious seeing. To cultivate conscious seeing is to see through eyes of peace. When we all feel more peaceful inside of ourselves, the peace and harmony in our world will grow. The values of home and family will again have their rightful place. I am convinced this is happening already. Our changing world provides evidence that indicates two trends.

First, old divisive structures like the Berlin Wall in Germany have come down. Countries such as Russia and South Africa are becoming freer, supporting individual rights and the right to self-determination. At the same time, there are still wars and famine. Suffering continues. People are without food and shelter. The duality of vision continues to create dramatic polarities.

Engaging these two polarities is vital for mastering the integration of thoughts, feelings, and emotions. In the preceding chapters you found ample practices to accomplish this. Our worldview is a metaphor for these polarities. Each one of us brings the exact circumstances, whether they be war, bankruptcy, divorce, death of a loved one, or even blinding eye conditions, that we need to fully experience integration. The integrative process within ourselves is a prerequisite for conscious seeing. Examples of world conflict are simply outer manifestations of unresolved inner conflict. Conscious seeing requires each of us to resolve these conflicts within ourselves first, and then watch as our own way of seeing is increasingly reflected in the larger global landscape.

What we've explored in this book is only the beginning. Whether you have already begun the practices or not, remember that conscious seeing is based on the principle of integration and wholeness. There is a purpose for matter coming together or breaking down. This is basic physics and explained in terms of the laws of nature. It is part of the process of evolution. Our lives are part of this constant change. There are moments of integration that lead to clearness and at other times to disintegration and blur or double vision.

The future of conscious seeing hinges on being aware of the duality of what you see in your world. Be wary of slipping into one or the other point of view. The pull toward polarity gives you a chance to deal with unresolved feelings and suppressed emotion. If you stay aligned with one polarity, you may limit the possibility for deeper integration. Your perception is tainted with a one-sided viewpoint and you stay stuck in your beliefs, fears, and unresolved emotion. Dualities exist in order for you to wrestle and learn from them. As you grow and develop, you come to understand the individual components that, when combined, allow you to reach higher and more sophisticated levels of integration. This is how you "become" conscious.

The ultimate goal is to observe both polarities of dualistic vision and find your own internal switches that lead to your reintegrating the parts of your being. This is when you see through your eye of vivencia, where you can stay present, fully conscious as you observe the presence of duality without being seduced toward one of the polarities.

Consciousness is already present within us and around us. It takes conscious seeing to be aware of consciousness. For the past two years I have had two polarities in my life that help me understand duality and being conscious. Part of my time I live in a small rustic cabin in British Columbia, Canada. The area is relatively remote, on an island. The only sounds I hear are the ocean, the movement of the trees, and the squawking of the eagles and seagulls flying by. I sit at my table overlooking the ocean. I have no television, newspapers, city or car noise, or supermarkets. Just the sounds of nature. In this environment, I hear the silence of my deepest consciousness. I cannot escape my inner feelings or emotions. I have a chance to practice my conscious seeing.

Being so close to nature I can look through my eyes and simultaneously connect with the ocean, trees, and wildlife while being with my inner nature. This is another form of duality. I walk in nature. I am in touch with myself. I become conscious of my seeing. My being still is part of my consciousness that I really enjoy.

There is another polarity I also dearly love. Within a two-hour time span I can be on a jet flying to a European city. To reach the airport I travel on a ship that shuttles me on my way to the bus that transports me to my flight. The moment I leave my cabin I am confronted with visual noise—newspapers, magazines, television, advertisements, people—and city noises, traffic, polluted air, to name a few. If I allow myself to slip into reactivity, my seeing can be pulled into an unconscious state. This is the direction of the polarity called noise and being upset by the outside world.

I have observed this reactive behavior enough in myself to know that my upset is an emotion that needs to be respected, felt, and experienced, not denied. If I deny my upset, I become emotionally out of balance. That imbalance, along with the constant noise and activity from the outside, leads me away from the inner peace I experience so profoundly on my island.

Through practicing the concepts I've shared with you in the preceding chapters, I can now find the peace of dwelling in my quiet inner environment even when I am in a busy city. I can stay centered and present even when there is a lot of activity and noise around me. Conscious seeing is staying present with what is and making choices that keep you in a balanced state of being.

Stay observant when you lose your integration. It is a big challenge to be always present in one's life. In the world our survival perceptions are being tested constantly, to help us discover when our sense of reality is based on a disintegrated state of seeing. Conscious seeing is when you are able to discern the differences between reality and illusion, and do so from your own, unique perspective. Remember, you are the author of your life when you are consciously seeing. You integrate your internal script or vision of your life with what is presented to you from the outside.

Our world includes twenty-four–hour shopping, drive-in banking, and eating on the run. Kellum says this kind of seeing lures us into an expectation of ease and accessibility. "The outward view is convenience."

Instead of stopping our work when our head hurts we can take a headache pill and continue working. If our eyes become unclear we get glasses and continue abusing them. We want to live long, look young, be beautiful, and accomplish all this and more with the minimum of effort. Conscious seeing demands a balance between convenience and the often hard work of self-responsibility, bringing us into ourselves, less dependent on others' vision of us.

A poignant example of this reality present in our world today is refractive or "corrective" laser eye surgery, touted as the cure-all for refractive errors. In 1998, 250,000 people in the United States alone had this surgery. Were these patients seduced into seeing the promised, clear, 100 percent eyesight? Can we believe everything we hear from the outside, like the slick advertisements from the ophthalmologists? What about the promised results in the long distance view, the farsighted one? The view of the future? What are the potential ramifications of such invasive surgery? Time will tell. Did any of these people who rushed into surgery consider the inner view of what caused their nearsighted condition in the first place? Probably not.

My point of view is that if you have exhausted all explorations of conscious seeing and your physical eyesight still remains unsatisfactory to you, then, as a last resort, consult with a physician to determine your suitability for the surgery.

We can choose to have this life be easy or challenging. We can be lazy or be accountable. You can choose to consciously see from the eye of vivencia. This doesn't mean your journey will be free of challenges. It means that life through your conscious seeing will reward you with the perfect plan for your unique nature. Opportunities to experience bliss and enlightenment are as available as your decision to say yes, to choose this path.

Now look at photograph 19 on page 133.

This is the way to feel and see peace on our planet. Our eyes provide the means to see all human beings as one large family, living peacefully and prosperously on our wonderful planet. Conscious seeing helps us restore our inner balance. It reacquaints us with the way our physical bodies were meant to function. When we see consciously, our souls have a place to emerge from the darkness of our modern lifestyles.

This is my blessing to you for having read this book.

# Suggested Reading

Bates, W. H. *The Bates Method for Better Eyesight Without Glasses*. New York: Jove/Harcourt Brace Jovanovich, 1978.

Bennet, H. Z. *The Lens of Perception*. Berkeley, Calif.: Celestial Arts Publishing Co., 1987.

Carter, R. *Mapping the Mind*. Berkeley, Calif.: University of California Press, 1998.

Damasio, A. R. "How the Brain Creates the Mind." *Scientific American* 281 (December 1999), no. 6:112–117.

Forrest, E. B. *Stress and Vision*. Santa Ana, Calif.: Optometric Extension Program Foundation, 1987.

Gottlieb, R. *Relieving Stress in Myopia, In Behavioral Aspects of Vision Care-Myopia Control*. Santa Ana, Calif.: Optometric Extension Program, 1921 E. Carnegie Avenue, Suite 3-L, 92705-5510, 1998. E-mail/Web site: oep@oep.org, www.oep.org.

Grof, S., with H. Z. Bennett. *The Holotropic Mind: The Three Levels of Human Consciousness and How They Shape Our Lives*. San Francisco: Harper Collins, 1992.

Grossman, M., and G. Swarthout. *Natural Eye Care: An Encyclopedia*. Los Angeles: Keats Publishing, 1999.

Harris, P. "Visual Conditions of Symphony Musicians." Journal of the *American Optometric Association* 59, no. 12 (December 1988): 952–959.

Johnson, D. R. *What the Eye Reveals*. Olga, Wash.: Rayid Publications, P.O. Box 438, 98279. Tel: (360) 376-6188; 1-800-743-0179; fax: (360) 376-3158; Web site: www.rayid.com.

Jung, C. G. *Memories, Dreams, Reflections*. New York: Vintage Books, 1965.

Kaplan, R. M. "Changes in Form Visual Fields in Reading Disabled Children Produced by Syntonic Stimulation." *The International Journal of Biosocial Research* 5 (1983), no. 1:20–33.

———. *Die Integrative Sehtherapie*. Freiamt, Germany: Arbor Verlag, 2000. Tel.: 07645.913050; fax: 07645.913055; E-mail: info@arbor-verlag.de.

———. *The Power Behind Your Eyes*. Rochester, Vt.: Healing Arts Press, 1994.

———. *Seeing Without Glasses*. Hillsboro, Ore.: Beyond Words Publishing, 1994 and 2001. Tel.: 1-800-284-9673; Web site: www.beyondword.com.

Kellum, R. B. *Capitalism and the Eye*. Ann Arbor, Mich.: UMI Dissertation Information Service, 1997.

Orfield, A. "Seeing Space: Undergoing Brain Reprogramming to Reduce Myopia." *Journal of Behavioral Optometry* 5 (1994), no. 5: 123–131.

Rojas, R. "The ISYS Model™ — A Three Dimensional Isomorphic Representation of the Nature and Structure of the Brain, the Mind, and Consciousness." Personal correspondence with author.

Schiffer, Frederic. *Of Two Minds: The Science of Dual-Brain Psychology*. New York: The Free Press, 1998.

Selye, H. *Stress without Distress*. New York: E. P. Dutton, 1980.

Wertenbaker, Lael. *The Eye: Window to the World*. New York: Torstar Books, Inc., 1984.

Zajone, A. *Catching the Light: The Entwined History of a New Species*. New York: Bantam, 1993.

# Conscious Seeing and Serving Others

My writing and photographs are one way to pass on my experiences. The other is to have you meet me via telephone, fax, E-mail, or personal consultations. In addition, I offer workshops and retreats where I train persons in iris reading and integrated vision therapy. This occurs in Europe and North America, and, as a certified vision educator, you can help others in conscious seeing. If you would like to know more, visit the Web page below. Otherwise, phone or write via E-mail. I would love to share more with you.

Dr. Roberto Kaplan
Voice and fax, North America: (604) 608-3519
Voice and fax, Europe: 0049 69 255-77003
E-mail: robertokap@sunshine.net
Web site: *www.consciousseeing.com*

## Products for Conscious Seeing

If you are interested in obtaining information about self-healing audiotapes, pinholes, color filters, or other products for conscious seeing, write, phone, or fax to:

### North America
Beyond 20/20 Vision®
P. O. Box 68
Roberts Creek, B.C. V0N 2W0
Canada
Voice: (604) 608-3519
Fax: (604) 608-3519

E-mail: *order@beyond2020vision.com*
Web site: *www.beyond2020vision.com*

## Europe
Institute Integrated Sehtherapie
31/7 Eckpergasse
1180-Wien, Austria.
Phone/fax: 0043 1-478-8437
Voice/fax: 0049 69 255-77003
E-mail: *robertokap@attglobal.net*
E-mail: *gabriela.jorg@nextra.at*
Web site: *www.integrativesehtherapie.at*

## Referral to a Vision Therapy Oriented Optometrist
Optometric Extension Program: *www.oep.org*
College of Optometrists in Vision Development: *www.covd.org*
Phone: 1-888-268-3770
Free referrals to providers of vision therapy:
*www.optometrists.org/eye_doctors.html*

# Glossary

**Amblyopia (lazy eye):** Reduced vision that is uncorrectable by glasses. It occurs when the brain "switches off" the messages coming from the eye.

**Astigmatism:** Refractive condition in which the cornea is "not round," so that there is no point focus but rather two or more focal lines, and the blurring of lines at a particular angle. This condition comes and goes and is possibly caused by stressful posture, physical distortions, and emotional factors. Metaphorically, it is the inability to accept, and is part of the survival personality.

**Camera eye:** That part of vision that occurs in the physical eye itself.

**Consciousness:** Realized awareness, perception that is known to oneself.

**Convex lens:** A lens that converges rays of light, used to compensate for farsightedness. It is also called a plus lens.

**Diopter:** A unit of measure of lens power. A one-diopter lens has the power to bring parallel rays of light to a point focus at a distance of one meter from the lens. Diopter = 1/focal length in meters. For example, a +3.00 lens is a plus lens, a converging lens of three diopters. Negative lenses are expressed with a minus sign.

**Eye of vivencia:** Vision associated with the part of the mind where we see from our true nature, with the masks removed.

**Flexible personality:** That part of the personality that is unrestricted and free to evolve in consciousness.

**Fovea centralis:** The point of keenest vision in the eye; a spot on the retina where cone cells are highly concentrated; the point of thoughts.

**Fusion:** The ability of the brain and mind to blend messages coming from both eyes.

**Hyperopia (farsightedness):** A state where the image of a close object falls behind the retina, resulting in blur. Emotionally it is an inability to be comfortable with intimate experiences. Hyperopia is usually compensated for by magnifying, or "plus," lenses.

**Integration:** The merging and blending of abilities and characteristics. It is the act of unifying rather than isolating, and denotes a state of high human understanding and consciousness.

**Looking:** Perceiving from the center of our focus and with understanding. Comes from a rational, logical mind-set. "Over-looking" is perceiving from a state of thoughts (thinking) where seeing, feeling, and "being" are suppressed or less emphasized.

**Macula ("macula lutea," literally "yellow spot"):** An oval, yellowish spot exactly in the center of the posterior part of the retina, corresponding to the axis of the eye, and the point at which the sense of vision is most perfect. See also fovea centralis.

**Mind's eye:** That part of vision associated with the brain and mind.

**Myopia (nearsightedness):** A refractive state of the visual system in which the image of distant objects falls in front of the retina, causing blur. Metaphorically, myopia is an inability to clearly perceive a large viewpoint. It is usually compensated for by contractive, or "minus," lenses.

**Presbyopia ("old age sight"):** The gradual loss of accommodative powers for near vision that usually occurs after age forty. It is compensated for by magnifying, or "plus," lenses.

**Refraction:** The bending of light as it travels between substances of different densities.

**Refractive error:** A numerical expression of how the eye fails to bring parallel rays of light to exact focus on the retina.

**Seeing:** That part of perceiving from our retina that is softer, more intuitive, and associated with feeling. Seeing is tuning in to how we feel about aspects of the invisible compared to what is directly in our view of perceiving (looking).

**Spherical lens:** A lens with spherical faces, with each face a smooth, polished surface with equal surface curvature in all its meridians. Such a lens brings light to a point focus. A spherical lens may have both faces convex or both concave, or one side may be a plane, or it may be a meniscus lens.

**Survival personality:** That part of the personality that is restricted because of fears, denials, and beliefs that keep one from being conscious.

**Toric lens (cylindrical lens):** A lens with at least one face that is not spherical, so it does not have the same curvature in all its surface meridians. It is a lens used for astigmatism.

# BEYOND WORDS PUBLISHING, INC.

## OUR CORPORATE MISSION
*Inspire to Integrity*

## OUR DECLARED VALUES
We give to all of life as life has given us.
We honor all relationships.
Trust and stewardship are integral to fulfilling dreams.
Collaboration is essential to create miracles.
Creativity and aesthetics nourish the soul.
Unlimited thinking is fundamental.
Living your passion is vital.
Joy and humor open our hearts to growth.
It is important to remind ourselves of love.

*To order or to request a catalog, contact*
Beyond Words Publishing, Inc.
20827 N.W. Cornell Road, Suite 500
Hillsboro, OR 97124-9808
503-531-8700 or 1-800-284-9673

You can also visit our Web site at *www.beyondword.com*
or e-mail us at *info@beyondword.com*.